Journalism
Principles and Practice

Tony Harcup

⑤SAGE Publications

London • Thousand Oaks • New Delhi

SAGE Publications Ltd
6 Bonhill Street
London EC2A 4PU

SAGE Publications Inc
2455 Teller Road
Thousand Oaks, California 91320

SAGE Publications India Pvt Ltd
32, M-Block Market
Greater Kailash - I
New Delhi 110 048

British Library Cataloguing in Publication data

A catalogue record for this book is available from the British Library

ISBN 0 7619 7498 9
ISBN 0 7619 7499 7 (pbk)

Library of Congress Control Number available

Typeset by Keystroke, Jacaranda Lodge, Wolverhampton
Printed in Great Britain by The Alden Press, Oxford

**To my mum, Beth,
and in memory of my dad, Fred**

Contents

Acknowledgements   ix
List of boxes   xi
Note to the reader   xiii

Chapter one   Who, What, Where, When, Why and How? An introduction to journalism   1

Chapter two   Constraints and influences on journalists   11

Chapter three   What is news?   29

Chapter four   Where does news come from?   43

Chapter five   The journalist as objective reporter   59

Chapter six   The journalist as investigator   73

Chapter seven   The journalist as entertainer   85

Chapter eight   Interviewing   93

Chapter nine   Writing news   105

Chapter ten   Writing features   115

Chapter eleven   Style for journalists   127

Chapter twelve   Beyond print: broadcasting and online journalism   141

Chapter thirteen   Conclusion: the challenge for journalism   151

Bibliography   159
Appendix One: NUJ Code of Conduct   169
Appendix Two: Some useful websites   171
Index   173

Acknowledgements

Thanks first of all to Julia Hall of SAGE, whose enthusiasm prompted me to come up with the idea for this book and who has been supportive throughout. She also came up with the title, which I concede is more effective than my unwieldy suggestion of *Who, What, Where, When and Why? Journalism in Context*.

If Julia helped make this book a reality, its origins go back much further. I am sure I have absorbed things from all my teachers, during what is now known as lifelong learning, but particular thanks must go to Chris Searle, Cathy Leman, Roger Worth, Trevor Cave, Colin Thorne and Max Farrar. Thanks too to Gill Ursell, John Short and the late Archie McLellan for helping a humble hack enter the world of academia. Together with other colleagues at Trinity & All Saints – in particular Derek 'Mac' McKiernan, Deirdre O'Neill, Michael Higgins and Fiona Thompson – they created a supportive and stimulating environment in which to work. Trinity & All Saints also facilitated my research by providing funds for literature and travel to interviews where necessary, for which I am grateful.

Over the decades I have worked alongside many journalists and talked about journalism with many more, and they have probably all contributed in some way to the ideas within this book. They are far too numerous for me to remember, let alone list, but honourable mentions must go to Keith Lomax, Gordon Wilson, Mat Hill, Julie Thorpe, Andy Comber, Sev Carrell, Quintin Bradley, Saeeda Khanum, Paul Breslin, Tony Lidgate, Helen Carroll, Sean Stowell, Tony Earnshaw, Ronnie Kershaw, Mark Hanna, Anne Creyke, Mike Glover, Richard North, Susan Pape, Peter Lazenby, Pete Johnson, Brian Kay, Vanessa Bridge, Tim Gopsill, Granville Williams, Colin Bourne, John Toner and Miles Barter. The contents of this book have also been informed by discussions with my journalism students, whose careers I continue to follow with admiration and even a little pride.

Journalism: Principles and Practice would not have been the same without the help of the following, all of whom gave generously of their time, their experiences and their ideas: Lindsay Eastwood, Paul Foot, Trevor Gibbons, David Helliwell, Jane Merrick, Abul Taher, Tony and Matt (*KDIS*), Martin Wainwright, Brian Whittle and Waseem Zakir. Heartfelt thanks to you all.

I am grateful to the following students for reading and commenting on the drafts of various chapters: Paddy Brennan, Rachel Crolla, Katie Cronin, Jenny Cuthbertson and Sally Symondson. Likewise to colleague Deirdre O'Neill.

Terry Wragg also commented on draft chapters and, throughout, has offered inexhaustible wisdom and unswerving support at home, for which much love and thanks.

Praise be to everyone at SAGE – especially Lauren McAllister and Seth Edwards, Jamilah Ahmed and Rosie Maynard, and the aforementioned Julia Hall – for treating an unorthodox idea as an opportunity rather than an inconvenience. The finished product owes much to you all, although responsibility for any errors or omissions rests with me.

Finally, a special vote of thanks goes to Bob Franklin for being unfailingly supportive and enthusiastic about my various attempts at bridging the division between academic and practitioner perspectives on journalism. You are an inspiration, mate.

Tony Harcup

List of boxes

Box 2.1 Constraints: legislation that restricts how journalists in England and Wales may gather information, what information they may have access to, and what may be published.   **22**

Box 3.1 News values: research suggests that potential items must generally fall into one or more of these categories to be selected as news stories.   **36**

Box 4.1 Sources: common sources of news stories.   **46**

Box 5.1 Wartime: words used by the UK press during the 1991 Gulf war.   **63**

Box 7.1 Media output: traditional and popular views.   **87**

Note to the reader

The unusual layout of this book is explained in Chapter One. If you start by reading the left-hand column on page two and continue with the untinted section through to page nine, all will be explained . . .

Chapter One

Who, What, Where, When, Why and How?

An introduction to journalism

Key terms

Commmunication

Churnalism

Journalism education

Public sphere

Fourth estate

Free press

Ideology

Agency

Ethics

What is journalism *for*? To pay the mortgage, if you ask many hacks. But journalism is about more than that. It is a form of **communication** based on asking, and answering, the questions Who? What? Where? When? Why? How? Of course, journalism *is* a job and journalists *do* need to feed their kids or pay off student loans. But being a journalist is not like working in a baked bean factory – journalists have a more *social* role that goes beyond the production of commodities to sell in the marketplace. Journalists *inform* society about itself and make *public* that which would otherwise be private.

Rather an important job, you might think. But public opinion polls frequently remind us that, in the league table of trustworthiness, journalists vie for bottom place with politicians and estate agents. Cynicism starts early. When 11-to-21-year-olds were asked how much they trusted journalists, just one per cent said 'a lot', 19 per cent 'a little', and a whopping 77 per cent replied 'I do not trust them' (*Observer* 2002). Despite this image problem, a never-ending stream of bright young and not-so-young people are eager to become journalists. Why?

Journalism can be one of the most exciting jobs around. You go into work not necessarily knowing what you are going to be doing that day. You get the chance to meet powerful people, interesting people, inspiring people, heroes, villains and celebrities. You get the chance to ask stupid questions. The chance to be one of the first to know something and to tell the world. The chance to indulge a passion for writing, maybe to travel, maybe to become an expert in a particular field. The chance to seek the truth and campaign for justice.

And then there's the excitement of seeing your byline in print, watching your report on TV, or hearing your words of wisdom on the radio. You can then do it all over again. And again.

Little wonder, perhaps, that so many people are prepared to make sacrifices for a career in journalism. Sacrifices such as paying for your own training before all but the lucky few will even be considered for a job; and then being paid less than many of the people whose complaints about low pay will feature in your news stories. When staff on a group of Lancashire weeklies went on

> **'The business of the press is disclosure.'**
> – *John Thaddeus Delane, 19th century editor of the Times.*

Communication

The basic questions of journalism highlighted in the title of this chapter – Who? What? Where? When? Why? How? – are echoed in an early model of the mass communication process, formulated by Harold Lasswell in 1948. For Lasswell, analysis of the media begins with the question: 'Who says what to whom, through what channel and with what effect?' (McQuail 2000: 52–3). This has been termed a 'transmission' model of communication, because it is essentially one-way, from sender to receiver. This and later versions of the transmission model have been challenged in recent decades as too simplistic, too linear, too mono-directional to explain the complexities of communication. It has been argued that an 'active audience' can filter messages through our own experiences and understandings, sometimes producing readings 'against the grain', or even suggesting multiple meanings.

Journalism

Journalists may indeed inform society about itself, and much journalism may be concerned with making public that which would otherwise be private, as suggested in this chapter. But such a formulation falls far short of an adequate definition. For a start, journalists also supply information, comment and amplification on matters that are *already* in the public domain.

Journalism is defined by Denis McQuail as 'paid writing (and the audiovisual equivalent) for public media with reference to actual and ongoing events of public relevance' (McQuail 2000: 340). Like all such definitions, this raises many questions – Can journalism never be unpaid? Can media be other than public? Who decides what is of public relevance? – but it remains a reasonable starting point for any analysis of the principles and practices of journalism. McQuail goes on to differentiate between different types of journalism: 'prestige' (or quality) journalism, tabloid journalism, local journalism, specialist journalism, 'new' (personal and committed) journalism, civic journalism, development journalism, investigative journalism, journalism of record, advocacy journalism, alternative journalism, and gossip journalism (McQuail 2000: 340).

strike in 2002 they used mops to hold up placards reading: 'Cleaners earn more than reporters'. The strike increased the starting rate for trainees on those papers from £10,486 a year to £13,060 – a huge percentage rise but still some way short of the £17,000 paid to trainee managers at McDonald's, that symbol of the low paid, fast food economy (*Journalist* 2002).

It was not an isolated example of low pay. A survey suggested the average salary among UK journalists as a whole was £22,500 a year, with one in ten earning less than £12,000 before tax. The hierarchy of average salaries was: national newspapers £40,000; television £35,000; magazines £22,500; radio £22,500; regional newspapers £17,500 (Journalism Training Forum 2002: 53–5). A trainee reporter told researchers:

> Young people with a strong enough passion for writing will suffer low wages for the chance to work in journalism. But it is a disgrace to the industry as a whole that they should have to. The industry cynically manipulates our ambition. (*Quoted in Journalism Training Forum 2002: 57.*)

Harsh. But fair? Another provincial press journalist seems to think so:

> Journalism is one of the worst paid professions, particularly for new starters, yet also one of the most popular. It strikes me that the latter point strangely justifies the former. (*Quoted in Journalism Training Forum 2002: 57.*)

Some wannabe journalists *are* put off when they discover the awful truth about pay. Others become disillusioned by work experience in newsrooms, observing that too many journalists seem to be chained to their desks in a culture of 'presenteeism', processing copy and checking things out – if at all – on the telephone or the internet.

Waseem Zakir, a business journalist with BBC Scotland, came up with the word 'churnalism' to describe too much of today's newsroom activity. He told me what he meant:

> Ten or 15 years ago you would go out and find your own stories and it was proactive journalism. It's

> *'Journalism largely consists in saying "Lord Jones Dead" to people who never knew that Lord Jones was alive.'*
> – GK Chesterton.

Such differentiation is rejected by David Randall, who recognises only the division between *good* and *bad* journalism:

> The bad is practised by those who rush faster to judgement than they do to find out, indulge themselves rather than the reader, write between the lines rather than on them, write and think in the dead terms of the formula, stereotype and cliché, regard accuracy as a bonus and exaggeration as a tool and prefer vagueness to precision, comment to information and cynicism to ideals. The good is intelligent, entertaining, reliably informative, properly set in context, honest in intent and effect, expressed in fresh language and serves no cause but the discernible truth. *(Randall 2000: viii.)*

Whether it is it as simple as that is a question we will explore in this and subsequent chapters.

Fourth estate

The notion of the press as a 'fourth estate of the realm' – alongside the Lords Spiritual (clergy sitting in the House of Lords), the Lords Temporal (other peers), and the House of Commons – originated in the 18th century and gained ground during the 19th century. Initially referring to the parliamentary press gallery, the term became a more general label for the press as a whole, locating journalists in a quasi-constitutional role as 'watchdog' on the workings of government. This is central to the liberal concept of press freedom, as Tom O'Malley notes:

> At the centre of this theory was the idea that the press played a central, if unofficial, role in the constitution. A diverse press helped to inform the public of issues. It could, through the articulation of public opinion, guide, and act as a check on, government . . . The press could only fulfil this function if it were free from pre-publication censorship and were independent of the government. *(O'Malley 1997: 127)*

become reactive now. You get copy coming in on the wires and reporters churn it out, processing stuff and maybe adding the odd local quote. It's affecting every newsroom in the country and reporters are becoming churnalists.

An ever-increasing workload may reduce the chances of doing the very things that made journalism seem so attractive in the first place. On top of all that, young journalists have to listen to the grumbles of more experienced hacks who insist 'it wasn't like this in my day'. As Jeremy Tunstall reminds us, the journalists of 100 years ago looked back fondly on a supposed 'golden age' of journalism circa 1870 (Tunstall 2002: 238).

Yet there is no shortage of people determined to become those 'day labourers of everyday life', journalists (Bourdieu 1998: 7). Even when disabused of any romantic illusions about travelling the world on huge expense accounts, pausing between drinks to jot down the occasional note, they are attracted by the fact that journalism remains an occupation in which no two days are exactly the same and where the big story may be only a phone call away. And by the fact that journalism *matters*.

If it didn't matter, why would there be so many laws restricting how journalists can do their jobs? Why would government and opposition alike spend so much time courting the media? Why would *Matlock Mercury* editor Don Hale have received numerous death threats? (Hale 2002) Why would Bill Goodwin, Martin Bright, Steve Panter and others have been threatened with jail for protecting their sources? (www.nuj.org.uk.) Why would a fatwa have been issued on Isioma Daniel, a young fashion journalist who wrote about the Miss World contest in Nigeria? (Isaacs 2002, Daniel 2003) Why would journalists such as Veronica Guerin, Martin O'Hagan, Naher Ali, Mario Coelho, Milan Pantic, and many others have been killed because of their work? Why would the International Federation of Journalists feel compelled to compile annual lists of journalists around the world killed in the course of their duties? More than 1,100 journalists and other media workers were killed in the decade up to 2003, and at least 20 died while covering the 2003 war in Iraq (IFJ 2003a, 2003b, 2003c, 2002).

> *'All human life is there.'*
> – old News of the World motto.

Public sphere

The public sphere rests on the idea of a space in which informed citizens can engage with one another in debate and critical reflection; hence its relevance to discussions of the media. Jurgen Habermas traces the rise of the public sphere in Europe in the late 17th and early 18th centuries and argues that increasing commercialisation led subsequently to the decline of the public sphere and the press as a space that enabled 'the people to reflect critically upon itself and on the practices of the state' (Stevenson 2002: 49). Today, according to this analysis, such reasoned public discussion has been replaced by 'the progressive privatisation of the citizenry and the trivialisation . . . of questions of public concern' (Stevenson 2002: 50). But Habermas has been accused of idealising 'a bygone and elitist form of political life' (McQuail 2000: 158).

Free press

Editors and owners alike are often heard extolling the virtues of a 'free press', a liberal model based on the idea that everyone is free to publish a newspaper without having to be licensed by those in power. Although publishers must act within the constraints of the law, they do not have to submit to censorship in advance. Newspapers are said to be in the business of truth-telling and serving only their readers. Thus, through the democracy of the free market, we get the press we both desire and deserve.

However, this concept of a press selflessly serving the public does not go unchallenged. Colin Sparks, for example, points to increasing concentration of owner-ship and to economic barriers on entry, keeping out competitors. He argues:

> Newspapers in Britain are first and foremost
> businesses. They do not exist to report the news, to
> act as watchdogs for the public, to be a check on the
> doings of government, to defend the ordinary citizen
> against abuses of power, to unearth scandals or to do
> any of the other fine and noble things that are
> sometimes claimed for the press. They exist to make
> money, just as any other business does. To the extent

The above evidence, and the fact that countless individuals come to 'know' about their communities via the work of journalists, supports the argument that **journalism** matters. But explanations of *how* and *why* journalism matters depend, like so many things, on *who* is speaking. Journalism is variously said to be the **fourth estate** of the realm, to be part of a **public sphere**, to support a **free press** or to inculcate us with the **ideology** of the ruling class. The reality is that journalism is probably all those things and more, because there is not *one* journalism.

This book

Individual journalists have their own tales to tell, their own beliefs about what they do, their own reasons for pursuing a career in whatever field of journalism they work in. I have interviewed a range of journalists for this book; their comments are taken from these interviews unless otherwise indicated. Here are some of those you will meet in subsequent chapters:

● Lindsay Eastwood, reporter for Yorkshire Television's *Calendar*. She began work on her local newspaper, the *Craven Herald*, straight from school. Lindsay moved to the *Watford Observer*, worked shifts on the nationals, and returned north to the *Yorkshire Evening Post* before switching to TV in 1998.

● Paul Foot, reporter for *Private Eye* and columnist for the *Guardian*. He joined the *Daily Mirror* in 1961 and worked on the *Daily Record* in Glasgow before moving on to *Private Eye* and *Socialist Worker*. For many years he had his own page in the *Daily Mirror* before falling foul of the post-Maxwell regime at the paper and returning to *Private Eye*.

● Trevor Gibbons, internet journalist for the BBC. He spent eight years as a sports journalist for *Open Rugby* magazine, then did a stint in public relations for the National Coaching Foundation and some freelancing for *Radio Leeds* before joining *BBC Online*.

> **'By journalism is to be understood, I suppose, writing for pay about matters of which you are ignorant.'**
> – Leslie Stephen, father of Virginia Woolf.

● David Helliwell, who was interviewed for this book while assistant editor of the *Yorkshire Evening Post*. He started out at the *Lancashire Evening Post* where he worked his way up

that they discharge any of their public functions, they do so in order to succeed as businesses. *(Sparks 1999: 45–6.)*

For Sparks, a truly free press – presenting objective information and a range of informed opinions while acting as a public forum – is 'an impossibility in a free market' (Sparks 1999: 59).

Ideology

By ideology is meant 'some organised belief system or set of values that is disseminated or reinforced by communication' (McQuail 2000: 497). Marxists believe that a ruling class ideology is propagated throughout western, capitalist societies with the help of the media. Ideology may be slippery and contested, but it is argued that the principle remains essentially as expounded by Karl Marx and Friedrich Engels in 1846:

> The ideas of the ruling class are in every epoch the ruling ideas: ie, the class which is the ruling material force of society, is at the same time its ruling intellectual force. The class which has the means of material production at its disposal, has control at the same time over the means of mental production, so that thereby, generally speaking, the ideas of those who lack the means of mental production are subject to it. The ruling ideas are nothing more than the ideal expression of the dominant material relationships, the dominant material relationships grasped as ideas; hence of the relationships which make the one class the ruling one, therefore, the ideas of its dominance. *(Marx and Engels 1965: 61)*

Ideological power has been described as 'the power to signify events in a particular way', although ideology is also 'a site of struggle' between competing definitions (Hall 1982: 69–70). To illustrate the point, Stuart Hall refers to media coverage of industrial action in the UK public sector in the late 1970s:

> [One] of the key turning-points in the ideological struggle was the way the revolt of the lower-paid public-service workers against inflation, in the 'Winter

from trainee reporter to deputy news editor, via crime reporter, before joining the *YEP* newsdesk team in 1996. He returned across the Pennines in 2003 to become editor of the *Gazette* in Blackpool.

- Jane Merrick, Lobby correspondent with the *Press Association* since 2001. After completing a postgraduate training course at the Centre for Journalism (Leeds) in 1998, she worked as a reporter for the *Mercury* news agency based in Liverpool and then for the *Press Association*, covering the North West patch, before moving to Westminster.

- Abul Taher, who was interviewed while news editor on *Eastern Eye* newspaper. Abul, who has an MA in Journalism Studies from Sheffield University, has also written on a freelance basis for the *Independent*, *Guardian*, and *Observer*. He has now joined the staff of the *Daily Mail*.

- Martin Wainwright, northern editor of the *Guardian*. Martin has been with the paper since 1976, having previously worked on the London *Evening Standard* and local newspapers in Bath and Bradford. He is also a frequent broadcaster.

- Brian Whittle, editor of *Cavendish Press*, a news agency based in Manchester. He started on the weekly *Harrogate Herald* at the age of 17 and went on to work for the Bradford *Telegraph and Argus*, the *Northern Echo*, the *Sun*, the *Daily Sketch*, the *Sunday People*, the *National Enquirer* and the *Daily Star* before launching his successful agency.

Another presence felt through-out this book will be that of the author. As a journalist for more than 20 years, I have first-hand experience of a range of news-papers, magazines and other media, both mainstream and alternative. As someone who teaches on vocational courses accredited by the National Council for the Training of Journalists (NCTJ) and the Broadcast Journalism Training Council (BJTC), I have first-hand experience of practical journalism training. As a long-standing member of the National Union of Journalists, I have engaged with the ethics and social role of journalism. And, as someone now employed in the university sector, I have some knowledge of the gap of under-standing that too often separates those who *study*

> **'Get it right. Get it fast. But get it right.'**
> – old Press Association motto.

of Discontent' of 1978–9, was successfully signified, not as a defence of eroded living standards and differentials, but as a callous and inhuman exercise of overweening 'trade-union power', directed against the defenceless sick, aged, dying and indeed the dead but unburied 'members of the ordinary public'. *(Hall 1982: 83)*

Viewed from this perspective, the 'news values' employed by journalists in the selection and construction of stories can be seen, not as the neutral expression of professional practice, but as ideologically loaded (Hall et al 1978: 54). Thus, for all the apparent diversity of the media, and taking into account various exceptions, the routines and practices of journalists *tend* to privi-lege the explanations of the powerful and to foreclose discussion before it strays too far beyond the boundaries of the dominant ideology (Hall et al 1978: 118).

An emphasis on the ideological content of journalism is frequently challenged for downplaying the agency of journalists and/or for failing to take account of the complex ways in which audiences may actually 'read' media texts.

Agency

Within the study of journalism, agency means the extent to which individual journalists can *make a difference* to media practices and content: 'To have agency is defined by the ability to be able to actively intervene' (Stevenson 2002: 226). To say that journalists have agency is not to deny that journalists operate in a world of constraints (see Chapter 2), but to argue that structural forces do not totally determine individuals' actions. Yet many academic critics of the media seem to allow little room for agency. Take Sparks' explanation for the 'lurid, sensational and sometimes offensive material' he finds in much of the press:

> None of these elements can be traced to the shortcomings of individuals. Newspaper proprietors may be, in the main, bullying reactionary bigots who force their editors to print politically biased material. But even if they were self-denying liberal paragons, it

media from those who *produce* media. As journalist David Walker notes: 'The academic literature of sociology, media studies or cognate disciplines nowadays goes almost entirely unread by journalists' (Walker 2000: 236–7). Another national newspaper reporter told researchers: 'The press in general does not value academic training and is fearful of being dissected' (Journalism Training Forum 2002: 46).

It is to help bridge this conceptual divide that I am adding to the growing literature on journalism – a literature too often polarised between journalists (practitioners) who feel academics have little to teach them, and academics whose focus on theory is in danger of denying journalists any degree of autonomy (or **agency**). This book makes explicit some of these different ways of exploring the principles and practices of journalism. In a dialogic approach, each chapter begins from a practitioner viewpoint but includes a parallel analysis from a more academic perspective. The practitioner perspective is in the left-hand untinted column, and the more academic treatment is in the right-hand tinted column. However, these two ways of seeing are not to be read in isolation, as each engages with the other.

Each chapter may be read in a number of ways: by reading the practioner section first, followed by the more theoretical section; by reversing the order; or by flitting between the two, following the highlighted words in the initial text to the relevant accompanying section – much in the way we might follow hyperlinks on a website. As well as providing useful practice in the journalistic art of keeping an eye on a number of things at once, this should also mean that the book will repay repeated visits.

The focus is on what might be termed the *basics* of journalism. The book does not attempt to go into too many of the specifics of, for example, being a foreign correspondent, a war correspondent, a sub, a sports reporter, a showbiz diarist, a consumer affairs editor, a motoring correspondent or most of the other specialisms that all have their own rules and folklore. Call me old-fashioned, but I believe the fundamentals of journalism must be grasped before more specialised roles can be either accomplished or understood.

would still make sense for editors to act in the same way, because that is the best business model available to them. Again, editors and journalists may well be moral defectives with no sense of their responsibility to society and to the people upon whose lives they so pruriently report. But even if they were saintly ascetics, it would still make sense for them to publish the same sorts of material, because that is what best secures the competitive position of their newspapers. *(Sparks 1999: 59)*

Little sense there of the flesh-and-blood journalists we will hear from in this book. Yet, if journalism matters – as is argued in this chapter – surely the actions of individual journalists matter too.

> **'Over the last 30 years journalism has become harder to enter, less secure, harder work and less financially rewarding – but I still love it.'**
> – radio journalist.

The experience of Edward Behr rings a bell that echoes down the years. As a young reporter, Behr went to work for the *Reuters* agency in Paris:

> In London, Agence France-Presse (AFP) correspondents rewrote Reuters' copy, as fast as they could, and the finished product ended up as part of the AFP news service. In Paris we shamelessly rewrote Agence France-Presse copy, serving it up as Reuters' fare. All over the world lesser news agencies were writing up *their* versions of Reuters' stories and serving them up as authentic Indian, Spanish, or Brazilian news agency stories. Somewhere, at the bottom of this inverted pyramid, someone was getting a story at first hand. But who was he, and how did he set about it? *(Behr 1992: 72.)*

He may not be a 'he', of course, but it is this reporter – the reporter who goes out and gets the story – who will be the focus throughout this book. Virtually anyone can cut and paste from the internet. Real reporting requires something more.

Journalism education

Many of the practices discussed here will be those of print journalism in general, and newspapers in particular, because newspaper journalism remains a good grounding for a career in TV, radio, magazine and online journalism. The practical emphasis will be on *core* journalistic skills and will reflect the priorities of the NCTJ, the BJTC, and those universities and colleges offering their own vocational training courses. But the book goes beyond practical instruction to encourage critical reflection and understanding.

There is a good deal of scepticism among journalists about the value of training. ITN political editor John Sergeant recalls spending his print journalism course 'writing fake copy for imaginary newspapers, to be judged by tutors who, we could sense, had failed in the profession' (Sergeant 2001: 130). But, disparaging though many older hands might be about training, anyone who has tried to get a job as a reporter on even the lowliest local weekly newspaper will know the value that most editors still place on new entrants having completed a bona fide journalism training course. Research suggests that 58 per cent of UK journalists have a journalism qualification, ranging from 42 per cent in magazines to 75 per cent in regional newspapers. The NCTJ accounts for almost two-thirds of the journalism qualifications held by today's journalists, with the remainder including the Periodicals Training Council (PTC), the BJTC, NVQs, in-house company schemes, and non-accredited university courses (Journalism Training Forum 2002: 34–5).

James Curran has accused media employers of wanting young journalists to be schooled in the routines of work through 'basic skills, relevant knowledge and an unquestioning attitude' – unencumbered by ideas of critical theory (Curran 2000: 42). This book is certainly aimed at supporting students and trainee journalists in the acquisition and application of reporting and writing skills to complement the other necessary elements of journalism training such as shorthand, media law, and a knowledge of public affairs. Yet, at the same time, it will introduce and engage with some of the more academic analysis that aids our understanding of how journalism works. To this end, the book is aimed at supporting *journalism studies* as well as *journalism training*. Taken together, the two elements might constitute what Michael Bromley refers to as *journalism education* (Bromley 1997: 339). By asking Why journalists do certain things – as well as the Who, What, Where, When and How – the study of journalism can offer insights to complement journalism training and encourage a questioning attitude and a more reflective practice.

While much of the material may be seen as culturally and historically specific to the UK in the 21st century, the discussion will include many points of wider relevance. Each chapter will raise questions that could form the basis of individual reflection and/or group discussion. Each chapter also suggests further reading that, together with the references listed in the extensive bibliography, will provide a wealth of stimulating material

> 'The news media avoid any discussion of media structure, leaving analysis of media ownership and advertising to the business pages and the trade press, where they are covered as issues that concern investors, not workers, consumers, or citizens.'
> – Robert McChesney.

to encourage further exploration of the issues discussed here.

The ethical dimension

There is a rapidly growing literature on the ethics of journalism, informed by ideas of right and wrong, good and bad (Harcup 2002b: 101), but you will not find a separate chapter on ethics in this book. That is not an oversight. A concern for ethical issues is not something to be compartmentalised, a curriculum item to be ticked off and conveniently forgotten. It is something with implications for *all* aspects of journalistic practice. Questions about ethical issues will therefore be raised at appropriate points throughout the text, just as ethical issues crop up throughout a journalist's working life, often when least expected.

Journalism is sometimes said to be a mirror reflecting society; on occasions, a distorting mirror. But journalism is not a simple *reflection* of everyday reality. As Walter Lippmann observed as long ago as 1922, reporting is not 'the simple recovery of obvious facts', because facts 'do not spontaneously take a shape in which they can be known. They must be given a shape by somebody' (quoted in McNair 2000: 71). That's where journalists come in. Journalism is not simply fact-gathering. It involves dealing with sources, selecting information and opinion, and telling stories – all within the framework of the constraints, routines, principles and practices discussed in the following chapters.

> 'We gentlemen or otherwise of the press may not be perfect but . . . we are now the principal source of light that exposes the corruption of unspeakable privilege to the people who pay for it.'
> – *Julie Burchill.*

Summary

Journalism is not simply another product but a process of communication, although not necessarily a one-way or linear process. Journalism is said to play a social role in informing society about itself, yet there is a gap of knowledge and understanding between vocational journalism training and academic journalism study. This book will describe the practices of practitioners while engaging with the principles that inform both practice and analysis. A number of theoretical models or concepts are introduced in this chapter.

Questions

What social role does journalism play?

What skills do journalists need?

Are journalists professionals or workers?

Why are journalists apparently so mistrusted by the public?

Why do media studies get such a bad press?

Further reading

One of the best introductions to journalism in general, and print journalism in particular, is Keeble (2001a), which combines valuable practical advice with contemporary examples and a questioning approach. Randall (2000) offers a thought-provoking introduction to the craft of journalism from the perspective of a reflective practitioner, while Bromley and O'Malley's (1997) collection of historical and contemporary accounts includes much to stimulate students, producers and consumers of journalism alike. McQuail (2000) is a comprehensive and comprehensible introduction to media and mass communication theories, including a glossary of almost 100 key concepts.

Notes

Sources for soundbites: Delane cited in Wheen 2002: xi; Chesterton 1981: 246; Stephen cited in Glover 1999: 290–91; radio journalist cited in Journalism Training Forum 2002: 57; McChesney 2000: 294–95; my emphasis; Burchill 2003.

Chapter Two

Constraints and influences on journalists

Constraints

Ownership

Routines

Audience

Advertising

Legislation

Regulation

Self-regulation

Codes of conduct

Public relations

Pseudo-events

Social composition

Socialisation

Propaganda

In the old movie *Five Star Final* a hack played by Edward G Robinson turns to his newspaper proprietor and lets him have it:

> Now you listen to me, Hinchcliffe. It'll be for the last time. I'm through with your dirty rag and I'm through with you . . . I want you to know that every human being that works for you knows what a diseased hypocrite you are. We all know what you are, but we take your money and do your work because we're afraid to starve. *(Lord and Morgan 1931)*

And with those words he rejects the **constraints** imposed on him by the paper's sensationalist plunge downmarket. He walks out and washes his hands of the whole dirty business.

Owners

Real life journalists have been known to do something similar. Sam Kiley spent 11 years as a foreign correspondent on the *Times* before resigning in 2001, exasperated by reports on the Middle East conflict being changed in line with the perceived views of the **proprietor**:

> Murdoch's executives were so scared of irritating him that, when I pulled off a little scoop by tracking, interviewing and photographing the unit in the Israeli army which killed Mohammed al-Durrah, the 12-year-old boy whose death was captured on film and became the iconic image of the conflict, I was asked to file the piece 'without mentioning the dead kid'. After that conversation, I was left wordless, so I quit. *(Kiley 2001)*

Another journalist who complained of constraints on the same newspaper was former East Asia editor Jonathan Mirsky. He says his coverage was hampered by the *Times*' desire to stay in tune with Rupert Murdoch's business interests in China, so everything was done to avoid upsetting the Chinese authorities:

> I saw the paper change from one keenly interested in reporting and analysing China to one so apprehensive that the editor spiked a piece by me on cannibalism during the Cultural Revolution . . . because he was having lunch that day at China's

> *'Those who declaim against Liberties taken by News Papers . . . know not what they say; it is this Liberty, that . . . protects all the rest.'*
> – London Evening Post, 1754.

Constraints

Journalism is not produced in a vacuum. Journalists work within a range of constraints and influences; structural factors that affect their output (McQuail 2000: 244). Media theorists argue that journalists 'have to make decisions at the centre of a field of different constraints, demands or attempted uses of power or influence' (McQuail 2000: 249). These range from legal constraints and regulatory codes of practice to the less visible influence of proprietors, organisational routines, market forces, cultural bias, patriotism, professional ethos, and a gender, racial or class imbalance in the workforce. Further constraints – time, sources, subjectivity, audience, style, advertisers – are addressed in David Randall's suggestion that every newspaper might consider publishing the following disclaimer:

> This paper, and the hundreds of thousands of words it contains, has been produced in about 15 hours by a group of fallible human beings, working out of cramped offices while trying to find out about what happened in the world from people who are sometimes reluctant to tell us and, at other times, positively obstructive. Its content has been determined by a series of subjective judgements made by reporters and executives, tempered by what they know to be the editor's, owner's and reader's prejudices. Some stories appear here without essential context as this would make them less dramatic or coherent and some of the language employed has been deliberately chosen for its emotional impact, rather than its accuracy. Some features are printed solely to attract certain advertisers. *(Randall 2000: 21.)*

Not that all influences are experienced as constraints; some pressures may be regarded as forces of liberation for journalists (McQuail 2000: 250). For example, codes of conduct laid down by regulators or trades unions may enable journalists to resist the excesses of employers or colleagues, representing 'a beacon for journalists to aim for' (Gopsill, quoted in Keeble 2001b: 15).

Journalists work in a field of conflicting loyalties, all of which have the potential to influence their work. They may feel a sense of duty towards their audience, editors, advertisers, proprietors, the

London embassy . . . Of course, the Murdochs do not need to tell their editors what to write about China on every issue; *they just know*. *(Mirsky 2001; my emphasis)*

Elsewhere in the same empire, a News Corporation executive reportedly told two journalists who lost their jobs after refusing to alter a story: 'We paid $3 billion for these TV stations. We will decide what the news is' (quoted in McChesney 2000: 275).

Andrew Neil, former editor of the *Sunday Times*, describes Murdoch's normal methods of control as rather more subtle, beginning with choosing editors 'who are generally on the same wavelength as him' (quoted in Sanders 2003: 134). He can certainly pick them, as demonstrated by the way the editorial line of all 175 Murdoch-owned newspapers on three continents just happened to agree with his own pro-war stance leading up to the 2003 conflict in Iraq (Greenslade 2003).

Murdoch has been an easy target for those who claim media owners wield too much power. But it is not only journalists taking the Murdoch shilling who feel proprietorial constraints, explicit or implicit. David Walker confesses:

> At the *Independent* I spilled much ink in editorials savaging his [Murdoch's] power and pricing strategy. But such criticism is vitiated by a lack of honesty about one's own organisation. How many *Independent* journalists, myself included, ever wrote in their own newspaper about the effects of ownership by Mirror Group Newspapers? *(Walker 2000: 241)*

The *Express* is another title that has published stories in harmony with the commercial interests of its proprietor. Owner Richard Desmond has also been accused of interfering in editorial matters by urging the inclusion of coverage critical of asylum seekers, prompting one of his business correspondents to issue a public attack on 'the continual interference of the proprietor in allegedly objective reporting' (quoted in Day 2001).

There is nothing new in media owners being accused of using *their* journalists to pursue certain agendas. It was in 1931 that Conservative party leader Stanley Baldwin launched his famous attack on newspaper proprietors:

> Their methods are direct falsehood, misrepresentation, half truths, the alteration of the speaker's meaning by

law, regulatory bodies, contacts, colleagues, fellow citizens, and to themselves and their families (Frost 2000: 61–4; Harcup 2002b: 103). Denis McQuail highlights 'the tension arising from the following oppositions at the heart of media-making':

- Constraint versus autonomy.
- Routine production versus creativity.
- Commerce versus art.
- Profit versus social purpose.

(McQuail 2000: 246.)

In Chapter 1 we heard the argument that a free press (social purpose) is impossible in a free market, because market forces (profit) work against the objective of supplying the public sphere with a reasoned discourse. But market forces are not the only pressures at work, as McQuail notes: '[The] relations between media organisations and their operating environment are governed not solely by naked market forces or political power but also by unwritten social and cultural guidelines' (McQuail 2000: 249). Even when analysed solely in economic terms, it has been pointed out that although media organisations will 'naturally gravitate towards oligopoly and monopoly market structures', if unchecked this process may have a negative impact on the journalistic product which could hit sales and advertising income (Doyle 2002: 125–6).

The constraints and influences discussed in this chapter need to be understood not as totalising systems imposing on journalists certain ways of doing things; rather they are a range of sometimes conflicting influences, some more powerful than others and some more powerful at certain times, with a *tendency* to influence journalists in certain ways. Constraints on journalists are subject to counter-pressures and can be negotiated and resisted as well as accepted.

Proprietors

Ultimately it is the owners who, 'through their wealth, determine the style of journalism we get,' argues Michael Foley (2000: 51). Media proprietors set the broad lines of policy for their organisations, and the combination of vertical and horizontal integration (synergy) may increase pressures on journalists to cross-promote other products

putting sentences apart from the context, suppression . . . What the proprietorship of these papers is aiming at is power, but power without responsibility – the prerogative of the harlot through the ages. *(Quoted in O'Malley and Soley 2000: 31)*

In 1949 Lord Beaverbrook told the Royal Commission on the Press that he ran the *Daily Express* 'merely for the purpose of making propaganda and with no other motive', and in the 1980s Robert Maxwell described the *Daily Mirror* as his personal 'megaphone' (Curran and Seaton 1997: 48 & 76).

Former *Mirror* journalist Paul Foot describes such proprietorial influence on journalism as 'absolutely insufferable'. Yet he did suffer it in the shape of Maxwell, and he managed to produce much challenging journalism in spite of it. Foot recalls how he pinned up a list of Maxwell's business friends and, whenever he was investigating one of them, made sure he had the story copper-bottomed and 'legalled' (checked by lawyers) before the subject would be approached for a comment:

> The minute you put it to him – 'is this true?' – he rings Maxwell. That happened on several occasions. So you have to have the story sewn up and prepared for when Maxwell says: 'Are you sure this is right?' *But we got most of the stuff published.*

A survey in the US found almost a third of local journalists admitting to softening the tone of a news story in line with their employer's interests, and one in five reporters had been criticised by bosses for stories damaging to their company's financial interests (Pew Research Centre 2000). In Italy, an employee of Silvio Berlusconi describes the atmosphere when the owner is also the country's Prime Minister:

> We never hear from him directly, editors don't cite his instructions. But there is a climate of self-censorship. We know we can only go so far. Lines exist and we do not cross them. *(Quoted in Carroll 2002)*

But for most journalists in most newsrooms, most of the time, proprietorial interference probably means little more than an editor's instruction to make sure you don't crop the owner's wife off a photograph or there'll be hell to pay. Many journalists go about their

> **'I did not come all this way not to interfere.'**
> – Rupert Murdoch.

or to keep their noses out of their company's business. However, it is also possible that the rise of the media conglomerate will reduce the influence of the individual 'press baron'. The situation in public service broadcasting is more complex than in commercial media, with bureaucratic and budgetary control rather than 'naked market forces'; nonetheless, public broadcasters operate in an increasingly competitive environment and so are not immune from market pressures (McQuail 2000: 259–61).

In their 'propaganda model' of how (US) media operate, Edward Herman and Noam Chomsky identify media owners as the first of five 'filters' through which the wealthy and powerful are able 'to filter out the news fit to print, marginalise dissent, and allow the government and dominant private interests to get their messages across' (Herman and Chomsky 1988: 166). The filters are:

- Wealth and concentrated ownership of dominant media firms.
- Advertising.
- Reliance on information from the powerful.
- Punitive action ('flak') against transgressors.
- Anti-communism.

(Herman and Chomsky 1988: 166–76)

This model has been dismissed by critics as a conspiracy theory, as too mechanistic, as failing to take account of resistance. Herman counters:

> [The] filters work mainly by independent action of many individuals and organisations . . . [The] propaganda model describes a decentralised and non-conspiratorial market system of control and processing . . . We never claimed that the propaganda model explained everything or that it illustrated media omnipotence and complete effectiveness in manufacturing consent. *(Herman 2000: 102–103)*

Routines

Journalists engage in routines, recurrent practices such as working to deadlines, keeping to word or time limits, ensuring that each newspaper or bulletin is exactly full, work without giving the wishes of the owner a second thought. Yet proprietors have influence not just by direct intervention or by establishing lines that will not be crossed. They set the tone, they decide which markets to target, they control editorial budgets, and they hire and fire the editors who are their representatives on Earth. Even editors' powers are constrained, as demonstrated when owners imposed a 'central subbing unit' on a group of weekly papers. Aaron Gransby, former editor of the *Harrow Observer*, explains what happened:

> The papers which came out of the unit were appalling, littered with errors and riddled with inconsistencies. No one seemed to understand the areas or the different editions . . . [The] outcome is worse newspapers, demotivated staff and a remarkable exodus of talent and experience. *(Gransby 2002)*

There are alternative models of media ownership. The publicly-owned BBC enshrines the Reithian principles of public service broadcasting (Briggs and Burke 2002: 160–3); the *Guardian* is owned by the Scott Trust, with a strict separation between financial and editorial matters (Franklin 1997: 98); and smaller-scale media may be run by ad-hoc groups, community organisations or workers' cooperatives (Harcup 1998: 106–8; Harcup 1994: 1–3). Journalists working for such media may escape the owner wishing to use them as a personal megaphone, but they cannot avoid the other constraints discussed in this chapter.

Routines

Deadlines, **routines** and the whims of the newsdesk tend to be more prevalent constraints. The constant pressure to meet deadlines – including the instant deadlines of rolling news – teaches journalists that an average story delivered on time is of more use than a perfect story that arrives late. Not that the deadline is always bad news. Many journalists welcome deadlines for providing the focus, and the adrenalin rush, necessary to get the job done.

Although the latest technology should mean that newspaper deadlines become later, in practice they have moved forward to cope with smaller staff numbers and the printing of fatter papers with ever more bulky supplements. Brian Whittle has observed

conforming to house style, making regular check calls to official sources, and covering 'diary' jobs. There is an occupational pressure on journalists to 'bow to the imperative of routine news copy production' (Manning 2001: 52). Although the unexpected may happen at any time, crises develop patterns so that, for journalists, even 'the unexpected becomes the predictable' (Curran and Seaton 1997: 276). Research has consistently found that 'content is systematically and distinctively influenced by organisational routines, practices and goals rather than either personal or ideological factors' (McQuail 2000: 244–5).

Advertisers

The interests of advertising can influence journalistic product, although such influence does not *normally* take the form of advertisers threatening to take their money elsewhere unless they receive favourable editorial coverage. Direct intervention by advertisers happens occasionally but a more prevalent influence is that the content patterns of media are matched to the consumption patterns of target audiences (McQuail 2000: 261). Commercial media operate in a 'dual product market' in which the media product sells *itself* to consumers and also sells its *audience* to advertisers (Sparks 1999: 53; Doyle 2002: 12). Mass circulation newspapers demand a mass readership for mass advertising, while the 'quality' press depend on delivering smaller target audiences for more niche advertising markets. The quest for these different audiences affects the journalism offered in such titles, as Colin Sparks notes:

> The popular press are under market pressure to try to reach the widest possible audiences, and thus must prioritise the kinds of material that will sell vast quantities. Quality newspapers are much less interested in maximising circulation, and are concerned to prioritise the kinds of material that will sell to particular kinds of people . . . The products that serve the richest audience are approximations to the newspaper of democratic mythology. The others are quite different commodities. *(Sparks 1999: 53 and 59)*

this trend from the perspective of a news agency selling news stories to the national newspapers:

> Now most pages are full by three o'clock in the afternoon. When I worked on the old broadsheet *Sun* in Manchester in the late sixties you could get a story in at half-past-three in the morning. You couldn't do that now.

Time is at even more of a premium on television, as Lindsay Eastwood discovered when she switched from newspapers to become a TV reporter:

> It takes so long to do everything. You've got to set up the story and organise camera crews, and it takes an hour to film a minute's worth of stuff. There's just so much faffing about and not actually doing the journalism, which I find very frustrating. You're still getting a shot of the house while all the newspaper reporters are knocking on the doors of neighbours, and I'm saying to the cameraman 'Come *on*'. Then you've got to get back to the studio to cut it before deadline.

Faced with a constant shortage of time, journalists make many decisions instantly, almost subliminally. A major regional evening paper might receive hundreds of news releases in a day, arriving by post, fax and email. News editor David Helliwell says most will receive just one or two seconds' attention before a journalist decides if it might make something. If not, it will be 'filed' in the bin. Spending five minutes pondering each one would bring the routines of the newsroom grinding to a halt.

Time constraints can result in inaccurate journalism, believes Martin Wainwright of the *Guardian*:

> You're doing stuff so quickly you don't have time to be absolutely sure about things, and more importantly the people you're talking to don't. So they will say things they believe to be true, about a developing situation, which then turn out not to be. It happened in the [Selby] rail crash when for a nearly a week everybody said 13 people had been killed. The police said 13 people had been killed. In fact it now turns out to be ten. A central fact of the whole story was wrong for nearly a week, and somebody coming across a newspaper from that week and not checking a week later will not get the truth.

Lack of time may also lead to journalists falling short of professional standards, as Michael Foley

Public relations

At the heart of public relations, according to Daniel Boorstin, is the 'pseudo-event', which he defined in the early 1960s as something planned rather than spontaneous, arranged for the convenience of the media, with an ambiguous relation to 'reality' (Boorstin 1963: 22–3). For Boorstin, the pseudo-event confuses the roles of actor and audience, object and subject. For example, a politician can *compose* a news story by 'releasing' a speech to the media, while a journalist can *generate* an event by asking an inflammatory question (Boorstin 1963: 40).

Since Boorstin described the rise of the pseudo-event, 'public relations staffs have expanded while journalists have been shrinking, creating news media's greater editorial reliance on press officers' (Franklin 1997: 19). Organisations ranging from local charities to multinational corporations now employ press officers who supply journalists with a stream of potential stories, comments and fillers. Press officers do not just supply information, they also play a role in controlling access. Writing in the context of music journalism, Eamonn Forde argues that the industry press officer has become increasingly powerful as a 'buffer zone', gatekeeping access to artists and screening journalists along the lines of 'the Hollywood approach to press management' (Forde 2001: 36–8). For Bob Franklin, the growing power and journalistic reliance on press officers comes at a price: 'they are not detached observers and reporters of the world, but hired prize fighters, advocates and defenders of whichever sectional interest employs them' (Franklin 1997: 20).

Such 'hired prize fighters' in the political arena – from Sir Bernard Ingham to Alastair Campbell – have been key to the process described as 'the packaging of politics' (Franklin 1994: 226). Former BBC Lobby correspondent Nick Jones is uncomfortable with political reporting based on unattributable conversations with politicians or advisers, and he has been ridiculed by Campbell himself as 'a nutter and obsessed with spin' (Gopsill 2001). But David Walker is critical of the self-conception of Jones and other Westminster journalists:

> They believe there is a single truth within and about politics. Battles over it form the staple of political reporting. Victory in this struggle for the single truth gives them their occupational justification. *(Walker 2002: 103)*

notes: 'Much that passes for unethical behaviour takes place because too few journalists are taking too many decisions quickly and without time to reflect. This is because proprietors have not invested in journalism' (Foley 2000: 49–50). Maybe. But the UK national paper enjoying some of the heaviest editorial investment is the *Daily Mail*, hardly a stranger to complaints of unethical behaviour or inaccurate reporting.

Even on the squeaky-clean *Guardian*, reporters can be constrained by being sent out when somebody else has apparently decided in advance what the story is. Wainwright again:

> During the foot and mouth crisis [of 2001] the newsdesk said to me: 'Can you go shopping and see the meat panic? And we do *want* a meat panic.' You're always coming up against that kind of pressure. It's a really pernicious aspect of modern journalism, that they don't trust people like myself who are here. They think they know what the story is because they've read it in the *Daily Mail* or heard it on the *Today* programme.

'A solicitor's letter produces a spectacular effect in a newspaper office – editors put work aside, 'executives' are summoned, anxious conferences convened.'
– Alan Watkins.

He adds that reporters sometimes feel pressure to 'deliver the goods' simply because the routines of page planning mean that a large space has been allocated in expectation of a major story:

> A colleague had it with drug dealers. The story collapsed but they [still] wanted a big thing about drug dealers. The way they'd designed it and thought about it, it had to be *big*. Lots of journalists I know complain about this and say 'they're not really interested in how *I* am seeing this'.

It is not unknown for a newsdesk to put pressure on a reporter to set aside personal or ethical considerations in the pursuit of a story. Even in organisations publicly committed to following ethical codes of practice, there may be an atmosphere of 'if you haven't got the story, don't bother coming back'. For example, journalists returning empty handed from 'death knocks' – calls on the recently bereaved to pick up quotes and pictures – may be ridiculed for being insufficiently aggressive (Harcup 2002b: 110). A sports reporter on the *Stoke Sentinel* lost his job after

Walker goes on to claim that this 'anti-ideological' ideology of political reporters – the battle for truth between journalists and spin doctors – takes no account of the possibility that media organisations might also be political players in their own right: 'the power held by journalists and the media organisations for which they work is unperceived or assumed away' (Walker 2002: 108).

Social environment

It has been argued that the news changes little when individual journalists are changed (Golding and Elliot, cited in Curran and Seaton 1997: 277). New recruits to journalism go through a process of 'assimilation of newsroom mythology and socialisation', and those who survive learn 'a way of doing things' that results in 'a conformity of production and selection' (Harrison 2000: 112–13). This professionalism 'can only be recognised by fellow professionals' (McQuail 2000: 257). Robert McChesney argues that most journalists are socialised into internalising their role as 'stenographers for official sources', with the result that: 'When a journalist steps outside this range of official debate to provide alternative perspectives, or to raise issues those in power prefer not to discuss, *this is no longer professional*' (McChesney 2002: 17; my emphasis).

However, the extent to which journalism is constrained in this way is questioned by Greg McLaughlin's study of reporting the Kosovo conflict. He found that, while many reporters may have internalised Nato's frame of reference, this did not entirely determine how stories were presented, and 'it would be wrong to dismiss as irrelevant the resistance of some journalists to Nato spin control' (McLaughlin 2002a: 258). Paul Manning similarly warns of downplaying agency:

> [There] is a danger that in envisaging the practice of news journalism as a production process, shaped by bureaucratic routines and organisational imperatives, we underestimate the extent to which particular journalists *do* make a difference. (Manning 2001: 53; emphasis in original)

refusing to seek an interview with one of his contacts whose son had died (Morgan 1999).

Audience

Journalists often have little direct experience of how audiences consume their work. BBC foreign correspondent David Shukman was invited to join a group of postal workers viewing two of his TV news reports about Angola. The stories – one about landmines and the other about corruption – were 'understood' by the viewers on one level, but only as more-or-less random happenings in a distant land. 'I never know which country is which,' said one of the group. Another added: 'It's in one ear and out the other' (Shukman 2000). In discussion, they were asked if they felt indirectly involved in the Angolan conflict; for example, by buying petrol or diamonds that originated there, thereby aiding one side or the other. Suddenly they engaged with the news stories on a different, more personal level, as Shukman notes:

> [It] had taken talk of the possible connections with Britain to raise real concern . . . The discussion had come alive. These were people who could follow the argument and did not want to be short-changed or patronised . . . For this group, foreign news, not always the favourite of the newsrooms, was becoming stimulating. *(Shukman 2000)*

His experience is interesting, given the tendency of some journalists to dismiss their audience as stupid (McQuail 2000: 263). In a survey of US journalists, three-quarters of broadcast reporters said that newsworthy stories were sometimes or often ignored because they were regarded as 'too complicated for the average person', a factor cited by just under half the print journalists. Almost eight in ten said they at least sometimes ignored stories that the audience might regard as 'important but dull' (Pew Research Centre 2000). In the UK, broadcast journalists reported a large turn-off factor during the 2001 general election and newspaper editors complained that sales went down whenever they put

> **'Forty years experience of "press self-regulation" demonstrates only that the very concept is an oxymoron.'**
> *– Geoffrey Robertson QC.*

If agency is a crucial consideration when discussing constraints, so too is the extent to which the social composition of the workforce influences journalistic practice. Anne Perkins asserts that, because relatively few women rise to the most senior editorial positions, 'a distorted image of women's lives protrudes from the newsstands' (Perkins 2001). But this assumption is challenged by Karen Ross, who studied women journalists in the UK:

> Gender *alone* will not make a difference in changing the culture of newsrooms or in the type of news produced, inasmuch as a journalist's sex is no guarantee that she or he will either embrace sentiments that privilege equality or hold specific values and beliefs that promote a more equitable and non-oppressive practice.' *(Ross 2001: 542; my emphasis)*

Similarly, it may indeed be 'shameful' that journalists – not to mention journalism professors – are overwhelmingly white, but can we assume that journalistic practice would be significantly altered merely by the presence of more black journalists? Or more journalists from working class backgrounds? Research is inconclusive but some studies suggest that journalists owe more of their relevant attitudes and tendencies to 'socialisation from the immediate work environment' than to their personal or social backgrounds (McQuail 2000: 267–9).

Nick Stevenson sounds a cautionary note about the tendency of media theorists to 'overstate the incorporating power of ideology' (Stevenson 2002: 46). Questioning assumptions that the social background of journalists leads automatically to a middle class perspective in their output, he argues not that class composition has *no* influence, but that there are ideological divisions and conflicts *within* classes, limiting the degree of 'ideological closure' achieved by the structural dominance of journalism by white middle class graduates (Stevenson 2002: 33). The prevailing atmosphere in such newsrooms, the extent to which dissent can survive and journalists have ideological room to breathe, cannot be divorced from the existence or otherwise of an effective collective forum, argues Paul Foot in this chapter. His point is

election news on their front page. 'People are just not interested,' said David Yelland of the *Sun* (Tomlin and Morgan 2001).

A study of UK television documentaries at the beginning of the 21st century found that in-depth factual coverage of developing countries had been replaced by holiday shows, travel challenges and docu-soaps in the pursuit of higher ratings (3WE 2002). As Charles Tremayne, controller of factual programmes at Granada Television, said in 2000: 'We're past the days of giving audiences what they should have – now it's all about what they want' (quoted in Philo 2002: 175).

Every now and then journalists will receive injunctions from on high to produce more human interest stories, based on the findings of surveys or focus groups. In the mid-nineties, for example, the *Yorkshire Evening Post* had a 'reader project' that for a while resulted in a 'softer' news focus, as David Helliwell recalls: 'It was trying to get away from the old council meeting style of reporting and to do something that was perceived as being more interesting, particularly to the newspaper-buying female public.' It wasn't a success and the paper quickly returned to a harder news agenda, but without losing all of its new-found interest in 'lifestyle' issues. This supposed 'feminisation' of journalism has been widespread as media compete for the female audience (Ross 2001: 541). As provincial newspaper editor Mike Glover notes:

> There have been trends and fads which have been absorbed over the years. The use of design and more lifestyle content have addressed the increased influence of women particularly in purchasing decisions. *(Glover 1998: 118)*

At the same time as (supposedly) attracting new readers, such lifestyle copy – entertainment, holidays, health, consumer stories and so on – has been used to attract additional **advertisers**.

Journalists are thought of as the active ones in the relationship with their audience, but audiences are not always passive. Take the reaction to the *Sun* front-page of April 19 1989, concerning the Hillsborough football disaster in which 95 Liverpool fans died. Under the banner headline THE TRUTH, the paper reported anonymous police officers accusing 'drunken

echoed by McChesney, who points out that rocking the boat can be a risky business for journalists. Like Foot, he advocates 'strong, progressive unions' as a bulwark to defend journalistic integrity against commercial pressures (McChesney 2000: 61 & 301–4).

Liverpool fans' of robbing the dead and attacking rescue workers. The reaction on Merseyside was based on the fact that so many people knew – via family, friends or personal experience – a different version of 'the truth'. Anger erupted on a *Radio Merseyside* phone-in, local newsagents put the paper under the counter or refused to stock it at all, and a Granada TV news crew turned up at a shopping precinct just in time to film people burning copies of the offending *Sun* (Chippindale and Horrie 1992: 286–9; Pilger 1998: 445–8). There was nothing passive about this particular audience:

> All over the city copies of the paper were being ripped up, trampled and spat upon. People carrying it in the street found it snatched out of their hands and torn to shreds in front of them; the paper entirely disappeared from Ford's plant at Halewood and dozens of landlords banned it from their premises . . . *Sun* readers in Liverpool had voted spontaneously with their feet and sales of the paper had collapsed . . . From sales before the disaster of 524,000 copies a day, the paper had crashed to 320,000 – a loss of 204,000, or 38.9 per cent. *(Chippindale and Horrie 1992: 289–92).*

The strength of reaction is notable precisely because it was so unusual. Slightly more frequent are audiences becoming volatile on a smaller, localised, temporary scale. For example, thousands of copies of a weekly paper in the small Yorkshire town of Morley were withdrawn from sale after readers reacted to anti-gay quotes in a front page story (Hold The Front Page 2002; PCC 2002b: 24).

Hostile audience reaction can also act as a potential constraint on *individual* journalists. The local newspaper reporter who gets something wrong – the spelling of a street name, the title of a local dignitary – is likely to get calls or letters from irate readers and will learn not to make that mistake again. The trickle of readers' letters can on occasion become a flood. Within a couple of days of questioning the behaviour of the mother of a murdered child, *Guardian* columnist Charlotte Raven received over 200 complaints (Mayes

> **'If it has fallen to my destiny to start a fight to cut out the cancer of bent and twisted journalism in our country with the simple sword of truth and the trusty shield of British fair play, so be it.'**
> – Jonathan Aitken, launching his ill-fated libel action.

2001b). That pales in comparison with the 2,000-plus emails received by her colleague Seumas Milne after he criticised US foreign policy in the wake of the attacks on the World Trade Centre (Mayes 2001a). Faced with such a barrage, laced with personal abuse and the occasional threat, it would be surprising if some journalists were not tempted to play safe in the future.

The Law

Playing safe may also seem an attractive option for journalists who come up against the power of the state, whether in the shape of moves to 'license' journalists, prosecutions for 'terrorist' reporting (Beaumont 2001), or good old-fashioned 'police brutality' (Covell 2001). The Taliban government even reportedly offered a £30,000 bounty to anyone killing a western journalist during the US bombing of Afghanistan (Traynor 2001).

But it is not only in far away countries, nor in such extreme ways, that the state acts as a constraint on journalists. We speak of enjoying a 'free press' in the UK, yet there are 50 to 60 laws restricting journalists' activities (see Box 2.1).

Viewers of TV news are given a clue about legal constraints whenever they see a reporter standing outside a court building, telling us about a brief hearing in which somebody has made their first appearance in the dock, ending with the stock phrase: 'Reporting restrictions were not lifted.' What restrictions? Those contained in the Magistrates' Courts Act 1980, limiting (with very few exceptions) reports of preliminary court hearings to ten points that should be committed to memory by every trainee journalist:

- The name of the court, and the names of the magistrates.

- Names, addresses, and occupations of the parties and witnesses, ages of the accused and witnesses.

- The offence(s), or a summary of them, with which the accused is or are charged.

- Names of counsel and solicitors in the proceedings.

- Any decision of the court to commit the accused, or any of the accused, for trial, and any decision on the disposal of the case of any accused not committed.

- Where the court commits the accused for trial, the charge or charges, or a summary of them, on which he or she is committed and the court to which they are committed.

- Where proceedings are adjourned, the date and place to which they are adjourned.

- Any arrangements for bail, including conditions, but not reasons for opposing bail.

- Whether Legal Aid was granted.

- Any decision of the court to lift, or not to lift, these reporting restrictions.

(Welsh and Greenwood 2001: 39)

Given the meagre fare offered above, it is remarkable how reports of high profile court appearances, lasting only a few minutes, are embellished. Extra information often includes the accused's clothing, facial expression and tone of voice, or the presence of the victim's weeping relatives in the public gallery. Jane Colston points out that, because Section 8 of the Magistrates Court Act 1980 applies only to reports of the proceedings themselves, it would not be a breach to say, for example, that large crowds assembled *outside* the courthouse (Colston 2002: 149). But what about reporting that the accused travelled in an armed convoy, amid tight security, with police marksmen on the roof of the court building? Does that not imply that the defendant is extremely dangerous and, therefore, probably guilty?

Journalists frequently push against legal constraints, stretching the boundaries of what they might report – *a little*. They usually get away with it. Sometimes, however, there are spectacular pratfalls. When the *Sunday Mirror* published an emotional interview with a victim's father while the jury in a high profile assault trial was still considering its verdicts, the case was immediately halted. The paper was fined £75,000 for contempt of court and ordered to pay costs of £130,000. Two lawyers were dismissed and the editor resigned (Media Lawyer 2002: 19–20; Hall 2002). Not a good day at the office. Journalists sometimes challenge the courts' interpretation of the law in a more formal manner. The journalists' trade rag *Press Gazette* frequently cites cases of reporters persuading

courts to lift orders banning publication of defendants' identities and other information that, arguably, should be in the public domain (*Press Gazette* 2002 and 2000a).

Laws that act as a constraint on journalists in England and Wales are listed in Box 2.1. The law in Northern Ireland is broadly similar to that in England and Wales, but Scotland has its own legal system (see Bonnington et al 2000, as recommended by Welsh and Greenwood 2001: 435).

Not even included in Box 2.1 is breach of confidence, based on common law rather than statute, which has been described by lawyer Joanna Ludlam as 'one of the most significant fetters on freedom of expression in the media' (Ludlam 2002: 89). Journalists have come up against this with increasing frequency in recent years, as governments, employers and celebrities alike have obtained injunctions preventing the media reporting 'confidential' information supplied by spies, employees, and even spouses or ex-lovers (Welsh and Greenwood 2001: 261–79 and 387–410; Ludlam 2002: 89–103; Grundberg 2002: 114–30).

The use of injunctions citing breach of confidence – by those who can afford to go to court – has drawn public attention to the issue of 'privacy'. Before the Human Rights Act 1998 (which became law in October 2000) there was no specific legal right to privacy in the UK. The Act incorporates the European Convention on Human Rights, Article 8 of which gives everyone 'the right to respect for his private and family life, his home and his correspondence'. But actions under Article 8 are weighed by the courts against the journalist's defence, enshrined in Article 10, that 'everyone has the right to freedom of expression' (Welsh and Greenwood 2001: 371). Courtroom battles between those citing Articles 8 and 10 are likely to be a recurring scene, with many 'victims' of the tabloids preferring to rush straight to the courts rather than trust the more sedate inquiries of the Press Complaints Commission (see below).

Apart from breach of confidence, the other main legal weapon in the hands of those with money is the law of libel. Ever-present during a journalist's working life is the possibility of being sued for libel because of defaming somebody. The risk is lower than it might be because potential litigants are put off by the horrendous costs involved, but it would be easier to avoid if there were a hard and fast rule of what defamation is.

Box 2.1 *Constraints*

Legislation that restricts how journalists in England and Wales may *gather* information, what information they may have *access* to, and what may be *published*.

Access to Justice Act 1999
Administration of Justice Act 1960
Adoption of Children Act 2002
Anti-Terrorism, Crime and Security Act 2001
Broadcasting Act 1990
Broadcasting Act 1996
Children Act 1989
Children and Young Persons Act 1933
Communications Act 2003
Contempt of Court Act 1981
Copyright, Designs and Patents Act 1988
Courts Act 2003
Crime and Disorder Act 1998
Crime (Sentences) Act 1997
Criminal Justice Act 1925
Criminal Justice Act 1987
Criminal Justice Act 1991
Criminal Justice Act 2003
Criminal Justice and Public Order Act 1994
Criminal Procedure and Investigations Act 1996
Data Protection Act 1998
Defamation Act 1952
Defamation Act 1996
Disability Discrimination Act 1995
Domestic and Appellate Proceedings (Restriction of
    Publicity) Act 1968
Employment Tribunals Act 1996
Family Law Act 1986
Financial Services and Markets Act 2000
Freedom of Information Act 2000
Human Rights Act 1998
Interception of Communications Act 1985

Judicial Proceedings (Regulation of Reports) Act 1926
Libel Act 1843
Local Government (Access to Information) Act 1985
Local Government Act 2000
Magistrates Courts Act 1980
Obscene Publications Act 1959
Obscene Publications Act 1964
Official Secrets Act 1911
Official Secrets Act 1989
Planning (Hazardous Substances) Act 1990
Planning (Listed Buildings and Conservation Areas)
    Act 1990
Police Act 1997
Police and Criminal Evidence Act 1984
Police Reform Act 2002
Political Parties, Elections and Referendums Act 2000
Proceeds of Crime Act 2002
Protection from Harassment Act 1997
Public Bodies (Admission to Meetings) Act 1960
Public Order Act 1986
Regulation of Investigatory Powers Act 2000
Rehabilitation of Offenders Act 1974
Representation of the People Act 1983
Representation of the People Act 2000
Sexual Offences (Amendment) Act 1976
Sexual Offences (Amendment) Act 1992
Sexual Offences Act 2003
Terrorism Act 2000
Trade Union Reform and Employment Rights Act 1993
Treason Felony Act 1848
Wireless Telegraphy Act 1949
Youth Justice and Criminal Evidence Act 1999

(Sources: Crone 2002; Welsh and Greenwood 2001, 2003; Addicott 2002; plus *Media Lawyer* No 37, Jan/Feb 2002, No 33, May/June 2001, and No 43, Jan/Feb 2003)

According to the courts, a statement is defamatory if it tends to expose someone to hatred, ridicule or contempt; if it causes someone to be shunned or avoided; if it causes someone to be lowered in the estimation of other people; if it disparages someone in their business or profession. The statement may not actually *have* such effects, only a tendency towards them in the eyes of a 'reasonable man' (Welsh and Greenwood 2001: 186).

> '*If one journalist betrays a source, others will be less willing to come forward in the future.*'
> – *Bill Goodwin.*

Considering the above definition, much of the work of journalists could be considered as defamatory were it not for the defences offered in law. The main ones are:

- Justification (proving that the report is true).
- Fair comment (an honest opinion, based on facts, without malice).
- Privilege (the right to fairly report parliament, council meetings, court cases and certain other proceedings affording either absolute or qualified privilege).

(Welsh and Greenwood 2001: 211–39)

Despite these defences, the libel courts are notoriously dangerous ground for journalists, and many news organisations err on the side of caution, settling out-of-court rather than risking huge damages in court. The net result is what has been referred to as a 'chilling' effect, whereby journalists avoid certain subjects or litigious individuals (Welsh and Greenwood 2001: 183; Dodson 2001). Robert Maxwell was one of the quickest on the draw when it came to issuing writs against anyone probing his business affairs, and he succeeded in preventing most – but not all – journalists from exposing his methods during his lifetime (Spark 1999: 147). Other powerful figures to make use of the law of libel against inquisitive journalists, only to end up being discredited, were Conservative politicians Jeffrey Archer, Jonathan Aitken and Neil Hamilton (Kelso 2001). Journalists cannot guarantee they will never be dragged through the courts by the rich and powerful, but Francis Wheen suggests a simple way of minimising the risk when he says: 'I don't like to go into print without checking my facts' (Wheen 2002: xi).

Sometimes journalists find themselves in court not because somebody wants to extract money or an apology, but because somebody wants to know the identity of a confidential source of information. That's what happened to Bill Goodwin after he took a phone call just three months into his first job as a trainee reporter with *The Engineer* magazine. A source told him about a company in financial difficulties. He called the firm for a response and the reply was a faxed injunction ordering the magazine not to publish anything about the company. Two days later he was in court facing an order to disclose the identity of his source or be sent to prison (Goodwin 1996).

Goodwin refused, citing Clause 7 of the NUJ Code of Conduct: 'A journalist shall protect confidential sources of information' (see Appendix One). Over the next seven years the case went before a succession of courts before he won at the European Court of Human Rights, which ruled in 1996 that an order to disclose a source could not be compatible with Article 10 of the European Convention on Human Rights unless there was an overriding requirement in the public interest (Welsh and Greenwood 2001: 286).

The Goodwin case is only one of the most celebrated such battles. Another journalist who defied the threat of imprisonment was the *Observer*'s Martin Bright, who had reported allegations by former MI5 officer David Shayler (himself later jailed) about a plot to assassinate Libyan leader Colonel Gaddafi. The police, who were already pursuing Shayler, demanded that Bright hand over his notebooks, copies of emails, dates of meetings with the ex-MI5 man, and details of any financial transactions. Bright said at the time:

> I wrote about alleged crimes by agents of the state, but instead of investigating a plot to kill a foreign leader, this government has chosen to attack the liberty of the press. No journalist can genuinely claim to represent the public interest if the police have access to everything they do. We will never know how many whistleblowers are silenced by the treatment of people like David Shayler. But as soon as journalists start handing over their notes no one will speak out.
> *(Bright 2000)*

Rejecting the police application, Lord Justice Judge warned against the dangers of stifling 'effective investigative journalism' by seizing journalists' working papers without 'compelling evidence' that such a move would be in the public interest (Welsh and Greenwood 2001: 284). Such cases will continue to be fought on their individual merits as journalists resist attempts to identify confidential sources and/or to seize film and photographs. Meanwhile, the safest way for journalists to be given leaked information remains the unmarked photocopy in a plain brown envelope delivered anonymously in the dead of night; nobody can reveal the identity of a source they do not know.

Before we leave the state, we should pause to consider the Defence, Press and Broadcasting Advisory Committee. That's where Whitehall mandarins meet representatives of the UK media, under the watchful eye of a Rear Admiral, and agree to restrain coverage of sensitive military or security issues. From time to time members of the committee will stir from their Earl Grey tea and cucumber sandwiches to issue a Defence Advisory Notice (better known as a D-Notice) requesting that some matter be ignored or played down. Entirely voluntary on the part of the media, it operates as 'an unofficial system of censorship involving public officials and senior media executives' (Curran and Seaton 1997: 367). In these days of so-called 'open government', the committee has its own website: www.dnotice.org.uk. D-Notices are a form of *self-censorship*; not to be confused with *self-regulation*, by which is meant the Press Complaints Commission (PCC).

Regulation and self-regulation

The PCC was set up by the newspaper industry itself to ward off statutory regulation. A voluntary arrangement with no powers to punish those who transgress its Code of Practice, the PCC operates by a system of 'customer complaints' (Harcup 2002b: 104). But only a tiny number of complaints are ever adjudicated. Of the 3,033 received in the year 2001 just 19 were upheld – a success rate significantly below one per cent (PCC 2002a; also see O'Malley 2002). The following year saw 2,630 complaints of which just 17 were upheld (PCC 2003). With the PCC, comments Catherine Bennett, 'we get all the benefits of a Code of Practice, with none of the burden of enforcement' (Bennett

2001). Yet, despite its toothlessness, the PCC does act as some kind of constraint on the activities of journalists. *Sun* editor Rebekah Wade told a committee of MPs in 2003 that the PCC had 'changed the culture in every newsroom in the land' (quoted in Rose 2003). Editors have no desire to be embarrassed by PCC rulings – which they agree to publish – and will not look favourably on journalists who attract too many complaints. Newspaper journalists as a whole, and those on tabloids in particular, also know that a recurrence of press 'excesses' – such as the perceived harassment of Princess Diana – may result in more stringent state regulation.

In contrast to the cosiness of newspaper and magazine 'self-regulation', broadcasters face the more serious business of *statutory regulation*, whereby misdemeanours can be punished with fines and even the withdrawal of licences. Lindsay Eastwood noticed the difference in regulatory regimes as soon as she left newspapers for television:

> TV is much stricter on things like intrusion, and taste and decency. You can't have people saying 'God' or 'Jesus Christ' in a vox pop, because if one person complains and it's upheld, it counts. They are quite careful at *Calendar* not to upset people, whereas newspapers are not bothered so much about flak. I think the difference is you can lose your licence with TV. They can shut you down, so there's a bit more at stake really.

Public relations

'It's now a very good day to get out anything we want to bury,' wrote government spin doctor Jo Moore in her notorious email sent at 2.55pm on September 11 2001, within an hour of the second hijacked plane hitting New York's World Trade Centre. Her memo, to senior colleagues in the Department for Transport, Local Government and the Regions, continued with the helpful suggestion: 'Councillors' expenses?' (Clement and Grice 2001). The department's press office duly rushed out news release number 388 concerning a new system of allowances for local councillors (DTLR 2001). As predicted, the councillors' expenses story was ignored by a media concentrating on recounting the rather greater horrors of the twin towers.

When her unwise words were leaked Jo Moore became something of a hate figure and subsequently lost her post. But wasn't she only doing her job? Isn't the whole **public relations** (PR) industry designed not simply to promote 'good news' about clients but to bury 'bad news'? Not according to the Institute of Public Relations, which promotes ethical practice and exhorts its members to 'deal honestly and fairly in business with employers, employees, clients, fellow professionals, other professions and the public' (www.ipr.org.uk). But Jo Moore was neither the first nor the last press officer to time the release of information to minimise coverage; Friday afternoons and the beginning of holiday periods seem to be particularly popular times. Others prefer disguising bad news with apparently good news, so that job losses become a footnote in a piece of puffery about an apparent expansion.

It might seem odd to discuss PR within a chapter concerned largely with *constraints* on journalists. After all, the work of the PR industry is visible in the media every day, and some short-staffed newspapers are only too grateful to be stuffed full of scarcely-rewritten news releases. But PR is not just about *releasing* information, it is also about *controlling* information. And controlling *access*. Many journalists have an ambivalent attitude to PR. On the one hand they maintain they are too hard-bitten to listen to PR departments, yet they are also quick to moan about bullying by political spin doctors, demands for copy-approval on behalf of celebs, or the freezing out of journalists who don't comply (Morgan 2002b; Helmore 2001; O'Sullivan 2001). Perhaps an ambivalent attitude is only natural. Although many press officers have good working relationships with journalists, based on trust and even grudging respect, the fact remains that they are *working to different agendas*.

Colleagues

If journalists have a social role in informing society about itself, does it matter that journalists are not particularly representative of that society? Jon Grubb, deputy editor of the *Nottingham Evening Post*, believes so:

> 'It's now a very good day to get out anything we want to bury.'
> – Jo Moore, September 11 2001.

For too long newspaper editorial departments have been dominated by white, middle-class staff. If newspapers want to truly connect with the community they must strive to better reflect the multi-cultural nature of their audience. This issue is not just about colour. We need more journalists with working-class roots. Until papers can understand the problems, hopes, aspirations and fears of all sections of the community they will find it difficult to win their hearts and minds. (*Quoted in Keeble 2001b: 143*)

Not just newspapers. Witness the prevalence of Oxbridge types at the BBC, particularly on more prestigious programmes such as *Newsnight*. Research suggests that the **social environment** in which journalists work 'does not reflect the diversity of the UK population, either in terms of ethnic mix or social background': 96 per cent of journalists are white and very few are from working class backgrounds (Journalism Training Forum 2002: 8). Journalism professor Peter Cole calls it 'shameful and disgraceful' that local papers in places such as Bradford, Oldham and Burnley have so few black journalists (Slattery 2002); and some training courses are now including race awareness workshops for journalists (Franceskides 2002). Ethnic minority journalists are sometimes seen as *representatives* of the entire black community, or the Muslim community; alternatively, they may be warned against dwelling on race (Younge 2002). White British journalists, in contrast, are not expected to represent 'the white community' – even assuming there is such an entity – or warned off 'white issues'.

As well as being very white, newsrooms had a rather blokey atmosphere in the past. However, the increasing proportion of women entering journalism in recent years has resulted in a more or less even split between the sexes (Journalism Training Forum 2002: 4). There may be more women in journalism but they are not always in the most powerful positions, as Anne Perkins notes: 'The higher up a newspaper hierarchy you travel, the fewer women there are to be seen' (Perkins 2001). Even a female national newspaper editor told researchers that 'much of journalism is still a boys' club, with women struggling for professional acceptance' (quoted in Journalism Training Forum 2002: 60).

Journalists are recruited from an even more limited pool now that so many have to pay for postgraduate journalism courses on top of normal undergraduate debt. Journalism can look like a closed door to 'outsiders', as only 30 per cent of journalists get their first job after seeing it publicly advertised; others approach employers on spec, are offered a job after work experience, or hear about vacancies through a range of informal means (Journalism Training Forum 2002: 33). Abul Taher, an ambitious young journalist, observes: 'The nationals recruit through their own network of contacts which makes it harder for some-one like me who is not very well connected'. In the words of a Fleet Street sub:

> Newspaper journalism fosters a culture of the clique. Anyone who does not fit into the prevailing clique's clearly defined pigeon-holes tends to be viewed with suspicion and ends up being marginalised or forced out. People may be tolerated for their usefulness, but few are promoted to the hierarchy, which remains a club that promotes only those who they recognise as younger versions of themselves. *(Quoted in Journalism Training Forum 2002: 60)*

The extent to which journalists internalise pre-vailing attitudes, and reproduce them in their work, is a matter for debate among academics and among some within journalism itself. The issue is at its most acute during times of conflict. Commenting on his own reporting of the Falklands war, Max Hastings – who went on to edit the *Daily Telegraph* and *Evening Standard* – quoted approvingly the words of his journalist father:

> When one's nation is at war, reporting becomes an extension of the war effort. Objectivity only comes back into fashion when the black-out comes down. *(Quoted in Williams 1992: 156)*

Veteran *CBS* news anchor Don Rather admitted that the work of US journalists – himself included – was compromised by 'patriotism run amok' in the months after the attack on the World Trade Centre on September 11 2001, preventing many from putting 'the toughest of the tough' questions to political and military leaders:

> It starts with a feeling of patriotism within oneself. It carries through with a certain knowledge that the country as a whole . . . felt and continues to feel this surge of patriotism within themselves. And one finds oneself saying: 'I know the right question, but you know what? This is not exactly the right time to ask it'. *(Quoted in Engel 2002)*

It is not necessarily a conscious process. While reporting Nato briefings in Brussels during the bombing of Serbia in 1999, *Sky News* correspondent Jake Lynch felt that most reporters had accepted the US/UK frame of reference:

> Journalists were prepared to accept the fundamental framing of the conflict which Nato was conveying, namely that this was all the fault of Slobodan Milosevic . . . [That] was *internalised*, unexamined, by journalists . . . *(Quoted in McLaughlin 2002a: 258, my emphasis.)*

Independent reporter Robert Fisk was rather more blunt about his colleagues' shortcomings: 'Most of the journalists at the Nato briefings were sheep. Baaaa Baaaaa! That's all it was.' In turn, 'mavericks' such as Fisk have been accused by fellow journalists of being too concerned with 'making tendentious political points' (quoted in McLaughlin 2002a: 263–4).

In war or peace, journalist colleagues can constrain each other by creating an atmosphere of conformity in which anyone who challenges the norm is ridiculed, forced out, marginalised or tolerated as the resident Jeremiah. But colleagues can also support individuals, whether those like Bill Goodwin threatened with the power of the state, or those facing pressure to act in unethical ways. That's why Paul Foot urges journalists to band together in their trade union rather than stand alone. 'You can only have an alternative to the control of the editorial hierarchy and the proprietor if you've got the discipline of being in a collective body behind you,' he argues.

Summary

The work of journalists is influenced by a range of structural factors such as legal constraints, regulatory regimes, the system of media ownership, organisational routines, shortage of time, market forces, advertising considerations, cultural bias, patriotism, professional ethos, and a gender, racial or class imbalance in the workforce. Constraints and conflicting loyalties lead to claims that individuals have little influence on journalistic output, while others argue that constraints can be resisted or negotiated. Influences such as codes of conduct also have the potential to liberate rather than constrain.

Questions

Would journalism in the UK be very different if Rupert Murdoch had stayed in Australia?

Why does the law place constraints on journalists?

Why should journalists protect confidential sources?

Do journalists' backgrounds and beliefs influence how they do their jobs?

What's the difference between a journalist and a spin doctor?

Further reading

Many constraints and influences are introduced in whistlestop but readable fashion by Keeble (2001b), who also discusses the response of journalists. Also highly readable is Knightley's (2000) classic study of journalism and censorship in wartime. O'Malley and Soley (2000) offer a historical account of press regulation and self-regulation, including case studies of how the Press Complaints Commission has handled particular issues. For legal constraints, Welsh and Greenwood (2003) is essential – make sure you consult the very latest edition – while Crone (2002) is a useful companion. McQuail (2000) reviews a range of relevant theories and research findings, and chapter 11 is particularly useful here. Tumber (1999) includes many relevant original readings, including Herman and Chomsky on their propaganda model and Golding and Murdock on the influence of economic power. McChesney (2000) offers a detailed and passionately argued case for journalism being far too important to be left to market forces.

Notes

Sources for soundbites: *London Evening Post* cited in Porter 2000: 191; Murdoch cited in Bailey and Williams 1997: 371; Watkins 2001: 114; Robertson cited in Foley 2000: 44; Aitken cited in BBC 1999; Goodwin 1996; Moore cited in Clement and Grice 2001.

Chapter Three

What is news?

Key terms

News pegs

News values

Relevance

Selection

Construction of news

Manufacture of news

Gatekeeping

'**D**og bites man isn't news. Man bites dog is.' So goes an adage probably as old as journalism itself. Like many such sayings, it conceals as much as it reveals. True, it tells us something about the value of novelty in news stories. But that is only part of the story when it comes to news, which is the lifeblood of journalism.

Asked why they watch the TV news, or read the news pages of a paper, people might say something about wanting to find out what is happening. Editors like to refer to the media as a window on the world or a giant mirror reflecting the world, warts and all. But it is not a simple reflection because news is mostly about what does not usually happen – that's why it is news. Few newspapers would be sold if they contained reports like this:

> Traffic flowed fairly smoothly along the A61 this morning, and police reported no accidents. Meanwhile, patients in the casualty departments of the city's hospitals were generally seen by doctors within two hours and nobody was forced to wait in a corridor overnight on a trolley. Finally, of the thousands of children on the streets yesterday, none were abducted, stabbed, or thrown off buses because they didn't have the correct change.

Pretty dull stuff, yet that is the kind of thing that happens every day. News, then, is a *selective* view of what happens in the world.

As the word implies, *news* contains much that is *new*, informing people about something that has just happened. But it ain't necessarily so. Some stories run for decades, not always justified with a new twist – examples include the Moors Murderers, the Yorkshire Ripper, and the Great Train Robbery. Other stories are recycled with a gloss of newness supplied by telling us that so-and-so 'spoke last night' or 'broke their silence about . . . ' some ancient scandal or other; or by the apparent discovery of some new information. Take this intro from a news story published 56 years after the events described:

> Government documents uncovered during a man's search for his lost father have revealed how thousands of Chinese servicemen who served Britain in the Second World War were forcibly repatriated in a climate of anti-oriental racism. (*SON'S HUNT FOR FATHER EXPOSES BETRAYAL OF WAR HEROES, Independent February 1 2002*)

News values

The news values in Box 3.1 are an attempt to update and develop an earlier taxonomy of news values produced by Norwegian academics Johan Galtung and Mari Ruge in the 1960s. Galtung and Ruge's influential list of 12 factors may be summarised as follows:

Frequency: an event that unfolds at the same or similar frequency as the news medium is more likely to be selected as news than is a social trend taking place over a long period of time.

Threshold: events have to pass a threshold before being recorded at all. After that, the greater the intensity, the more gruesome the murder, the more casualties in an accident, then the greater the impact on the perception of those responsible for news selection.

Unambiguity: the less ambiguity, the more likely an event is to become news. The more clearly an event can be understood, and interpreted without multiple meanings, the greater the chance of it being selected.

Meaningfulness: the culturally similar is likely to be selected because it fits into the news selector's frame of reference. Thus, the involvement of UK citizens will make an event in a remote country more meaningful to the UK media. Similarly, news from the US is seen as more relevant to the UK than is news from countries which are less culturally familiar.

Consonance: journalists may predict that something will happen, thus forming a mental 'pre-image' of an event which in turn increases its chances of becoming news.

Unexpectedness: the most unexpected or rare events – within those that are culturally familiar and/or consonant – will have the greatest chance of being selected as news.

Continuity: once an event has become headline news it remains in the media spotlight for some time because it has become familiar and therefore easier to interpret. Continuing coverage also justifies the attention an event attracted in the first place.

Composition: an event may be included as news less because of its intrinsic news value than because it fits into the overall composition or balance of a newspaper or news broadcast.

Reference to elite nations: the actions of elite nations are seen as more consequential than the actions of other nations. Definitions of elite nations will be culturally,

The new element is the 'peg' that the story hangs on, but news pegs are not always as strong as they could be. Witness the flurry of news stories in August 2001 about the fatal floods that occurred 49 years earlier in Devon, the flimsy peg being that a radio documentary on the topic was about to be broadcast (RAF RAINMAKERS BLAMED FOR 1952 FLOOD, *Guardian* August 30 2001). Or the front-page splash telling the story of a killing that took place a year earlier, and the resulting five-month-old court case: THE PHONEY GRAFFITI WAR AND THE KILLING THAT SHOCKED AN ESTATE (*Guardian* September 5 2001).

Most news is newer than that, of course. But many stories in the national media are a week or two old, having been passed up the journalistic food chain from the local weekly paper to a regional evening and then, maybe via a freelance news agency, on to the national stage – where the 'when' of the five Ws will be buried somewhere near the bottom in the hope that any whiff of staleness will be overlooked. The majority of local stories will not make it that far, though. The opening of a shopping centre, the death of a child in a simple road accident, or the fire in a warehouse are all good local stories that are unlikely to achieve national coverage on their own merits, without additional elements.

> **'There is no news tonight.'**
> – BBC announcer on Good Friday, 1930.

A good story

If news isn't necessarily new, and if it isn't a mere reflection of reality, what exactly is it? News may be about animals, places or the weather, but it is mostly about *people*. People *doing* things. Things like: fighting, saving, killing, curing, crashing, burning, looting, robbing, rioting, stealing, kidnapping, rescuing, giving, marrying, divorcing, striking, sacking, employing, resigning, conning, suing, investigating, arresting, quizzing, freeing, loving, hating, kissing, bonking, hunting, chasing, escaping, fleeing, creating, destroying, invading, deserting, voting, leading, following, reporting, negotiating, accepting, rejecting, changing, celebrating, commemorating, inventing, making, breaking, selling, buying, treating, operating, comforting, mourning, leaving, arriving, delivering, succeeding, failing, winning, losing, searching, finding, giving birth, surviving, dying, burying. As well

politically and economically determined and will vary from country to country, although there may be universal agreement about the inclusion of the US.

Reference to elite people: the actions of elite people may be seen as having more consequence than the actions of others, and the audience may identify with them.

Reference to persons: news has a tendency to present events as the actions of named individuals rather than a result of social forces.

Reference to something negative: negative news could be seen as unambiguous and consensual, generally more likely to be unexpected and to occur over a shorter period of time than positive news.

> *(Galtung and Ruge 1965: 65–71;*
> *Harcup and O'Neill 2001: 262–4)*

Additional news values have been suggested by other academics. Allan Bell, for example, adds the importance of *competition*, increasing the desire for a scoop; *co-option*, whereby a story that is only tangentially related can be presented in terms of a high profile continuing story; *predictability*, that is, events which can be pre-scheduled for journalists are more likely to be covered than events which turn up unheralded; and *prefabrication*, meaning that the existence of ready-made texts (news releases, cuttings, agency copy) will greatly increase the likelihood of something appearing in the news as journalists will be able to process the story rapidly (Bell 1991: 158–60).

While the news values identified by Galtung and Ruge and others may be 'predictive of a pattern' of which events will and will not be reported, they cannot provide a *complete* explanation of all the irregularities of news composition (McQuail 2000: 343). Further, as John Hartley points out, identifying news values may tell us more about *how* stories are covered than *why* they were chosen in the first place (Hartley 1982: 79). It is also argued – notably by Stuart Hall – that lists such as the above fail to address what lies behind news values in terms of *ideology* (a concept introduced in Chapter 1). For Hall:

> 'News values' are one of the most opaque structures of meaning in modern society . . . Journalists speak of 'the news' as if events select themselves. Further, they speak as if which is the 'most significant' news story, and which 'news angles' are most salient are divinely

as doing, news can be about people *saying* things, whether in the form of speeches, announcements, publications, accusations, or replies to journalists' questions. News can also be about somebody being *set to* do something or even *set to* say something. Any of the above *may* become news if the raw ingredients have the makings of a good story for your audience. It will depend on who is doing or saying something, where, when, and in what circumstances. It will also be influenced by what other stories are around to compete for limited time or space.

'News stories are what people talk about in the pub, or wherever they gather,' says Brian Whittle. He should know. As the editor of a thriving news agency, his income depends on spotting stories that his customers – the regional, national and international media – will pay for. He continues:

> Six people killed in a bus crash on the M56, that's hard news. You can't get any bigger hard news story than what happened in America [the attack on the World Trade Centre on September 11 2001]. But a lot of other stories are a result of lateral thinking. When a story's been around for a few days, you're looking for where the next development will be – so good instinct will result in a good story.

Evidence of his instinct for a good story can be seen in the framed front-page splashes adorning the walls of his Manchester office: CATWOMAN 'SEDUCED' BOY OF 15 . . . PAEDOPHILE WALKS FREE . . . 18,000 POLICE TO FAIL DRIVING TESTS . . . BOY, 9, WRECKS TEACHER'S LIFE . . . MCCARTNEY'S £5,000 BABY HUSH MONEY . . . and so on, all stories likely to be mentioned by people chatting in the pub or next to the water cooler.

Somebody else who knows a thing or two about telling stories is the writer Michael Frayn, whose career has combined journalism with novels and plays:

> Very deep in both journalism and fiction and life in general is the concept of a *story*. Why are some things a story and others just a sequence of events? All journalists recognise a story, and that's why they begin to tell it, but it's very difficult to say what a story is.
>
> (*Quoted in Armitstead 2002; my emphasis*)

> **'Isn't it amazing that the amount of news that happens in the world every day always just exactly fits the newspaper?'**
> – *Guardian advert.*

inspired. Yet of the millions of events which occur daily in the world, only a tiny proportion ever become visible as 'potential news stories': and of this proportion, only a small fraction are actually produced as the day's news in the news media. We appear to be dealing, then, with a 'deep structure' whose function as a selective device is un-transparent even to those who professionally most know how to operate it. (*Hall 1973:181*)

Viewed from such a perspective, news offers a highly selective version of events influenced by the 'ideological structure' of prevalent news values (Hall 1973: 235). Robert McChesney gives the example of journalists' emphasis on individual 'events' and 'news hooks' (or pegs) meaning that 'long-term public issues, like racism or suburban sprawl, tend to fall by the wayside, and there is little emphasis on providing the historical and ideological context necessary to bring public issues to life for readers' (McChesney 2000: 49–50). Furthermore, news values tend to privilege individualism, regarding it as 'natural', whereas civic values are deemed 'marginal' (McChesney 2000: 110). This is what is meant when critical commentators argue that, far from being neutral, news values provide journalists with ideologically-loaded 'maps of meaning' used to make sense of the world for an audience (Hall et al 1978: 54).

Construction

In Chapter 1 we heard Walter Lippmann argue that facts must be given a shape if they are to become news, and this is what academics mean when they refer to the *construction* or even the *manufacture* of news. It is not that facts are invented by journalists (except in rare cases) but that the identification, selection and presentation of facts in a news story is a social construct viewed through a 'cultural prism' (Watson 1998: 107). Maggie Wykes argues that 'the construction of news simultaneously constructs for audiences a framework of interpretation as it presents the "facts"' (Wykes 2001: 187). Studies suggest that journalists frequently construct news stories within the framework of earlier stories or even, according

In his first novel, written in the mid-sixties, Frayn came up with the notion of news as a series of 'standard variables and invariables' that could just as easily be written by computer, changing only the names and the local details (Frayn 1995: 37–8). His novel also included market research into what readers wanted:

> The crash survey showed that people were not interested in reading about road crashes unless there were at least ten dead. A road crash with ten dead, the majority felt, was slightly less interesting than a rail crash with one dead, unless it had piquant details – the ten dead turning out to be five still virginal honeymoon couples, for example, or pedestrians mown down by the local JP on his way home from a hunt ball. A rail crash was always entertaining, with or without children's toys still lying pathetically among the wreckage. Even a rail crash on the Continent made the grade provided there were at least five dead. If it was in the United States the minimum number of dead rose to 20; in South America 100; in Africa 200; in China 500.
> *(Frayn 1995: 69)*

It may have been a spoof but it was informed by the author's first-hand knowledge of how **news values** and the **construction** of stories can render news predictable. As predictable as the annual stories about A-levels getting easier or the pictures of female tennis players showing their knickers at Wimbledon every summer. Formulaic and predictable some news may be but, unlike in Frayn's novel, we have not lost the connection between real journalists and real events featuring real people. Which brings us back to the issue – essential for any trainee journalist to grasp – of what news *is*.

To begin at the beginning. 'Man bites dog' stories are certainly unusual but not unknown. Take this intro from a report of a court case: 'A drunken teenager who was said to have "growled like an animal" as he sank his teeth into a police dog's neck has been put on probation for two years' (*Yorkshire Evening Post* November 4 2000). Or this unlikely headline: WOMAN BITES DOG IN SAVAGE PIT BULL ATTACK (*Independent on Sunday* June 17 2001). The rarity and surprise factors involved in such stories make them newsworthy. As with this twist-in-the-tale: 'A pensioner ended up in hospital in Zurich after being bitten by a dog . . . owner. The 74-year-old woman was attacked by

to Jack Lule (2001), through the retelling of enduring myths – points that will be considered when we examine how news is written (Chapter 9).

However, a focus on how events and facts are constructed into news items offers only a partial explanation of the processes at work. The concept of 'pseudo-events', introduced in Chapter 2, suggests that 'many items of news are not "events" at all, that is in the sense of occurrences in the real world which take place independently of the media' (Curran and Seaton 1997: 277). Some commentators go even further in divorcing the news from real life. Exploring media-hypes such as the 'flesh-eating virus' stories that swept the UK (and elsewhere) during 1994, Peter Vasterman argues that lists of selection criteria such as those produced by Galtung and Ruge are flawed in their presumption that journalists actually report *events* at all:

> News is not out there, journalists do not report news, they produce news. They construct it, they construct facts, they construct statements and they construct a context in which these facts make sense. They reconstruct 'a' reality. *(Vasterman 1995)*

Gatekeepers

The concept of gatekeeping is associated with a David Manning White study of how a wire editor at a US morning newspaper selected stories for inclusion during one week in 1949. White concluded that the choices were 'highly subjective' and based on the editor's own 'set of experiences, attitudes and expectations' (White 1950: 72). The gatekeeping approach has been challenged for assuming that there is a given reality out there in the 'real world' that newsgatherers will choose either to admit or exclude (McQuail 2000: 279). A study by Walter Gieber suggested that the personal attitudes of journalistic 'gatekeepers' were of less importance than the mechanical and bureaucratic processes involved in producing and editing copy (Gieber 1964: 219). For Gieber:

> News does not have an independent existence; news is a product of men [sic] who are members of a news-gathering (or a news-originating) bureaucracy . . . [The] reporter's individuality is strongly tempered by extrapersonal factors. *(Gieber 1964: 223)*

another female pensioner in a row about the dog's attitude' (*Ananova* July 4 2001; ellipsis in original).

Sometimes 'dog bites man' stories are also deemed newsworthy enough for selection, usually because there are additional factors involved. Maybe it is the unusual, not to say horrific, nature of the attack itself, as in: DOG BITES OFF MAN'S GENITALS (*Guardian* September 2 2000). Perhaps a local child is involved: TODDLER IN MUM'S ARMS IS SAVAGED (*Yorkshire Evening Post* November 6 2000). There could be legal action over a ruined career: GOLFER BITTEN ON FINGER BY DOG SUES OWNER FOR £1M (*Independent* December 3 2002). Or the legal action might result from the fact that the biting has been done by a police dog: MAN BITTEN BY POLICE DOG SUES (*Yorkshire Post* February 20 2001). The *Washington Post* took the police angle further by reporting that a police dog in Prince George's County, Maryland, USA, had hospitalised more than 40 people during its career (cited by Pandora, *Independent* December 31 2001). These additional elements offer further clues to the existence and operation of what are called news values.

News values

If news isn't necessarily new, and if 'dog bites man' stories can occasionally make the headlines alongside more lurid tales of 'man bites dog', then coming up with a foolproof definition of news is clearly easier said than done. News values have been deconstructed by academics but rather fewer journalists have either the time or the inclination to stand back and subject the selection process to such critical scrutiny. John Sergeant says: 'It is often distressing to argue about news stories, because usually journalists rely on instinct rather than logic' (Sergeant 2001: 226). Recruits to journalism tend to pick up a sense of newsworthiness and develop their 'nose' for a story by consuming news and by absorbing news values from senior colleagues.

It can be a fairly subjective process. Fleet Street editor Alastair Hetherington notes that, when it comes to the value of a particular story, most journalists instinctively ask the simple question: 'Does it interest me?' He adds that interesting stories are likely to involve significance, drama, surprise, personalities, sex, scandal, crime, numbers, and/or proximity

The gatekeeping model has subsequently been developed by Pamela Shoemaker to take account of multiple levels of decision making and wider factors:

> The individual gatekeeper has likes and dislikes, ideas about the nature of his or her job, ways of thinking about a problem, preferred decision-making strategies, and values that impinge on the decision to reject or select (and shape) a message. But the gatekeeper is not totally free to follow a personal whim; he or she must operate within the constraints of communication routines to do things this way or that. All of this also must occur within the framework of the communication organisation, which has its own priorities but also is continuously buffeted by influential forces from outside the organisation. And, of course, none of these actors – the individual, the routine, the organisation, or the social institution – can escape the fact that it is tied to and draws its sustenance from the social system. *(Shoemaker 1991: 75–6)*

(Hetherington 1985: 8–9). The *Guardian*'s Martin Wainwright measures a potential story against whether it interests himself or 'increasingly as I get older, would it interest my children?'. Although newsworthiness may be hard to define, we can get a fairly good idea about how news values work by examining stories that make it into the news. A recent study of the UK national press suggests that, although there are exceptions to every rule, potential news items must generally satisfy one or (ideally) more of the requirements listed in Box 3.1 to be selected as news stories (Harcup and O'Neill 2001).

Although the news values listed in Box 3.1 are based on a study of the UK national press, similar considerations come into play when journalists select stories for broadcast, online and local or regional media. But how do they operate in practice?

The power elite: stories concerning powerful individuals, organisations or institutions

Virtually every action of the Prime Minister seems to be considered newsworthy, from Cabinet reshuffles at one end of the spectrum to their choice of clothing at the other. This is less so for the Prime Minister's senior colleagues and so on down the pecking order of government and opposition, through the backbenches, in diminishing order of newsworthiness. Whereas the Prime Minister's holiday plans are usually enough to generate a news story, Cabinet colleagues might have to make a policy announcement or a blunder to grab the headlines, while a lowly constituency MP will be of interest to the national media only if they are embroiled in some kind of scandal, row, rebellion or defection. Locally, even the most somnolent constituency MP will be considered one of the power elite, as will the leader of the council, and many of their comments and actions will be reported in the local media. As with individuals, some institutions or organisations are deemed to be newsworthy because of their positions of power and/or influence – examples include Nato, the Vatican, the European Commission, the Bank of England, Oxbridge universities and Eton.

Celebrity: stories concerning people who are already famous

Celebrities are newsworthy and it has ever been thus. The evidence is the fading sign still adorning the wall of the old *Harrogate Advertiser* building – 'List of visitors Wednesday' – which dates back to when the local paper began as little more than a weekly list of the rich and famous who came to stay in the North Yorkshire spa town over 150 years ago. However, today's journalists are often heard complaining that good stories are squeezed out by an increasing media obsession with celebs on the A, B, C and D-lists. Brian Whittle dismisses many of today's news editors as 'daleks who only rate a story if it features a third-rate celebrity'. He recalls one of his former news editors defining a good news story as 'ordinary people doing extraordinary things', before adding with a hint of sadness: 'I think some of that's been lost.' If you come up with a story about somebody who is famous you will have a better chance of having it used than if the same story concerns an 'ordinary' person.

Entertainment: stories concerning sex, showbusiness, human interest, animals, an unfolding drama, or offering opportunities for humorous treatment, entertaining photographs or witty headlines

Stories and pictures with the capacity to entertain or amuse an audience are looked upon favourably by editors. Indeed, some stories have little else going for them. Why else, for example, would the *Daily Express* devote almost the whole of one of its prime news pages to a woman saying that a tree-trunk resembled the face of her dead pet dog? (BARK THAT SAYS ZOE WILL ALWAYS BE HERE, *Daily Express* November 6 2001.) See also the overweight pet stories that appear with alarming frequency, such as CHARLIE THE FLABRADOR (*Daily Mail* October 25 2001) or KING OF THE FAT CATS (*Daily Mirror* October 31 2001). A sex angle is also popular with editors, and court cases or employment tribunals involving sex have a greater chance of being covered than those without. Other reliable entertainment stories likely to trigger a response are those based on lists, be they the 1,000 best records, the 100 greatest films, the top 50 songs ever written, or comparisons of who is 'out' and who is 'in', such as OFFICIAL – BRITNEY IS WORLD'S NUMBER ONE CELEB (*Sun* June 21

Box 3.1 *News values*

Box 3.1 Recent research suggests that potential items must generally fall into one or more of these categories to be selected as news stories (Harcup and O'Neill 2001: 279).

- **The power elite**
  Stories concerning powerful individuals, organisations or institutions.
- **Celebrity**
  Stories concerning people who are already famous.
- **Entertainment**
  Stories concerning sex, showbusiness, human interest, animals, an unfolding drama, or offering opportunities for humorous treatment, entertaining photographs or witty headlines.
- **Surprise**
  Stories with an element of surprise and/or contrast.
- **Bad news**
  Stories with negative overtones such as conflict or tragedy.
- **Good news**
  Stories with positive overtones such as rescues and cures.
- **Magnitude**
  Stories perceived as sufficiently significant either in the numbers of people involved or in potential impact.
- **Relevance**
  Stories about issues, groups and nations perceived to be relevant to the audience.
- **Follow-ups**
  Stories about subjects already in the news.
- **Media agenda**
  Stories that set or fit the news organisation's own agenda.

2002). But hard news, even tragic news, may also be judged on whether it is entertaining – not in the sense of being amusing but of offering an unfolding drama, with plot twists featuring characters we come to know. For example, there is little suspense or drama about the dozens of children killed on our roads each year, and they receive relatively little media coverage. But there is huge coverage of the intense drama attached to a police hunt for a missing child: the smiling picture, the plotting of the last movements, the release of CCTV footage, the emotional appeals, the discovery of a body, the placing of flowers with heartfelt messages, the arrest of a suspect, the howling mob outside court. Journalism as entertainment is discussed further in Chapter 7.

> **'News is anything that makes a reader say "Gee whiz!"'**
> – Arthur MacEwen, editor of the San Francisco Examiner.

Surprise: stories with an element of surprise and/or contrast

This is where the 'man bites dog' stories come in along with other surprising, shocking or unusual events ranging from the 12-year-old who becomes a mum to the one-legged man who skywalks on the wing of an aeroplane. There is also a great value placed on contrast, as in the vicar who runs off with somebody else's wife or the policeman arrested for distributing porn by email.

> **'News is what newspapermen make it.'**
> – Walter Gieber.

Bad news: stories with negative overtones such as conflict or tragedy

Death, tragedy, job losses, factory closures, and falls from grace are all examples of somebody's bad news being good news for journalists. Sometimes journalists might almost *create* bad news by seeking hostile reaction to an incident or comment in the hope of starting – and reporting – a 'row'. Or, if they are really lucky, a 'war of words'.

Good news: stories with positive overtones such as rescues and cures

Positive stories are far more prevalent than is suggested by the cynical claim that the only good news is bad news. Somebody somewhere always seems to be winning a dream prize, going on the trip of a lifetime, or getting straight As when they open their exam results. Neighbours are frequently hailed as heroes for leaping into action to rescue people from burning houses. Miracle cures are also more common than their name suggests, as in the following front-page lead: BACK FROM THE BRINK: COMA GIRL JENNIFER MAKES A MIRACULOUS RECOVERY (*Yorkshire Evening Post* February 2 2002). The *YEP*'s David Helliwell explains:

> Hard news is often bad news so we want to break up the court stuff, the police stuff, industry or whatever with something a little bit lighter. A bit more light and shade among the death and destruction.

Another miracle is described in a national front-page splash: 'OUR MIRACLE: MUM TELLS OF ESCAPE AS 100MPH GALES BATTER UK: A mum told how her two children narrowly escaped death when a tree uprooted by storm-force winds crashed on to their gran's car' (*Daily Mirror* January 29 2002). Such miraculous escapes are a recurrent theme in news stories. A classic of the genre took up a whole news page of the *Daily Mail* – LUCKIEST BOY ALIVE: THE TODDLER WHO CLIMBED THROUGH A WINDOW AND FELL 25FT . . . STRAIGHT INTO THE ARMS OF A PASSING DOCTOR (June 27 2001) – duly illustrated with photographs of the boy, his relieved mother, and the window in question.

Magnitude: stories perceived as sufficiently significant either in the numbers of people involved or in potential impact

Magnitude comes into play when a journalist rejects a potential story with the words: 'Not enough dead' (quoted in Harrison 2000: 136). Martin Wainwright recalls how he decided to go to the scene of the Selby rail crash in 2001:

> I heard about that on the news early in the morning and went out there when I knew that there were going to be more than just a couple of people killed. *It's got to be that level.*

But magnitude is relative. So television news may lead on seven deaths in UK storms and treat 500 people feared dead after an explosion at a Nigerian arms depot as a brief item fourth in the running order (*Channel 5 News*, 9pm, January 28 2002). Had the figures been reversed, seven deaths in Nigeria would probably not have been of sufficient magnitude to warrant inclusion at all – unless they were Brits (see Relevance, below) – while 500 deaths in the UK would have cleared the schedules for rolling news broadcasts from the scene.

Relevance: stories about issues, groups and nations perceived to be relevant to the audience

As we have just seen, 500 deaths in Nigeria are perceived as being of less interest to a UK audience than a fraction of that number in the UK or of Britons abroad. 'It's a question of the impact on people,' says a BBC news editor, explaining why a coach crash in India did not make the news despite the fact that 60 people had drowned (quoted in Schlesinger 1987: 117). In the gallows humour typical of newsrooms, this is sometimes referred to as McLurg's Law, after a legendary editor who ranked events by how far away they occurred (Schlesinger 1987: 117). But it is not simply a question of geographical distance. In the UK we get more stories about the USA than, say, Belgium because, although the latter is nearer and a partner in the European Union, we share more language and cultural reference points with the former. Away from international news, the concept of relevance affects selection about topics. That's why bulletins on *BBC Radio One*, aimed at young people, have so many news items about drugs or the entertainment industry; why the *Guardian*, which is bought by many teachers (and students), has so many stories about education; and why the *Daily Mail*, aimed at middle class and 'aspirational' working class readers, features a large number of stories about mortgages and property prices. Relevance works at a micro-level as well as the national and international level, so a local newspaper in a seaside town might have lots of stories about the menace of seagulls whereas an equivalent publication in a rural area

> '**One European is worth twenty eight Chinese, or perhaps two Welsh miners worth one thousand Pakistanis.**'
> – McLurg's Law of public interest.

inland will be more concerned with the price of sheep, and a big city newspaper wouldn't touch either.

Follow-ups: stories about subjects already in the news

'News is not news until someone else reports it,' is how Phillip Knightley sums up the attitude of too many editors (Knightley 1998: 197). News organisations feed off each other, picking up stories that dominate the headlines for days or weeks before disappearing whence they came. Remember the dangerous dogs menace? At least one perceptive reader does: 'It's terrible that children got hurt, but I'll bet there were no more than at any other time . . . No one thinks about them now, not now they're off the front pages. They're just dogs again' (quoted in O'Neill 2000: 278). But most follow-up stories are less hysterical, and journalists are understandably concerned to 'move the story on' to discover new information or introduce new angles. Follow-ups have a number of advantages for journalists, including the fact that background material is readily available, that contacts have already been identified, and that certain developments may be able to be predicted and therefore planned for.

Media agenda: stories that set or fit the news organisation's own agenda

Sometimes news stories seem to be selected less for any intrinsic newsworthiness than because they fit the agenda of the news organisation, whether to promote certain commercial or political interests or to engender a sense of audience loyalty and identification. Examples of the former were discussed in Chapter 2, while examples of the latter range from a local paper running a campaign to encourage readers to carry organ donor cards to the *Sun*'s stories openly supportive of fuel protesters, complete with a 'save our truckers' logo: WHITE VAN JAM: TAX DEMO TO CRIPPLE CAPITAL (*Sun* March 18 1999). The *News of the World*'s controversial campaign to 'name and shame' paedophiles encouraged readers to identify with the paper as being on their side against the 'perverts' and authorities alike. And when the *Daily*

Mail published a series of news stories attacking the BBC's coverage of the Queen Mother's death in 2002 it seemed to have more to do with promoting the paper's agenda of moral outrage than with reporting a 'row' that had any existence outside the confines of its pages. The *Mail*'s political attitudes are frequently visible in its news stories as well as its comment pages, as memorably satirised in this spoof splash:

> Middle-class newspaper readers might as well top themselves at once, according to a series of reports published every day in the *Daily Mail*. The only reason to stay alive, according to experts, is to see whether the *Mail* runs an even more depressing report the next day, suggesting that it is only a matter of time before economic ruin strikes every man, woman and child in Britain, reducing them to eating their pets and begging for loose change from asylum seekers who (cont. p94) *(Private Eye, June 28 2002)*

The news values listed above interact with each other, and the more buttons pressed by an event the more likely it is to become news. But even events that satisfy several of the above criteria do not automatically become news. First they must be noticed, weighed up, selected and constructed.

Selection

This role in selecting the news has led to journalists in general, and those working on newsdesks in particular, being described as **gatekeepers**. The gatekeeper allows some events to pass through to become news while others are turned away. From a newsdesk perspective, David Helliwell explains what he looks for when a reporter brings in a story:

> For a front page story you definitely need some sort of drama, some action or excitement, and you need something that's going to draw the reader in. Preferably you would be looking at something that is people-led. If you were looking at a robbery, for example, we would only consider it a good front page robbery if we had some detail, some colour, so you got to know who was involved, who the victims might be. Not just a flat police statement that 'two masked men

sped off in a westerly direction with an undisclosed sum'. Whatever it is – be it crime, industry, business, whatever – we would always try to make it as human as possible.

Take this splash about two 18-year-olds jailed for seven years for robbing an elderly woman – YOUNG THUGS CAGED: TERROR ATTACK ON PENSIONER (*Yorkshire Evening Post* October 6 2001) – illustrated with photographs of the two robbers. Helliwell says the pictures helped elevate the story to page one:

> Getting the pictures from the police, always a tricky business, definitely lifts it. People love to see who you're talking about. Even if we didn't have the pictures it would have been a strong page lead early on in the paper. It's the viciousness of what they did, the things they said to her, the judge's comments, and the seven years each which are pretty heavy sentences. Even in this day and age these things are fairly rare.

> 'News is what a chap who doesn't care much about anything wants to read. And it's only news until he's read it. After that it's dead.'
> – *Evelyn Waugh.*

However, just as most crimes reported to the police are not covered by the media, most court cases also pass unreported. This is for logistical reasons as well as ideas of newsworthiness, because newspapers have cut back on court reporters while broadcasting and online media only cover high profile cases. Most coverage relies on news agency reporters ducking and diving in and out of cases looking for one with an interesting line or two, as Jane Merrick explains:

> A murder trial wasn't enough, it had to have two or three different angles. The agency was geared to the tabloids, because they were the ones who would buy most of our stuff, so it was very much human interest. One of the first court cases I did was a woman who had killed her lover's wife, but that wasn't enough to make a good story for the papers. I think she was in the chorus line and the victim was the lead singer in this amateur play, so that was the extra line.

Even at a local level, except in the smallest of towns, the bulk of court cases do not get covered by the media at all. Helliwell again:

> We have someone covering Crown Court full-time and on many days there are two people there, covering 12

courts. Like many other papers, the days of covering Magistrates Courts are virtually gone. We go up for things we know about but not on spec. I'm sure there are cracking stories that we miss, but so much gets adjourned that in terms of producing copy it's just not worth it. Similarly with employment tribunals. We look out for the sexual discrimination cases because a lot of the others are just too dull or too technical. A dispute over procedure isn't going to make a good lead for us. We check out sexual discrimination, unfair dismissal, or if it is a big local employer. Every now and then there will be a race equality organisation accused of discrimination. People love that. It's human nature that people love the hypocrisy of it.

Reading such an item on screen, Helliwell may find himself tutting or shaking his head, a sure sign that a reporter has delivered a good story. As with court cases or tribunals, so with the selection of other news. Yes, even hard-bitten hacks can respond to stories with feelings of shock, surprise, outrage, sadness, joy or amazement at the human condition. 'That's the big test if you're on newsdesk,' he explains. 'If it moves something in you then it will move somebody else, and that's what you want.'

That's news. In the next chapter we will find out where it comes from.

Summary

News is a selective version of world events with a focus on that which is new and/or unusual. However, not all news is new, much of it is predictable, and some does not concern 'events' at all. Journalists identify, select and produce news items according to occupational norms including the concept of what will interest a particular audience. Implicitly or explicitly, journalists measure potential news items against a range of criteria that have become known as news values. Academics have produced lists of such news values based on studies of journalistic output. Other theoretical models associated with the study of news include news as a social construct; journalists as gatekeepers admitting or excluding events; and news values being imbued with the dominant ideology of society.

Questions

Where do news values come from?

Do news values change over time?

Who are the gatekeepers?

Is the news predictable?

Does *the manufacture of news* mean it is not true?

Further reading

Both Randall (2000) and Boyd (2001) have practical chapters discussing news from the point of view of an experienced print and broadcasting journalist respectively. Harrison (2000) includes a study of TV news values while Harcup and O'Neill (2001) present the results of a content analysis of news values at work in the UK national press. The latter also explore academic interpretations of news values. Extracts from many such studies – including Galtung and Ruge, Schlesinger, Shoemaker, and Gans – are reprinted and introduced in Tumber (1999). Stuart Hall's classic analysis of news values as ideology is also extracted in Tumber, but it is worth seeking out the full version from the original, chapters three and four of Hall et al (1978).

Notes

Sources for soundbites: BBC cited in Allan 1997: 325n; *Guardian*, 8 June 2001; MacEwen cited in Boorstin 1963: 20; Waugh 1943: 66; McLurg's Law cited in Schlesinger 1987: 117; Gieber 1964: 223.

Chapter Four

Where does news come from?

Key terms

News sources

Contacts

Calls

Source considerations

News access

Primary definers

Power

Journalist-source relationship

'**H**ave you seen those awful Harvey Nichols posters?' asked Jane, a friend who had been offended by adverts for the opening of a Harvey Nichols shop in Leeds. I hadn't. She described the huge hoardings featuring a black woman wearing a dog-lead and collar, accompanied by the weak pun: 'Harvey Nichols Leeds (not follows)'. Jane felt it was a degrading image of women in general, and black women in particular, made worse by the juxta-position with unrelated posters promoting a local 'zero tolerance' campaign to combat violence against women.

'I don't know if you might be able to make it into a story,' she added. The answer was yes, it could be a story if somebody complained. So she duly fired off an angry letter to the Advertising Standards Authority (ASA). It turned out that the model in the dog-lead was not black at all but Jodie Kidd in heavy make-up. However, it was a newsworthy story because the complaint meant there was a 'row' involving a high profile upmarket store popular with celebs including the Princess of Wales. It might not have been the kind of thing to impress journalist David Randall – who dismisses 'row' stories as 'the great contagion and con-trick of journalism' (Randall 2000: 41) – but it reflected genuine anger.

Having gathered some more outraged comments from locals and councillors, along with a dismissive response from the store's PR people, I filed copy to the national and local papers. Many gave it a good show the next day, accompanied by pictures and obligatory puns such as: HOT UNDER THE COLLAR (*Daily Express*), HARVEY NICKS 'DOG GIRLS' UNLEASH A ROW (*Daily Mail*), TOP STORE IN THE DOGHOUSE AS 'RACIST AND SEXIST' POSTER UNLEASHES PROTESTS UP NORTH (*Guardian*), and STORE FAILS TO FIND FOLLOWING AMONG LEEDS LADIES WHO LUNCH (*Daily Telegraph*; all October 10 1996). In the way of these things, the story was followed-up by the broadcasting media before finally becoming the property of newspaper colum-nists, who contributed their philosophical twopence-worth based on a pile of cuttings.

Then it was forgotten, except by me. As every freelance knows, where there is a story there is a potential follow-up. Three months later, when the ASA declared the ads to be harmless fun, I dusted off the original story and bashed out fresh copy that was used in brief by several papers. Had the verdict gone

Sources ✓

Sources are central to the practice of journalism. Sources are the people, places or organisations from whom potential news stories originate; and the people, places or organisations to whom journalists turn when checking potential stories. Allan Bell argues that 'the ideal news source is also a news actor, someone whose own words make news' (Bell 1991: 193–4). He lists the following 'news actors' as the major sources of news: political figures, officials, celebrities, sportspeople, professionals, criminals, human interest figures, and participants such as victims or witnesses (Bell 1991: 194). Journalists may like to say that sources are everywhere but most of the time they opt to use a narrow range of sources, argues Bell. He points to a series of research studies suggesting that, to a very large extent, 'news is what an authoritative source tells a journalist'; alternative sources, including minorities and the socially disadvantaged, 'tend to be ignored' (Bell 1991: 191–2).

When assessing sources a journalist's over-riding consideration is *efficiency*, according to Herbert Gans: 'Reporters who have only a short time to gather infor-mation must therefore attempt to obtain the most suitable news from the fewest number of sources as quickly and easily as possible' (Gans 1980: 128). He has identified six interrelated 'source considerations' used by journalists to evaluate sources of news. They may be summarised as follows:

Past suitability: sources whose information has led to stories in the past are likely to be chosen again and to become regular sources (although journalists could eventually become bored of them).

Productivity: sources will be favoured if they are able to supply a lot of information with minimum effort by the journalist.

Reliability: journalists want reliable sources whose information requires the least amount of checking.

Trustworthiness: journalists evaluate sources' trustworthiness over time and look favourably on those who are honest and do not limit themselves to self-serving information.

Authoritativeness: everything else being equal, a journalist will prefer a source in an official position of authority.

Articulateness: sources capable of expressing themselves in articulate, concise and dramatic soundbites or

against Harvey Nichols this follow-up would no doubt have been bigger news. But such is life.

Sources

Journalists are surrounded by **sources** of potential news stories or features. A conversation with a friend, a poster on a wall, an unexpected juxtaposition – all might result in a story if you keep your eyes, ears and mind open.

Veteran *Yorkshire Evening Post* reporter Peter Lazenby is one of those journalists who seems to be able to find stories wherever he goes. Shopping in a local super-market one weekend, he spotted a card on the community notice-board offering a reward of several hundred pounds for the return of a lost parrot. Thinking it must have been 'one hell of a parrot' to be worth so much, he called the number and discovered that it was indeed a rare breed of parrot. But it had not been lost. It had been stolen by members of an international smuggling syndicate who were abducting exotic birds to order and delivering them in a private aeroplane to wealthy collectors. Not a bad story to bring home with the groceries on what was supposed to be a day off. In this sense, a good journalist is never off-duty.

As news agency editor Brian Whittle explains: 'Sources of news are everywhere.' Some sources will be routine points of contact for journalists while others may be one-offs. Some will be proactive, approaching journalists because they want **news access** for their views or information, while other sources may not even be aware that they *are* sources. A good journalist will look for leads from a range of sources and will certainly not rely on stories arriving 'gift-wrapped' courtesy of the PR industry (Thom 2002). Some of the most common sources of news are listed in Box 4.1.

> **'Sources of news are everywhere.'**
> – Brian Whittle.

Contacts books

The sources listed in Box 4.1 will form the backbone of any journalist's contacts book. Contacts books come in many shapes and sizes – electronic or paper – but what they have in common is that they can be the

quotes will be favoured when journalists need somebody to be interviewed.

(Gans 1980: 129–31.)

For Gans, this process means that 'journalists are repeatedly brought into contact with a limited number of the same types of sources' (Gans 1980: 144). This apparent homogeneity of sources is reinforced by the fact that journalists use other journalists and other media as one of their main sources of ideas and validation. Pierre Bourdieu refers to this as the 'circular circulation of information', arguing that journalists *consume* so much news because 'to know what to say, you have to know what everyone else has said'. For Bourdieu, this results in 'mental closure' (Bourdieu 1998: 23–4).

Are journalists' sources really drawn from as narrow a range as suggested above? If journalism *does* tend to privilege a narrow range of 'resource-rich institutions' (Cottle 2000: 433), then it does not *have* to do so. Studies of the alternative press suggest that it may not be the routines of news production themselves that determine the choice of sources but the ethos of the organisation, thus allowing for the alternative press to select 'a different cast' of sources and voices (Cottle 2000: 434–5; see also Harcup 2003: 360–67).

News access

The question of who gets 'on' the news is important to considerations of the public sphere, and journalists' tendency to rely on official sources is frequently said to benefit the powerful (Cottle 2000: 427; McQuail 2000: 288; McChesney 2000: 49). Unequal access to the news has damaging social effects, argues Stuart Hall:

> Some things, people, events, relationships *always* get represented: always centre-stage, always in the position to define, to set the agenda, to establish the terms of the conversation. Some others sometimes get represented – but always at the margin, always responding to a question whose terms and conditions have been defined elsewhere: never 'centred'. Still others are always 'represented' only by their eloquent absence, their silences: or refracted through the glance

Box 4.1 *Sources*

Box 4.1 Common sources of news stories.

Academic journals	MPs and MEPs
Adverts	News agencies
Airports	News releases
Ambulance service	Noticeboards
Anniversaries	Official reports
Armed forces	Other media
Arts groups	Parish newsletters
Campaigns	People
Chambers of Commerce and/or Trade	Police
Charities	Political parties
Churches, Mosques, Synagogues, Temples	Post offices
Colleagues	Posters
Community groups	PR companies
Companies	Press conferences
Consumer groups	Pressure groups
Council departments	Professional bodies
Council meetings	Public inquiries
Council press officers	Pubs
Councillors	Quangos
Court hearings	Readers/viewers/listeners
Cuttings/diary	Regeneration projects
Email lists	Regional development agencies
Entertainment industry	Regulatory bodies
Eyes and ears	Residents' groups
Fire brigade	Schools
Government departments	Scouts, Cubs, Guides, Brownies, Woodcraft Folk
Government News Network	Solicitors
Health authorities	Sports organisations
Heritage groups	Support groups
Hospitals	Theatres
Inquests	Trade associations
Lateral thinking	Trade press
Leaks	Trades unions
Letters	Transport companies
Libraries	Universities
Motoring organisations	Web

difference between meeting the deadline or missing the boat.

A contacts book will normally list organisations on an alphabetical basis, adding names, titles, main switchboard telephone numbers, direct lines, mobile numbers, fax numbers, email addresses, and home numbers where possible. Out-of-hours numbers are particularly important, as you may be working on stories early in the morning or late in the evening when most work numbers are useless. Cross-referencing is advised, to increase your chances of finding the right name and number in a hurry. And don't rely on being able to remember who somebody is and why you have their number in your book. Even Mr Memory would struggle to remember all the people a journalist will speak to in an average year, so add titles and a brief note to aid recall.

You will also need to build up a range of individual contacts, people associated with particular interests or issues. Having such contacts listed in your book – categorised under their job, their hobby, their area of expertise – can help you find that vital comment, that missing piece of information or that fresh angle much more quickly than if you have to start from scratch each time. People listed in your contacts books will vary enormously depending on the type of organisation you are working for, the geographical or specialist patch you are covering, whether you work mainly on features or news, and how you develop your own particular niche of interest or expertise.

> '**The good reporter is able to . . . find at least two good stories during a twopenny bus ride.**'
> – FJ Mansfield.

Useful people contacts are likely to include some of the following: academics; actors; agents; alternative health practitioners; anglers; architects; artists; astrologers; astronomers; athletes; authors; barristers; biologists; builders; business people; carers; cavers; celebrities; chefs; chemists; clairvoyants; climbers; collectors; comedians; community leaders; computer whizkids; councillors; counsellors; criminologists; cultural critics; dentists; designers; detectives; dieticians; disability campaigners; DJs; doctors; economists; engineers; environmentalists; estate agents; explorers; farmers; feminists; film directors; film stars; financial experts; footballers; gardeners; gay activists; golfers; historians; hoteliers; imams; international experts; judges; magistrates; market traders; midwives;

or the gaze of others. If you are white, male, a businessman or politician or a professional or a celebrity, your chances of getting represented will be very high. If you are black, or a woman without social status, or poor or working class or gay or powerless because you are marginal, you will always have to fight to get heard or seen. This does not mean that no one from the latter groups will ever find their way into the media. But it *does* mean that the structure of access to the media is systematically skewed in relation to certain social categories. *(Hall 1986: 9; emphasis in original)*

Such media representations do not necessarily remain unchanged over time (Schudson 1989: 280), and black and gay voices are now heard more frequently than when Hall wrote the above words. I have suggested elsewhere that the example of the alternative press may have prompted mainstream media to use a wider range of non-official and community-based sources (Harcup 1994: 29; Harcup 1998: 114). However, notwithstanding that relationships between journalists and sources may be complex and subject to change over time – and that there will be occasions when the voices of the powerless take centre stage – there remains a *tendency* for the powerful to enjoy 'routine advantages' in news access (Manning 2001: 139). For example, Gary Younge notes that black 'community leaders' still tend to be regarded as authoritative sources only when rioting breaks out: 'While rarely summoned to the microphone in more peaceful times, they are in great demand when it comes to condemn wayward members of their community' (Younge 2001). News access is discussed further in Chapter 5

< *passivity.*

Primary definers

For some cultural critics, notably Stuart Hall, the 'skewing' of access to the media privileges the dominant forces in society by allowing them to establish the parameters of debate on social issues. Politicians, employers, the police and so-called experts become 'primary definers' of events whose 'primary definition sets the limit for all

millionaires; models; musicians; nurses; pet owners; pilots; police officers; political activists; priests; psychiatrists; psychologists; rabbis; ramblers; refugees; restaurateurs; sailors; scientists; shopkeepers; singers; social workers; sociologists; soldiers; solicitors; sports people; supporters; surgeons; teachers; transport experts; trawler captains; TV stars; undertakers; vegetarians; vets; vicars; victims; writers; zoologists. Also, don't forget to list other journalists with whom you might be able to swap favours.

On a quiet news day you could simply go through your contacts book and call some of the people to whom you have not spoken for a while. You never know, you might pick up a story or two. A contacts book is a living thing and you need to feed it by constantly adding fresh contacts from stories you are working on. Similarly, if you call somebody only to be told they are dead or retired, update your contacts book accordingly. Finally, make a back-up copy. Everyone agrees this is sound advice but too few journalists get around to it until the bitter experience of losing a contacts book makes them realise what a good idea it would have been.

The calls

A reporter's first job of the day is to find out what is happening on their patch, as Brian Whittle explains:

> As far as newsgathering goes we still do the old-fashioned things. So we get up early and do the calls. By the time I come into the office I've watched the telly, read at least a couple of national papers and a couple of locals. You're immediately tuned in to what's going on and you hit the floor running.

'The calls' – regular inquiries to a range of agencies – are a staple of newsgathering. Minimum calls will be the police, the fire brigade and the ambulance service, noting down anything of interest that has happened since the last time the calls were made, including updates to ongoing stories. Weekly papers might do calls once a day; daily papers will make several rounds of calls a day; and broadcast newsrooms and agencies will usually do the calls hourly or even more frequently. Journalists covering coastal areas will find the coastguard and lifeboat services included in their rounds of calls, while those covering areas popular

subsequent discussion by framing what the problem is' (Hall et al 1978: 59). According to this analysis, journalists play the role of 'secondary definers', circulating the interpretations of the powerful not because of any conspiracy but because 'the hierarchy of credibility' reflects the social power structure (Manning 2001: 138). The concept of primary and secondary definition has been criticised for neglecting the potential of media themselves to become primary definers (Critcher 2002: 529) and for downplaying some of the complexities of relationships between journalists and sources (Schlesinger 1990: 66–7; Manning 2001: 15–17 and 137–9; Kuhn 2002: 52–8).

Power

The journalist-source relationship has been described as resembling both a dance and a tug-of-war (Gans 1980: 116–7). McQuail says that the growing role of PR spinning means that 'it has probably become harder for the media to make any independent assessment of their own of the value of information provided to them in such volume' (McQuail 2000: 291). Larsake Larsson's study of relationships between reporters and local politicians found an interplay based on 'the exchange of information for media exposure', in which sometimes the journalist would have the upper hand and at other times the politician (Larsson 2002: 27). However, although journalists might highlight negative news, on a day-to-day level the agenda seemed to be set not by the journalists but by their sources:

> The local media obtain the bulk of their [municipal] news from matters addressed in municipal administrative and decision-making processes. Municipal news stemming from journalistic initiative is less common, since journalists' working conditions seldom permit independent inquiry and agenda building. They are forced, in a sense, to choose between the dishes offered on the municipal buffet table. Only rarely do they venture into the kitchen to see what the host may have hidden in the cupboard.
> ... [The] media stay within the news selection frames determined by the organisations they report. (Larsson 2002: 29)

This 'framing' of media coverage may on occasions be achieved by those outside the social power structure. For

with walkers or cavers may check with the mountain rescue service. A final round of calls will be made just before deadline. When I worked Saturday shifts for a Sunday paper I even had to ring the region's prisons asking if there had been any escapes or incidents, just in case.

Time was when calls used to involve journalists gathering at the local police station when a police officer would deliver a daily briefing on the latest crimes and misdemeanours by reading from the log of incidents. It still happens like that in some places, but most calls these days are on the telephone, many to recorded voicebanks updated by press officers.

The system of routine calls is very much a one-way flow of information – obviously so in the case of voicebanks. Although journalists will occasionally find out about crimes from members of the public or personal observation, the vast majority of crime stories that make the news have been supplied by the police. It has been argued that this gives the police a privileged position as one of a number of **primary definers** able to influence how certain issues are reported and debated. This question of **power** relations between journalists and sources has been explored at length by academics while journalists have been more concerned with the practicalities of getting the story. For journalists, making regular calls to the police and other emergency services is both a valid and a valuable way of generating copy. Calls provide a regular supply of stories ranging from nibs (news in brief) to leads; calls can be carried out routinely by any competent reporter even without any relevant personal knowledge or contacts; and calls provide insurance against the ignominy of missing something big happening on your patch. The calls will continue to be an important method of newsgathering.

Sources of news

Organisations contacted during the calls may be among the most prolific sources but they are only a few of the places where news comes from. Common sources, listed in Box 4.1, are introduced below.

Academic journals

Research by academics, published in peer-reviewed journals, is a frequent source of news stories. The

example, covering farmers' protests in Brittany prompted one journalist to express ethical concerns:

> After ten days we wonder if we are not being manipulated. They called us out for a photo opportunity. We got the feeling of giving backing to demonstrators. Without us, they do not exist. *(Quoted in Neveu 2002: 65)*

Yet it ought not to be forgotten that journalists retain the power to choose between sources, and to include or exclude certain perspectives, within the context of the constraints discussed in Chapter 2.

journalist's job is twofold: to spot a potential story among the qualifications and caveats beloved of academics, and to render the story intelligible and interesting to lay readers. There are almost daily examples, ranging from the quirky to matters of life and death.

Adverts

An advert for a high-powered job might alert you to the fact that the previous incumbent has left – maybe they resigned or were sacked. And when a state school felt the need to appeal for money in *Private Eye*'s classified ads it prompted widespread coverage about the state of the education system.

Airports

As well as being arrival and departure points for celebs galore, airports can generate stories both positive (record journey times, new routes) and negative (accidents, noise, battles over runway extensions).

Ambulance service

A routine call to the ambulance service may provide early warning of accidents, explosions, and even the occasional birth on the way to hospital.

Anniversaries

Journalists love anniversaries, especially those with a five or, even better, a zero at the end. Births, marriages, deaths, inventions, disasters, and wars starting or ending are just some of the occasions given the anniversary treatment.

Armed forces

In peacetime the armed forces can generate stories through manoeuvres, recruitment campaigns and pictures of 'local boys' overseas, plus the occasional mysterious death or case of bullying that comes to light. During times of conflict military briefings become events in their own right.

Arts groups

Apart from providing information about forthcoming events, arts groups can generate rows about funding or controversial subject matter.

Campaigns

Campaigners who want to influence public opinion on subjects ranging from animal rights to real ale are likely to come up with opinions or events that might generate news stories.

Chambers of Commerce and/or Trade

As spokespeople for business such organisations can be useful sources of stories or comments about anything from interest rates to Christmas shopping.

Charities

Because charities need publicity to generate public donations, many are geared up to the needs of journalists, suggesting heartrending stories complete with photogenic victims, human or animal.

Churches, Mosques, Synagogues, Temples

Religious organisations may make the news by holding events, by having internal rows or by attacking the views of others.

Colleagues

People you work with are likely to be parents, patients, residents, commuters and consumers, among other things. As such, they may come across events with the potential to become news.

Community groups

A good source for rows and reactions, especially of the not-in-my-backyard variety.

Companies

Behind the self-serving PR puffery, genuine business stories involve real products, real jobs and real profits or losses.

Consumer groups

Consumer stories range from the miss-selling of pensions to the discovery of a mouse in a sandwich. When groups of consumers band together they can become a valuable source.

Council departments

You will get some good exclusive stories if you bypass the council press office to establish direct relationships with officers actually doing the work in departments such as housing or highways.

Council meetings

Meetings tend not to be covered in the 'parliamentary gallery' style of old but they can still provide good copy as well as a chance to hang around and chat to councillors, officers and any members of the public who turn up to lobby on a particular issue. The bulky documents accompanying most agendas may also have some gems buried deep within.

> 'What an examination of published stories and their sources reveals is that news . . . is mainly a one-way traffic – 'them' telling 'us' what they want us to know.'
> – Brian Whittaker

Council press officers

Sizeable local authorities employ teams of press officers, many recruited from the newsrooms of local newspapers. They *react* to journalists' queries, coming up with information, quotes and contacts while acting as a buffer between decision-makers and journalists. And they *proactively* distribute stories in the form of well-written news releases or well-timed telephone calls. David Helliwell of the *Yorkshire Evening Post* says that council press officers with an eye for a good story should be able to get daily page leads in local evening papers because 'they know what will turn us on'. He adds: 'Sometimes they knock out stories *before* the meeting, which is slightly disturbing.'

Councillors

As with MPs, Euro-MPs and members of the assemblies in Scotland, Wales and Northern Ireland, councillors often have something they want to get off their chest. Most councillors have other day jobs, so work and mobile numbers are essential.

Court hearings

'You ignore the courts at your peril,' explains Brian Whittle, 'because you get the best human interest stories from them.' Court reporters dip in and out of several courtrooms looking for cases that fit the news values discussed in Chapter 3. Hence the importance of good contacts with court staff, police, solicitors, and the Crown Prosecution Service. Some reporters, especially those working for agencies, will also go after background material on defendants and 'after-match quotes' from victims and relatives.

Cuttings/diary

One story often leads to another, particularly if reminders are added to the newsdesk diary. Cuttings from previous articles are a major source of background information, but beware assuming that everything in a cutting is necessarily accurate. Certain myths seem to be recycled because they were published once and other journalists have not bothered to check. The Press Complaints Commission has warned that 'too many journalists now seem to act in the belief that to copy from 10 old stories is better than to write a new one with confirmation by proper fresh enquiry' (PCC 1992: 2).

Email lists

Adding yourself to a number of specialist email lists will undoubtedly lead to lots of spam but might also generate story leads.

Entertainment industry

An increasingly important source for today's media, as discussed in Chapters 3 and 7, although the line between puffery and journalism is sometimes dangerously anorexic.

Eyes and ears

Keep your eyes and ears open as you go about your life and you will be surprised at how many stories you can spot.

Fire brigade

One of the staple agencies for journalists' calls, checking with the fire brigade will provide early warning of house fires, motorway pile-ups and heroic rescues.

Forward planning services

For a subscription fee, such services will supply constantly updated details of forthcoming events along with contact details – all searchable by geographic area or specialist interest.

Government departments

As for council departments but on a national level.

Government News Network

The Government News Network (GNN), formerly part of the Central Office of Information, produces vast numbers of news releases on behalf of government departments and agencies on a regional and national basis. It also handles ministerial and royal visits.

Health authorities

Outbreaks of serious disease, funding crises, hospital closures and health promotion initiatives are all example of news stories that may emanate from health authorities.

Heritage groups

Campaigns to protect everything from historic woods to old gasworks can come up with some lively stories.

Hospitals

A hospital is not going to tell you about patients left overnight on trolleys, or given inappropriate treatment – those stories will come from other sources. But hospitals are a source of 'good news' stories about cures, new treatments, and general triumph-over-tragedy.

Inquests

The coroner's court provides a regular supply of tragic stories for the local media with the most high profile or unusual making it into the nationals. A major advantage for journalists is that most inquests are relatively brief encounters compared with criminal trials. Occasionally a large number of similar cases might indicate a story bigger than just the immediate tragedy.

Lateral thinking

Lateral thinking involves making connections and having a good memory. When Brian Whittle heard about a new report linking BSE in cows and CJD in humans – in contrast to reassurances by politicians – he remembered an earlier story about a woman who had died from suspected CJD after working in a butcher's:

> I sent a reporter and photographer to see the husband who had been left to bring up three kids on his own. They not only got a marvellous interview, he also gave them the most amazing picture. When she was dying in hospital he had taken a Polaroid picture of a nurse handing her the baby.

The picture was splashed across the front page of the *Daily Mirror* beneath the banner headline THE PROOF and a statement from the Prime Minister: 'I should make it clear that humans do not get mad cow disease' (*Daily Mirror* March 21 1996). 'It was lateral thinking, asking where there was a victim to illustrate this story, and that picture went half way round the world,' adds Brian Whittle.

Leaks

Leaks of information, whether from close contacts or anonymous whistleblowers, can lead to exclusive stories. The protection of such sources is discussed in Chapter 2, while Chapter 6 examines some stories that originated from leaks.

Letters

Letters pages should not be overlooked as a source of news. They contain opinions, questions, information and allegations that might repay further investigation. Sometimes a letter might become a news item in its own right.

Libraries

Hard though it is for some people to believe, not everything is available on the internet. Libraries retain a useful role in providing access to reference books, company reports, local history archives, indexes of local societies, community noticeboards and, by no means least, helpful librarians.

Motoring organisations

Organisations such as the RAC and the AA are always coming up with comments or surveys that make the news, and they are also good sources of reaction for anything to do with cars, roads or transport generally. However, given that people join for the recovery service rather than to have a mouthpiece, don't assume they speak for all motorists. The Environmental Transport Association (ETA) may provide a 'greener' viewpoint.

MPs and MEPs

MPs, Euro-MPs and members of regional and national assemblies need to maintain their profile with voters so they can usually be relied upon to make sure journalists know what they are up to. This means lots of dull statements and pseudo 'photo opportunities' among the more genuinely newsworthy items. At a national level, political correspondents spend a lot of time talking to backbench MPs, picking up gossip and gauging feeling.

News agencies

News agencies are the foot soldiers of journalism at a national and international level, allowing media organisations to cover stories in areas where they have few or no staff. Brian Whittle's agency, covering the ten towns of Greater Manchester, will be called by staff reporters of the national papers every day to see what stories might be happening on their patch: 'By nine o'clock in the morning we know what's going on in the region because we will have talked to the police forces, the ambulance, the fire brigade.' They will also have trawled through the local media, particularly the weekly newspapers, looking for stories with the potential to be turned around for the nationals. Agencies keep an eye on register offices and churches for signs of 'secret' celebrity weddings coming up. And if a London newsdesk needs somebody door-stepped at the other end of the country, it will usually be an agency reporter who gets the job, as Jane Merrick recalls:

A lot of our work was actually finding people at the centre of the story. So, rather than just going along to a court case and reporting it, we would find the accused's husband and see if he wanted to talk. A lot of it is going through the electoral roll and finding out where people live. You have to do a lot of running around.

News releases

News releases, aka press releases, can be good, bad or indifferent. Some sections of the media are alarmingly full of scarcely-rewritten news releases from councils, businesses, charities, universities and so on. Some news releases are pointers to genuine news but many are a waste of everybody's time. Even the worthwhile ones should be treated more as a starting-point than an end, and there may well be a better story if you read between the lines. Also, a simple phone call may avoid the embarrassment of reporting that something has happened just because a news release said it was going to happen – when it may have been cancelled.

> 'One study after another comes up with essentially the same observation . . . the story of journalism, on a day-to-day basis, is the story of the interaction of reporters and officials.'
> – Michael Schudson.

Noticeboards

Notices in shop windows, offices, libraries, colleges and elsewhere may tip you off about public meetings, petitions, planning applications or lost parrots.

Official reports

When confronted with an official report, don't simply rely on the executive summary. Newsworthy lines may be buried in the main text, demonstrating the value of cultivating friendly experts who will be able to help you understand such documents.

Other media

Newspapers monitor other papers plus TV, radio, Ceefax and news sites on the web. And, in turn, each medium monitors other media. The *Guardian*'s Martin Wainwright says:

The pyramid of stories starts maybe with a parish magazine, then a weekly paper, say the *Wharfedale Observer*, picks it up. The *Yorkshire Evening Post* picks it up from the *Wharfedale*, then the *Yorkshire Post* picks it up, and we pick it up if it's got a national interest.

Not that the story will simply be lifted. Not always, anyway. Different outlets require different treatments. To illustrate the point, Brian Whittle spreads on his desk a copy of one of the weekly papers on his patch, the *Knutsford Guardian*. He is excited by the potential of a story about some newts that have held up work on a traffic scheme:

> That's not the story at all. The real story is, this is one of the worst accident blackspots in the country, with a couple of people killed each year or even more, and they can't put this improvement scheme in because of a pond of great crested newts. The way we'll develop that is to go and see the wife of the latest victim, who will say to us 'who is more important, my husband or a pond of bloody newts?' And, if you do the pictures properly, you've got a page lead in one of the nationals.

> 'You have to be careful not to get to know them too well – it's a matter of maintaining a sound mistrust.'
> – Swedish reporter on political sources.

It happens at a political level too, with politicians' performances on the heavyweight broadcasting programmes being monitored for signs of splits or subtle changes of direction, as well as the latest comment on the controversy of the day. Jane Merrick explains:

> If they say something on TV you can use it. There are probably about four hours of political programmes on a Sunday, for example, and out of that there'll maybe be two quotes which will make a story. It's a daily cycle. If you're on the late shift you wait for the first editions of the newspapers to come in at about 10.30pm. Some newspaper will have been briefed about a story so you phone up the Home Office at 11 o'clock at night and they say yes it's all true, or no comment.

And so it goes on, with those newspapers influencing the next morning's *Today* programme (Radio Four) and the *Today* programming influencing TV news, the London *Evening Standard*, and the following morning's national newspapers.

Parish newsletters

There may be some spectacular rows lurking within their pages. Failing that, you might find stories ranging from an upcoming fete to a shortage of vicars.

People

Potential stories can be suggested by people you meet while at work, rest and play. This can range from somebody mentioning that they have just seen a police car parked in their street to rather more substantial fare. As a student journalist on work experience, Abul Taher was researching an education story about the influence of Islam on British campuses when he came across a stronger story:

> The leader of an Islamic extremist group made a passing remark that a lot of British Muslim students had gone to fight jihad in Bosnia, Afghanistan and Kashmir for the cause of Islam. I immediately latched on to that and he provided me with details of three students from Queen Mary and Westfield College abandoning their studies to go to jihad. I checked with the college, and the story made it as an exclusive in the *Guardian* and generated a lot of response from other media. This was two years before September 11. The source was really a chat with someone.

Police

Probably the single most important source for journalists, particularly in the local and regional media, is the police. Regular calls to police voicebanks and police stations, followed up where necessary with calls to the press office or preferably the investigating officer, result in an endless stream of stories about brutal killings, bungling burglars, callous thieves and have-a-go heroes. In addition to providing this rollcall of crimes, the police will sometimes tip-off the media about operations, allowing for dramatic pictures of dawn raids and drugs busts. Police may organise press conferences with victims' relatives. Experienced crime correspondents will develop their own networks of sources within the police, bypassing the press office where possible.

Political parties

Contacts within parties can be a fruitful source of stories about rows and splits, while party spokespeople will be more keen to let you know about the selection of candidates or the launch of policy initiatives.

Post offices

A post office, particularly in a rural area, can be a focus for information and gossip on local people and events.

Posters

The Harvey Nichols story discussed in this chapter is just one example of posters prompting news stories. Another occurred when a Bradford journalist noticed that posters near his office had been covered with white paint over a picture of Anna Kournikova wearing a bra. Enquiries with locals revealed that some Muslims were behind the action because they objected to the tennis player showing too much flesh – and the story made the national media.

PR companies

Journalists and PR people love to hate – or at least poke gentle fun at – each other. But the fruits of the PR industry's labours are there for all to see in the media every day, so the reality is that PR *is* a major source for many journalists. The role of public relations is discussed further in Chapter 2.

Press conferences

Fewer press conferences take place these days as most journalists are too busy to go and collect information that could be faxed or emailed. But police press conferences, for example during murder hunts, remain an important source of news. Press conferences are also likely to be held to announce the results of official inquiries or to unveil new appointments, and they give you a chance to question senior figures who may not otherwise be available. As with news releases, it is sometimes best to read between the lines and remember that the best angle might not even be mentioned from the platform. Try to get there early and hang around at the end, talking to other journalists as well as the participants. You might pick up a useful tip.

Pressure groups

As with campaigns, except that pressure groups tend to be more long-term. Note how often the English Collective of Prostitutes is referred to in stories about prostitution, not because it necessarily represents the views of most women on the game but because it is both quotable and easily accessible to journalists in a hurry.

Professional bodies

Stories from professional bodies may include disciplinary hearings or criticism of government policy. They are also seen as authoritative sources on anything to do with their profession.

Public inquiries

Public inquiries can produce good copy, but remember to look beneath the surface. It was only by skim-reading hundreds of pages of official documents at a public inquiry into a 1990s draught that reporter Peter Lazenby discovered that a suggestion to evacuate the entire city of Bradford had been raised at a meeting between Yorkshire Water and the city's emergency planners because the water supply could not be guaranteed. It was just one line in a set of old minutes towards the bottom of a mountain of paper, but it made that night's headlines.

Pubs

Publicans and regulars can be mines of information about the community and, if you get chatting, they might tell you about anything from charity events to the death of a local character. Peter Lazenby delights in telling young journalists that more cracking news stories started out being scribbled on wet beermats than will ever be uncovered by reporters sitting at their desks. Not everyone has the personality to pick up a story in a pub, of course, and many of today's bars are not exactly conducive to chatting; but the point remains that off-diary stories come from *talking* to people.

Quangos

A quango is a 'quasi-autonomous non-governmental organisation' operating at arms-length from ministers. Quangos can be sources of news by virtue of the work they do, how they spend their money, and by controversial appointments.

Readers/viewers/listeners

Journalism cannot exist without an audience and many members of the audience will suggest stories by popping into the office, telephoning, sending letters or emails, or by collaring a reporter at some public event. Some will tell you about personal gripes, some will describe impossibly complicated disputes, and some will tell you that government agents are using lamp-posts to beam poison rays into their bedroom at night. But others will come up with excellent stories. How you treat people will influence whether they come back to you next time.

Regeneration projects

A huge amount of public money is spent on regenerating run-down areas or former industrial sites and such projects can provide both 'good news' stories and allegations of miss-spent funds.

Regional development agencies

These agencies bring together regional 'stakeholders' and can come up with stories on inward-investment, planning issues and regeneration.

Regulatory bodies

Ofwat (water), Postcomm (mail), Ofgem (energy) and all the rest are regular sources of stories about customer complaints, rising prices, excess profits and directors' pay. Media regulators adjudicate on complaints from the public on matters such as taste and decency.

Residents' groups

See community groups.

Schools

Schools can provide good news stories about achievements such as productions, sporting feats and exam passes. They can also be the focus of tragic news, especially when trips go wrong.

Scouts, Cubs, Guides, Brownies, Woodcraft Folk

As organisations dependent on attracting new members, youth groups are likely to let you know about events, exchange trips and so on. They also make the news because of changes in traditional activities, songs or uniforms.

Solicitors

'Solicitors are very good sources because they represent people who have been done down,' says Paul Foot of *Private Eye*. It may be in their clients' interests to gain publicity for an appeal against a miscarriage of justice, a civil action for wrongful arrest, or a compensation claim for an industrial disease. Solicitors can become valuable long-term contacts, as Jane Merrick explains:

> There are three or four solicitors in Liverpool – and it's probably the same in most other cities – who tend to deal with the big cases. So it's a question of knowing them well enough, keeping them warm so they'll speak to you and contact you about cases. They like to see their names in the paper.

Sports organisations

Apart from accounts of the winning, the losing and the taking part, you might also find stories about lack of facilities or the sale of playing fields.

Support groups

Groups set up to support people with particular conditions or diseases can come up with great human interest stories.

Theatres

Events, celebs, subject matter and funding are all ways in which a theatre may prompt a news story.

Trade associations

The views of a particular industry might be newsworthy, particularly if it is calling for a change in government policy to prevent closures and job loses.

Trade press

As with academic journals, the trade and specialist press contain many stories of potential interest to the general reader, as long as you can identify and translate them. Journalists on specialist publications can also be interviewed as authoritative sources; for example, editors of railway or aviation magazines are often interviewed as experts after rail or air crashes.

Trades unions

Unions can be an excellent source of stories not just about industrial disputes but everything from pensions scandals to sexual harassment. The bigger unions have well-resourced research departments able to provide journalists with useful background material.

Transport companies

Cancellations, strikes, fares increases, punctuality figures, franchise bids, 'journeys from hell' and crashes are all obvious news stories. Once in a blue moon you might even come across the occasional good news story from a transport company – an announcement of new investment, perhaps, or the opening of a new route.

Universities

Universities are a source of a huge range of stories, whether it is ground-breaking research, an unusual degree scheme or an ethical argument about accepting funding from a tobacco company. Universities are also where you will find experts in everything from aeronautics to the zodiac.

Web

In addition to news from around the world there are countless potential stories lurking on the web in sites that are unusual, amusing, quirky, informative, provocative, dangerous, disgusting or just plain nasty. Some useful websites are listed in Appendix Two.

From sources to stories

Although not exhaustive, the above list covers the major sources used by reporters to originate or check stories. How journalists obtain and evaluate information from sources is discussed further in Chapters 5 and 6. If you watch the TV news, listen to a radio bulletin or read a newspaper with this list in mind, you should be able to come up with a fairly good idea of where most stories are likely to have come from.

Some sources are less visible than others. Former Fleet Street journalist Simon Winchester recalls

> **'The responsibility for truth is left to the source, more often than not'.**
> – Denis McQuail.

reporting 'the troubles' in Northern Ireland and being given off-the-record briefings by the oxymoronic chaps at military intelligence. Winchester would pass on the contents of the briefing to his audience, telling the nation that the young man shot dead by British soldiers the night before was a leading paramilitary. Only later did he realise that 'most of what I gaily rebroadcast was, if not a pure figment of the imagination of some superheated British army intelligence officer, then to a very large degree, wishful thinking' (Winchester 2001). This underlines the value to a journalist of maintaining a *questioning* attitude, no matter who you are dealing with.

Putting unattributable briefings with spooks to one side, the strongest news stories come from journalists *talking* to people. Even a story that originates from a news release or a cutting will be improved by talking to people. Making an extra call or knocking on that extra door might make the difference between having the same story as everyone else or coming up with a fresh angle or a new piece of information. There is no substitute for speaking to the people directly involved in a story, where possible. That can sometimes require you to be tough and single-minded. But it does not excuse the behaviour witnessed by Edward Behr in newly-independent Zaire, as thousands of Belgian women and children waited to be airlifted to safety:

> Into the middle of this crowd strode an unmistakably British TV reporter, leading his cameraman and sundry technicians like a platoon commander through hostile territory. At intervals he paused and shouted, in a stentorian but genteel BBC voice, 'Anyone here been raped and speaks English?' *(Behr 1992: 136)*

Such insensitivity might get the story, but at what cost? As journalists we have a duty to ourselves, to our sources and to our fellow citizens to pause for reflection from time to time. Without some sense of humanity and empathy, what is the point of our journalism?

Summary

Journalists need sources to provide information that may be turned into news and to check information provided by other sources. Journalists are surrounded by sources of potential news stories, although many academic studies suggest that a high proportion of stories come from a relatively narrow range of sources. Information on sources is collected in contacts books, and some sources such as the police are contacted on a regular basis because they are major suppliers of potential news. Journalists tend to evaluate sources based on their previous experience. It has been suggested that some sources have the power to virtually guarantee access to the news and to frame debate on social issues.

Questions

Why do journalists need sources?

Why do sources need journalists?

Who has more power, the journalist or the source?

Why do some people or organisations get in the news more than others?

What is the effect of journalists using the media as a source?

Further reading

For practical advice on the sources of news, Keeble (2001a) and Frost (2002) are both worth dipping into. Manning (2001) is the best option for an up-to-date review of relevant research and more theoretical frameworks on journalist-source relationships. Tumber (1999) offers useful extracts, while Hall et al (1978) is worth reading for the concept of primary definers.

Notes

Sources for soundbites: Whittle interview with the author; Mansfield 1936: 82; Whittaker 1981: 32; Schudson 1989: 271; Swedish reporter cited in Larsson 2002: 25; McQuail 2000: 291.

Chapter Five

The journalist as objective reporter

Key terms

Objectivity	Opinion
Subjectivity	Truth
Impartiality	Bias
Balance	Agenda setting
Neutrality	Moral panic
Strategic ritual	Common sense
Facts	Hegemony

More cracking news stories have started life scribbled on wet beermats than will ever be uncovered by reporters sitting at their desks poring over piles of press releases. This distinctly old school philosophy, featured in Chapter 4, came to mind when I noticed an unusual beermat beneath my pint. Advertising a regional Sunday sports newspaper, *Yorkshire Sport*, it read: 'Heavily censored. Totally biased. It's the perfect read.' Where does that leave the notion of the journalist as objective reporter?

Objective reporting has been defined as:

- Balance and even-handedness in presenting different sides of an issue.

- Accuracy and realism in reporting.

- Presenting all main relevant points.

- Separating facts from opinion, but treating opinion as relevant.

- Minimising the influence of the writer's own attitude, opinion or involvement.

- Avoiding slant, rancour or devious purposes.

(Boyer 1981, cited in Watson 1998: 98)

Objectivity in the eye of the beholder

But concepts such as **objectivity** and **impartiality** need not apply when it comes to much reporting of sport, it seems. I know, because for the last few years I have written a magazine column following the fortunes of the local rugby league team. It is intended as a supporter's view so, although I have a media pass allowing me to get into games without paying, I eschew the neutral space of the press box in favour of the more partisan terrain of the terraces. This comes across in my copy which, though accurate and devoid of devious purposes, is certainly slanted, opinionated and even on occasion rancorous. Anybody who has ever been to a passionate sporting occasion will know that objectivity – indeed, **truth** – can be a relative thing. Our view of what is going on is influenced by those around us, along with whatever personal and collective baggage we've brought along to the occasion. So supporters of different teams, and journalists 'representing' different communities, might have markedly different opinions

Objectivity

Objectivity hinges on separating independently verifiable 'facts' from subjective values (Schudson 1978: 293). The concept is associated with the Enlightenment project of rationality and the pursuit of scientific knowledge. Such grand thinking has been challenged in recent years, with some postmodernist theorists dismissing as naïve empiricism the idea that there is a truth that exists 'out there' in the world, independent of discourse, just waiting to be discovered. This view was perhaps expressed most (in)famously in Jean Baudrillard's assertion that that the 1991 Gulf war did not exist; that it was a media spectacle (cited in Kieran 1998: 23).

A commitment to objectivity in journalism can be defined as meaning that 'a person's statements about the world can be trusted if they are submitted to established rules deemed legitimate by a professional community' (Schudson 1978: 294). Michael Schudson explains this 'objectivity norm' further:

> The objectivity norm guides journalists to separate facts from values and to report only the facts. Objective reporting is supposed to be cool, rather than emotional, in tone. Objective reporting takes pains to represent fairly each leading side in a political controversy. According to the objectivity norm, the journalist's job consists of reporting something called 'news' without commenting on it, slanting it, or shaping its formulation in any way. *(Schudson 2001: 150)*

But journalism was not always expected to be objective, and the above norm was not a constituent part of those 18th century publications such as the *Craftsman* and the *Gentleman's Magazine* that helped establish the press as 'a genuinely critical organ of a public engaged in critical political debate: as the fourth estate' (Habermas 1992: 60). Before the 1830s newspapers were expected to be partisan and 'objectivity was not an issue' (Schudson 1978: 291). The emergence of the US 'penny press', with many papers being politically neutral or indifferent, brought a new range of news values privileging factual coverage of human interest stories over analysis or opinion (Allan 1997: 304–5). The gradual adoption of objectivity as a normative standard of news reporting may have been encouraged by the development of wire services such as Associated Press (AP) from 1848. AP had a market imperative to

of what they have witnessed. They have, in a sense, been to different games.

But that's sport. We might expect sports journalism to be informed by the subjective, even though we trust journalists to be accurate when giving us the score. At the end of the day, it's not a matter of life and death – it's just entertainment. News reporting is different. Isn't it? Up to a point. Consider the following *news* reports of Rupert Murdoch's ill-fated attempt to buy Manchester United football club, taken from the front pages of rival newspapers:

> GOLD TRAFFORD
>
> £565m Sky deal makes Utd most valuable team in the world . . . Skyly delighted . . . Thrilled Manchester United fans were buzzing with excitement over BSkyB's amazing takeover bid yesterday . . .
> *(Sun September 7 1998)*
>
> RED DEVIL
>
> Fury at tycoon Rupert Murdoch's plan to buy Manchester United reached fever pitch last night. Reds fans begged the world famous club not to sell out and called on supporters to boycott Murdoch's Sun newspaper and satellite TV stations . . . *(Daily Mirror September 8 1998)*

No prizes for guessing which newspaper is part of the Murdoch empire and which is one of its main commercial rivals. Truth can be a relative concept even in the *same* newspaper. Take the *Sun*'s coverage of the launch of the euro currency. The front page of its main edition proclaimed: 'The euro is born. And thank goodness Britain is not part of it' (DAWN OF A NEW ERROR, *Sun* January 2 2002). But the Irish edition, under the same picture of the 'Page 3 girl of the year', had a different slant – DAWN OF A NEW ERA – and enthused that 'Ireland's new euro currency is set to be a huge hit with the public' (*Sun* January 2 2002).

> 'We shall give a correct picture of the world . . . wherever human nature or real life displays its freaks and vagaries.'
> – James Gordon Bennett, founder of the New York Herald, 1835.

Unlike broadcasting organisations, newspapers have no statutory requirement to be impartial, whether between the commercial interests of rival proprietors or between rival political policies or parties. General elections would not be the same without **agenda setting** headlines such as LABOUR'S TAX LIES EXPOSED (*Daily Express* March 23 1992) and A LABOUR

concentrate on the bare facts, compressed into the intro, so it could sell stories to newspapers with widely divergent politics. This strategy of unadorned reportage helped AP staff overcome the unreliable nature of the new technology and placed a premium on brevity (Allan 1997: 306).

But Schudson says the journalist's commitment to separating facts from values may have had more to do with the rising status of reporters in relation to their employers in the late 19th and early 20th centuries, and with a professional debate about objectivity in the years after the First World War. Therefore, 'a self-conscious, articulate ideology of objectivity can be dated to the 1920s' (Schudson 2001: 159–60). In the UK, as Chris Frost notes, the move towards a less partisan style of reporting gathered momentum only during the early part of the 20th century, culminating in the imposition of a statutory obligation to be impartial on the fledgling broadcasting industry (Frost 2000: 159).

Impartiality

The words 'impartiality' and 'objectivity' are sometimes used interchangeably, but impartial reporting is normally defined as being neutral, while objective reporting is taken to be the reporting of verifiable facts. According to McQuail, impartiality means 'balance in the choice and use of sources, so as to reflect different points of view, and also neutrality in the presentation of news – separating facts from opinion, avoiding value judgements or emotive language or pictures' (McQuail 2000: 321). For Frost, impartial reporting means that a journalist is *aiming* at the truth, whereas true objectivity would require giving the *whole* picture – a task as impossible for the journalist as it is (in an analogy borrowed from Hartley) for the cartographer (Frost 2000: 38). Like a map, a news report is still a selective and *mediated* representation of reality.

Balance and neutrality have themselves been challenged by some journalists who advocate their abandonment in situations where to be impartial would mean standing 'neutrally between good and evil, right and wrong, the victim and the oppressor' (Bell 1998: 16). This raises inevitable questions about *who* defines 'good

GOVERNMENT WILL LEAD TO HIGHER MORTGAGE PAYMENTS (*Daily Mail* April 7 1992). Despite the fact that broadcasting organisations are required by law to be impartial, TV and radio journalists' election coverage can still be influenced by a press agenda focusing on certain issues (tax, crime, Europe) to the exclusion of others (homelessness, poverty, jobs). And the clockwatching 'balance' between the Labour and Conservative parties also tends to marginalise the Liberal Democrats and other parties.

Objectivity in wartime

If objective reporting of elections is problematic – the country being divided – then what of objective reporting of warfare, when a country is supposedly united against a common enemy? That truth is the first casualty of war has become a truism, but objective reporting has repeatedly gone to the wall in the name of national unity. British Prime Minister Lloyd George alluded to this in 1917, during a private conversation about the battlefield horrors of the First World War:

> If people really knew, the war would be stopped tomorrow. But of course they don't know and can't know. The correspondents don't write and the censorship would not pass the truth. *(Cited in Knightley 2000: 116–17)*

Are we any better informed today? Research suggests that tabloid headlines such as GO GET HIM BOYS (*Daily Star* January 16 1991) and the obsession of TV news with 'smart bombs' and 'Star Wars' technology painted only a partial picture of the 1991 Gulf war, rendering invisible some of the salient issues (including oil supplies), not to mention Iraqi civilian casualties (Philo and McCloughlin 1993: 146–55). The choice of words themselves told a story (see Box 5.1).

Reflecting shortly after that war, BBC reporter John Simpson identified a gap in UK television's saturation coverage of the conflict: 'As for the human casualties, tens of thousands of them, or the brutal effect the war had on millions of others . . . we didn't see so much of that' (quoted in Philo and McCloughlin 1993: 155). Nor did we hear very much about the 'undeclared war' waged against Iraq in the decade that followed. Figures released quietly by the Ministry of Defence in

and evil' and whether journalists who *do* take sides automatically abandon any claims to be able to report events *objectively*. It could be argued that such journalism, although not neutral, is actually *more* objective because the audience knows where the journalist is coming from. Viewed this way, *Socialist Worker* would be more objective than *BBC News* because the political and cultural assumptions of the former are made explicit – and can therefore be taken into account by the audience – whereas the political and cultural assumptions of the latter remain implicit.

Truth

Truth has become an increasingly slippery notion in recent years as the apparent certainties of modernity have come under challenge. Yet for many journalists the truth is still out there in the shape of 'facts that are verified and explained' (Seib 2002: 4). Either you can get to this truth or you can't; and if you can't, it's probably because somebody is trying to stop you. Such 'general truth claims' have been replaced in much cultural analysis by a foregrounding of the subjective experience (Dovey 2000: 25) or by a wider claim that the concept of there being *a* truth is merely a monologic *version* of truth produced from within a discourse that is white, male, and elitist (Allan 1998: 124–6). Even reporters witnessing an event for themselves may be carrying all sorts of personal or cultural baggage that can impact on what they see as 'true' and what they recognise as 'the facts' (Keeble 1998: 182). Despite such claims, truth is not that difficult a concept to grasp, argues Matthew Kieran:

> In journalism, as distinct from fiction, there is a truth of the matter and this is what objectivity in journalism aims at . . . Where reporting turns away from the goal of truth and journalists treat events as open to many interpretations, according to their prejudices, assumptions, news agenda or the commercial drive toward entertainment, the justification and self-confessed rationale of journalism threatens to disappear. *(Kieran 1998: 34–5)*

Box 5.1

Box 5.1 (Wartime: words used by the UK press during the Gulf war, as listed in the *Guardian* January 25 1991, cited in O'Sullivan et al 1998: 80)

we have	*they have*
Army, Navy and Air Force	A war machine
Reporting guidelines	Censorship

we	*they*
Take out	Destroy
Neutralise	Kill
Dig in	Cower in their foxholes

we launch	*they launch*
First strikes	Sneak missile attacks

our boys are	*they are*
Loyal	Blindly obedient
Young knights of the skies	Bastards of Baghdad
Desert rats	Mad dogs

	their missiles cause
our missiles cause	Civilian casualties
Collateral damage	

Agenda setting

The term agenda setting was coined by Maxwell McCombs and Donald Shaw in their study of media coverage and voter attitudes in the 1968 US presidential election campaign. They found that the media exerted a 'considerable impact' on voters' judgements of what were the salient issues of the campaign (McCombs and Shaw 1972: 323–4). On the basis of this and similar studies it is argued that, although the media might not be able to tell us what to *think*, they have an influence on what we think *about*. But agenda setting has been dismissed as 'at best a hackneyed half-truth' on the grounds that it downplays the existence of multiple agendas by media organisations and voters alike (Wilson 1996: 30). McQuail notes that the direction of flow in the agenda setting model could be reversed, raising the possibility that, rather than *setting* the agenda, the media merely *reflect* the attitudes of voters. For him, agenda setting remains a 'plausible but unproven idea' (McQuail 2000: 456). Much the same could perhaps be said about the many theories of media effects, including the shift of recent years towards privileging 'the instability of meaning and the interpretative horizons of the audience' (Stevenson 2002: 29).

November 2000 showed that 84 tonnes of bombs had been dropped on southern Iraq by British aircraft over the previous two years (Norton-Taylor 2000). This silent bombing campaign passed almost unnoticed by the UK media, which awoke only to cheer on occasional 'spectaculars' with headlines such as US LAUNCHES AIR STRIKES ON BAGHDAD (*Daily Telegraph* February 17 2001) and WE BOMB BAGHDAD (*Sun* February 17 2001). Note the use of 'we' in the latter example – a tiny word with huge meanings.

> **'Comment is free, but facts are sacred.'**
> – CP Scott, editor of the Manchester Guardian, 1921.

'The way wars are reported in the western media follows a depressingly predictable pattern,' wrote Phillip Knightley as US and UK forces geared up to attack Afghanistan in the wake of September 11:

> Stage one, the crisis; stage two, the demonisation of the enemy's leader; stage three, the demonisation of the enemy as individuals; and stage four, . . . the atrocity story. *(Knightley 2001)*

Moral panics

A moral panic could be described as the periodic response of 'right thinking people' to someone or something perceived as 'other'. Stanley Cohen researched the Mods and Rockers youth subcultures of the 1960s, and summarised moral panics thus:

> A condition, episode, person or group of persons emerges to become defined as a threat to societal values and interests; its nature is presented in a stylised and stereotypical fashion by the mass media; the moral barricades are manned by editors, bishops, politicians and other right-thinking people; socially accredited experts pronounce their diagnoses and solutions; ways of coping are evolved or (more often) resorted to; the condition then disappears, submerges or deteriorates and becomes more visible. Sometimes the object of the panic is quite novel and at other

Such coverage prepares the public for battle 'by showing that the enemy is evil, mad and a danger to the civilised world' (Knightley 2002). Stephen Dorril traced the leaking of intelligence dossiers containing truths, half-truths and untruths about Iraq to 'trusted journalists and newspapers' in the UK and US (Dorril 2002a). 'If the history of the media teaches us anything,' he concluded, 'it is that the "war on terrorism" is a ripe opportunity for disinformation and the creation of provocative incidents which the press reports with casual disregard for the truth' (Dorril 2002b). What Paul Foot calls 'war fever' seemed to infect many – but not all – UK newsrooms before and during the US-led invasion of Iraq in 2003. The *Sun* reported the start of the war with the headline SHOW THEM NO PITY . . . THEY HAVE STAINS ON THEIR SOULS (*Sun* March 20 2003). *Sun* journalist Katy Weitz promptly resigned from the paper because, she explained, 'I want to be proud of the work I help to produce, not shudder in shame at its front-page blood lust' (Weitz 2003).

But it is not only those who support their own government's war efforts who sometimes discard the cloak of objectivity. Reflecting on his role in reporting conflicts around the world, veteran journalist James Cameron wrote:

> It never occurred to me, in such a situation, to be other than subjective, and as obviously as I could manage to be . . . I always tended to argue that objectivity was of less importance than the truth, and that the reporter whose technique was informed by no opinion lacked a very serious dimension. *(Cameron, quoted in Bailey and Williams 1997: 356)*

He felt that a journalist's attitude should be up front and open to scrutiny or counter-argument. Similarly, George Orwell argued that the reader could be freed of the influence of a journalist's 'bias' only if the reader were made *aware* of it (cited in Pilger 1998: 525). Certainly there is no mistaking the attitude of John Pilger, writing in the *Daily Mirror* about the bombing of Afghanistan under the headline THIS WAR OF LIES GOES ON:

> There was, and still is, no 'war on terrorism'. Instead, we have watched a variation of the great imperial game

> '**To journalists, like social scientists, the term "objectivity" stands as a bulwark between themselves and critics.'**
> *– Gaye Tuchman.*

times it is something which has been in existence long enough, but suddenly appears in the limelight. Sometimes the panic passes over and is forgotten, except in folklore and collective memory; at other times it has more serious and long-lasting repercussions and might produce such changes as those in legal and social policy or even in the way society conceives itself. *(Cohen 1972: 9)*

In a classic study of the phenomenon of mugging in the 1970s, Stuart Hall and colleagues concluded that a moral panic about what was perceived as a race-specific crime was created by a mutually reinforcing circle between powerful 'primary definers' (police, judges, politicians and so on) and the media to effect 'an ideological closure of the topic' (Hall et al 1978: 75). This shorthand equation of black youths with mugging in the 1970s is echoed three decades on in the media's readiness to associate Muslims with terrorism (Karim 2002: 102; Seib 2002: 114; Richardson 2001: 229). However, as with agenda setting, it is possible that media coverage of a 'moral panic' *reflects* rather than *creates* a public demonisation of a particular social grouping at a particular time.

Strategic ritual

It may be that Tuchman's strategic ritual of objectivity is more concerned with ritual than with objectivity, because the journalist retains the power to select who to quote and what evidence to include. Just as, when writing this book, *I* have chosen who to interview, which publications to cite, and what issues to address. But I have not acted in a vacuum and journalists act within the context of the influences and constraints discussed in Chapter 2.

In the Harvey Nichols story discussed in this chapter, it could be argued that I followed the strategic ritual and that the story was 'true'. It could also be argued that the story had little independent objective existence, because most of the opinions or actions that helped 'stand up' the story were *solicited* by me after receiving the initial tip-off. My fingerprints were all over the story that appeared in the next day's papers, yet they could not be detected with the naked eye.

of swapping 'bad' terrorists for 'good' terrorists, while untold numbers of innocent people have paid with their lives: most of one village, whole families, a hospital, as well as teenage conscripts suitably dehumanised by the word 'Taliban'. *(Pilger 2001)*

Some journalists who reject Pilger's campaigning style nonetheless question the professional commitment to objectivity when covering bloody conflicts. ITN reporter Michael Nicholson adopted an orphaned girl he met while covering the Bosnian war. He says:

> No, I don't believe in this so-called objectivity. You can still report the facts. You can still be as close to the truth as any person can be and still show a commitment, an emotional anguish. I don't see them to be contradictory. *(Quoted in McLaughlin 2002b: 154)*

Former BBC correspondent Martin Bell has called for 'a journalism of attachment'. While accepting that 'the facts are sacred', Bell wants journalists covering conflicts to accept the 'moral responsibility' that they can *affect* the events they are reporting (quoted in McLaughlin 2002b: 178). Christiane Amanpour of CNN argues along similar lines without necessarily rejecting the concept of objectivity itself:

> I have come to believe that objectivity means giving all sides a fair hearing, but not treating all sides equally. Once you treat all sides the same in a case such as Bosnia, you are drawing a moral equivalence between victim and aggressor. And from there it is a short step toward being neutral. And from there it's an even shorter step to becoming an accessory to all manners of evil; in Bosnia's case, genocide. So objectivity must go hand in hand with morality. *(Quoted in Seib 2002: 53)*

> '*The more one is aware of political bias, the more one can be independent of it, and the more one claims to be impartial, the more one is biased.*'
> – *George Orwell.*

Taking such arguments a stage further are the few journalists who step aside from their reporting role and appear as witnesses at international war crimes tribunals. BBC correspondent Jacky Rowland was cross-examined by former Yugoslav president Slobodan Milosevic when she testified at the Hague in 2002 about events in Kosovo three years earlier. Afterwards, she explained why she defied fellow

The formula of presenting conflicting versions in a story means that journalists – rarely experts in a particular subject – do not normally have to decide between competing truth claims. As Keeble notes, reporters use sources to distance themselves from stories (Keeble 2001a: 44). Sometimes journalists *do* privilege one source, or truth claim, over another. For example, in this chapter I have quoted ACPO as giving 'the facts' about crime and asylum seekers. But is their account more objectively true than the more lurid press headlines? Yes, in the sense that the ACPO version is based on crime statistics. But can such figures be regarded as objective when they are based only on *reported* rather than *actual* crime? By following the strategic ritual and stating where information is from and when it is disputed, journalists can absolve themselves from the responsibility of deciding who is right and who is wrong on such issues. As one journalist put it: 'We don't deal in facts but in attributed opinions' (quoted in Gans 1980: 246).

Common sense

Journalists use their common sense to assess whether something has the ring of truth about it. But common sense itself can be seen as socially, culturally and historically constructed, rendering it highly questionable as an 'objective' test. Useful here is the concept of hegemony, the way in which a dominant class is said not merely to rule a society but also to exert moral and intellectual leadership, albeit contested (Gramsci 1971: 57). Hegemony goes beyond mere manipulation of opinion to saturate society and become regarded as 'common sense' (Williams 1980: 37–8). This does not mean that common sense contains *no* truths; rather, that common sense is 'an ambiguous, contradictory and multiform concept, and *to refer to common sense as a confirmation of truth is a nonsense*' (Gramsci 1971: 423; my emphasis).

journalists' arguments that she had compromised her impartiality and posed a threat to future war correspondents:

> I believe that journalists are essentially witnesses to the events they report on. My testimony to the Hague tribunal was an extension of this . . . When I met the witness who was due to take the stand after me – a woman who had lost eight members of her family in an alleged massacre by Serbian police – I felt that a journalist's arguments for not testifying looked rather weak.
>
> *(Rowland 2002)*

Adhering to traditional journalistic objectivity while remaining true to a sense of moral responsibility can be a difficult ethical balancing act. Philip Seib points to another tribunal at which a reporter's notebooks – containing sensitive information on confidential sources – were scrutinised in public. Risking 'burning' a source in this way may dissuade other sources from speaking to journalists in the future: 'That is a substantial price, but some journalists may judge it to be reasonable given the substance of a war crimes trial' (Seib 2002: 86).

Objectivity on the home front

From enemies without to 'the enemy within', Prime Minister Margaret Thatcher's characterisation of the coalminers who staged a year-long strike against pit closures in 1984/5. Much media coverage of the miners' strike was framed by a few key themes, with three phrases being repeated throughout the dispute: uneconomic pits, picket line violence, the drift back to work (Philo 1991:37–42; Hollingsworth 1986: 242–85). In contrast, another group of workers found their battle largely ignored a decade later. More than 300 Liverpool dockers were sacked for refusing to cross a picket line in 1995, and for two years their campaign for reinstatement won support and considerable media coverage in other countries but few headlines in the UK. One docker told me matter-of-factly that the government had imposed a 'news blackout' – it was the only explanation he could come

> **'Between elections, if you're relevant and intelligent and know how to popularise an issue, you can help set the agenda.'**
> – Rupert Murdoch.

Subjective

Reflexivity and the foregrounding of subjective experience may have become increasingly fashionable in the media (Dovey 2000), but for the most part news journalism remains a bastion of the authoritative-sounding 'objective' approach. This is a deeply undesirable state of affairs for cultural theorist John Fiske, who argues that journalists would better reflect 'reality' if they became more like the writers of TV soaps:

> Objectivity is authority in disguise: 'objective' facts always support particular points of view and their 'objectivity' can exist only as part of the play of power. But, more important, objective facts cannot be challenged: objectivity discourages audience activity and participation. Rather than being 'objective', therefore, TV news should present *multiple perspectives* that, like those of soap opera, have as unclear a hierarchy as possible . . . [The] reporters should be less concerned about telling the final truth of what has happened, and should present, instead, *different ways of understanding* it and the different points of view inscribed in those different ways. So, too, they should not disguise their processes of selection and editing, but should open them up to reveal news as a production, not as transparent reportage. *(Fiske 1989: 194; my emphasis)*

It is not easy to imagine what such a form of journalism would look like in practice. But we might find out sooner rather than later if Stuart Allan is right when he says that there is no reason to expect objectivity – as a historically-specific concept – to continue as a guiding principle of journalism (Allan 1997: 319).

up with for the dearth of coverage. But most editors do not need to be *told* to ignore 'boring' industrial disputes in favour of celebrity gossip, as John Pilger notes:

> Because the myths of the 'market' have become received wisdom throughout the media, with millions of trade unionists dismissed as 'dinosaurs', the dockers' story has been seen as a flickering curiosity of a bygone era. That their struggle represented more than half of all working people caught up in the iniquities of casual or part-time labour, making Britain the sweatshop of Europe, was not considered *real news*.
> *(Pilger 1998: 354; my emphasis)*

Objectivity, then, is not simply concerned with *how* a particular story is covered, but also with *what* is selected as a potential story – and what is ignored.

It sometimes seems as if issues come from nowhere to dominate headlines for a few weeks before disappearing again; mugging, devil dogs, a mysterious flesh-eating bug, video nasties, juvenile crime, paedophiles, and asylum seekers are just some examples of what have become known as **moral panics**, during which professionals with expert knowledge of a field are often appalled by the media's apparent lack of objectivity or regard to the facts. For example, in February 2001 – after more than a year of hostile press coverage claiming that asylum seekers had brought a crime wave to parts of Kent – the Association of Chief Police Officers (ACPO) noted:

> In Dover, continual interest from the media, locally and nationally, has been focused on the 'apparent' *increase* in crime since asylum seekers have been in the town. In line with general trends in Kent, the local commander was able to report an actual *reduction* in all aspects of reported crime over a three year period. This generally resulted in the national media not reporting anything as this was not what they had been told by some locals and was *not what their editors wanted.* (ACPO 2001: my emphasis)

We heard in Chapter 2 how headlines about asylum seekers in the *Express* caused disquiet among some of the paper's own journalists. Even a brief item about the publication of a new dictionary was headlined NOW

ASYLUM SEEKERS INVADE OUR DICTIONARY (*Daily Express* September 26 2002). Similar themes are to be found in the *Daily Mail*: ASYLUM: YES, BRITAIN IS A SOFT TOUCH! (February 1 2001) and PATIENTS LOSE GP'S SURGERY TO ASYLUM SEEKERS (September 5 2002) being just two of many similar examples. The *Mail*'s agenda of moral outrage was introduced in Chapter 3. It has long been accused of abandoning notions of objectivity in favour of peddling a particular 'Middle England' world view, exemplified by an ideal of aspirational, property-owning Conservative voters who believe in 'family values'. In the words of a former *Daily Mail* journalist: 'You kind of know what the obsessions are, and you very much know you've got to do a story in a specific way' (quoted in Beckett 2001). It is claimed that this approach goes beyond overtly political stories to inform the *Mail*'s broader coverage:

> [The] softer daily stories about animals, the self-improvement features, the straight-faced serialisations of apocalyptic new age speculations – these also emphasise, in a more gentle fashion, the importance of aspiration and domesticity, the need to distrust official explanations, the dangerousness of the world outside your neat home. *(Beckett 2001)*

Objectivity as a 'strategic ritual'

The above examples might suggest that objective reporting is honoured more in the breach than in the actuality. But this does not mean the concept of objective reporting has no resonance for working journalists. In my experience, *most* journalists, *most* of the time, *do* attempt to be objective; albeit their objectivity can be very different depending on the culture, market and ownership of the news organisation they work for. According to Gaye Tuchman, objectivity can be seen as a **'strategic ritual'** that journalists use as a defence mechanism. She identified four routine procedures that allow journalists to claim objectivity for their work:

1 The presentation of conflicting possibilities.

2 The presentation of supporting evidence.

> 'The truth, as all honest journalists know, is that newspapers are full of errors.'
> – Ian Mayes.

3   The judicious use of quotation marks.

4   The structuring of information in an appropriate sequence.

(Tuchman 1972: 299–301)

Journalists might see themselves as satisfying their professional commitment to objectivity by taking the following steps before publishing:

● Looking at both sides of a story.

● Assessing conflicting claims.

● Assessing the credibility of sources.

● Looking for evidence.

● Not publishing anything believed to be untrue.

● In short, seeing if the story stands up.

In the light of this formula, let's revisit the Harvey Nichols story discussed in Chapter 4. The initial source was known to me as someone reliable, so I immediately took her call seriously. My experience told me it was a potentially newsworthy story because of the high profile nature of the Harvey Nichols store. After looking at the offending posters to confirm what I had been told, I suggested to my source that there might be a story if someone actually complained. From her I obtained copies of several letters of complaint sent to the company and the Advertising Standards Agency. I also spoke to Harvey Nichols' PR people to get their side of the story and consulted cuttings for background on the firm. I approached a senior councillor on the local authority women's committee to ask whether she would be proposing that the council itself made a formal complaint. She gave some strong quotes and said that she would indeed be proposing such a course of action. So I had some complainants, meaning the Advertising Standards Authority would have to investigate the issue; I had opinion from someone in a position of some authority; I had background information on the company involved; and I had a comment from the company, disputing claims that the posters were offensive. The story stood up.

If a story stands up it will be written with the journalist taking care to give both sides. The journalist will make it clear when claims are disputed, will attribute information and opinion to external sources,

> **'The truth is that most of us know just what we mean by the truth.'**
> – John Diamond.

and will not mix what appear to be facts with the journalist's own comments. At least, that is what *usually* happens. Things are not always quite that simple. For a start, aren't there often more than *two* sides to a story? And even looking at 'both sides' is not always adhered to.

One of my first assignments on one local paper was to report on residents' complaints about a group of Gypsies – the usual allegations of theft, defecation and general lowering of the value of property. Eyebrows were raised in the newsroom when I said I was going to ask the Gypsies themselves for their version of events. It seemed that a comment from the police or local authority was thought to be sufficient to balance the story. I persisted and not only got a better story – the Gypsies threatening to move their caravans onto hallowed town centre grassland if they continued to be hounded from pillar to post – but also found out that many of them were actually 'locals', having been born in the area (*Harrogate Advertiser* September 23 1989). It was not rocket science, it was just journalism. But it remains unusual to see Gypsies or asylum seekers quoted in response to allegations against them. Given social prejudices against such groups, is it not *more* rather than *less* important for journalists to get their side of the story?

Checking the facts

Journalists routinely assess conflicting claims, weigh the credibility of sources, and check the facts by looking for evidence. However, as suggested in Chapter 4, sources are not equal. If the police say that three people have been killed in a road accident, then journalists will report that 'fact' without first feeling the need to drive to the scene, count the bodies and feel for a pulse. But if a motorist calls the newsroom with the same story, then a reporter will check it out – by calling the police – before reporting it. Checking the facts of a story begins with comparing what we have been told with what we 'know' of the world; with our knowledge and experience; asking whether, at a **common sense** level, it has the ring of truth about it? If it doesn't, a potential story might be dropped as not worth further effort. If a potential story survives this first test we might check the facts further by looking at published sources, by observing at first hand, by talking to people involved, and/or by talking to independent observers or experts. Useful here is the 'three-source' guideline whereby an allegation should normally be corroborated with two additional and reliable sources of information (Brennen 2003: 123).

Despite such routines, journalists frequently publish things that turn out to be untrue. Inaccuracies might appear because sources do not (yet) know the full story. Initial reports after the attack on the World Trade Centre on September 11 2001 suggested that 10,000 people had been killed (*Sun* September 12 2001; *Daily Mail* September 13 2001). For weeks journalists were still reporting that up to 7,000 people had died, but by November 2001 New York police put the death toll at 3,702 (Lipton 2001). A year after the attacks the official death toll had been reduced to 2,801 in New York, 184 at the Pentagon, 40 in Pennsylvania, plus the 19 hijackers, with doubts remaining over 35 to 40 of the New York total (Lipton 2002).

Inaccuracies might appear in stories because a journalist has made an assumption and not bothered to check, because an inaccurate cutting has been relied on, or because of a shortage of time to check. Foreign correspondents complain that they are under such time pressure, filing reports for different news outlets, that they barely have time to go outside and see for themselves what is happening; they end up simply regurgitating information fed back to them from London (Harcup 1996). Inaccuracies might appear because an inaccurate story has been 'lifted', as when the *Beijing Evening News* inadvertently reprinted a spoof article from the satirical website *The Onion* (Ananova 2002). Inaccuracies might appear because a journalist has misused or mis-understood statistics – or has failed to question such misuse by a source. And innacuracies might appear because a source lies, as when 13 art students claimed to have spent their £1,000-plus exhibition grant partying on Spanish beaches (STUDENTS USE GRANT FOR HOLIDAY, *Daily Express* May 19 1998), only to reveal that they hadn't spent a penny, had faked the holiday snaps in Yorkshire, and that the resulting media

> **'Who you gonna believe, me or your own eyes?'**
> – Chico Marx.

spectacle had been 'a talking point about what is art' (STUDENTS' WORK OF ART WAS CHEAP FORGERY, *Times* May 20 1998).

There is an old tabloid motto that 'It's all right flying a kite, but remember to keep hold of the string'. Yet there are occasions when the kite soars into the sky with the journalist desperately trying to cling on. This is particularly the case when a reporter comes under pressure to *make* a story stand up. I once came across a tabloid hack trying desperately to find non-existent irate white parents to condemn their local authority serving curry for school dinner, just because his editor had already thought up a possible headline: WE'LL HAVE NAAN OF THAT! Thankfully, such pressures on journalists are less than those felt by the researchers on daytime TV programmes who resorted to supplying *fake* guests to comply with producers' ever more bizarre requirements (Arlidge 1999). Pure invention remains the exception in journalism, although Abul Taher observes:

> There is a lot of cutting corners, dishonesty about sources and interviews. A lot of people end up doctoring the truth for a good story. It's a job that is a daily ritual of moral and intellectual compromise.

A compromise it may be but, however imperfectly, most reporters seem to retain some sense of objectivity in their everyday routines. Jane Merrick gives a not untypical journalist's response when asked about objective reporting:

> When I sit down to write a story I never think 'is this objective?' But I'm always aware of being fair and balanced and having both sides of a story. I'm not sure you *can* be objective. I've never really thought about it, to be honest.

The key thing is to be *fair*, argues Jon Snow of *Channel 4 News*:

> **'Don't believe anyone, not even us.'**
> – slogan of Radio B92, Belgrade.

> I don't think there's such a thing as a neutral journalist. Human beings are moved by what they see, either against it or for it, admiringly or despairingly, or whatever it is. And I think those qualities are essential, otherwise what the journalist

reports becomes an unnatural event . . . I'm against neutrality. But I'm for fairness at the same time. Complete fairness. You've got to recognise what your dispositions are, and balance them by allowing other points of view. *(Quoted in Roy 2002: 38)*

For Martin Wainwright, objectivity means approaching stories with an open mind, giving all sides their say, including as much contextual information as possible. And trying to show what underlies people's actions. This leads him to be critical of the more **subjective** 'heart-on-sleeve' style of journalism associated with the likes of James Cameron and John Pilger:

All my experience as a journalist teaches me that situations are always complicated, and there very seldom is *one* source of evil. Very emotional journalism has some limited use in waking people up to a bad situation, but when it comes to actually telling people what's going on and why it's happened I do think you need to be as dispassionate as possible. The less of the journalist the better, I think. Some people say it's more dangerous to pretend to be objective and actually not be, and they say nobody is objective because you can't be. That's all true. But *you can have a very good shot at being objective*, I'm sure you can. It's a counsel of despair to say we've all got to be subjective.

Some of the ways in which journalists check facts will be considered further in the next chapter.

Summary

Objective reporting is commonly understood to involve separating verifiable facts from subjective feelings. Journalists' use of objectivity has been described as a 'strategic ritual' to distance themselves from stories; a defence against charges of bias and lack of professionalism. This formula involves presenting conflicting possibilities and supporting evidence, with attributed opinion and information, in an appropriate sequence. The objectivity norm and the related concept of impartiality have been challenged for being impossible to achieve; for ignoring the existence of multiple perspectives; and for being undesirable in conflicts between right and wrong. Nonetheless, most journalists appear to retain some sense of objectivity when assessing sources and checking facts to establish whether a story stands up.

Questions

Is there a distinction between objectivity and impartiality?

How would impartiality change our newspapers?

If objectivity is impossible to achieve, does it make any sense to aim for it?

Which gets closer to the truth, subjective journalism or objective journalism?

How might journalists feature different narratives and multiple perspectives?

Further reading

Frost (2002) provides a brief practical account of the basics of reporting and fact-checking, Randall (2000) has a useful chapter on dealing with numbers and statistics, and Boyd's (2001) manual covers broadcasting's statutory requirement to impartiality. Edited collections with readable and illuminating contributions on the subject of objectivity include Kieran (1998), Bromley and O'Malley (1997), and Tumber (1999). Pilger's (1998) eloquent if holier-than-thou critique of the world amounts to a sustained challenge to most of what passes for objective journalism in the mainstream media. McLaughlin (2002b) has an interesting discussion of objectivity, conflict and the 'journalism of attachment', based in part on interviews with war correspondents. For a more theoretical perspective, Stevenson (2002) explores various Marxist explanations of the media – touching on objectivity, hegemony and moral panics – as well as the postmodernist challenge to the concept of 'the truth'. Critcher (2002) subjects the concepts of moral panic and agenda setting to critical scrutiny within the context of the *News of the World*'s 'name and shame' campaign on paedophilia.

Notes

Sources for soundbites: Bennett cited in Allan 1997: 304–5; Scott cited in O'Malley and Soley 2000: 23; Tuchman 1972: 297; Orwell cited in Pilger 1998: 525; Murdoch in Channel 4 1998; Mayes 2000: ix; Diamond 2001: 4; Marx, *Duck Soup*, 1933; B92 cited in Seib 2002: 99.

Chapter Six

The journalist as investigator

Key terms

Investigative journalism

Constraints

Facts

Entertainment

Democracy

Structural forces

The figure of the investigative journalist is a familiar one from movies such as *All the President's Men*, *Defence of the Realm* and *The Insider*. Funnily enough, Paul Foot had watched *The Insider* the night before I turned up at his home to interview him for this book. Its portrayal of the intense relationship between journalist and source clearly struck a chord. 'That's the key to all this, the source,' he told me almost as soon as I walked through the door. *The Insider* tells the true story of how journalist Lowell Bergman (played by Al Pacino) persuaded tobacco scientist Jeffrey Wigand (Russell Crowe) to defy a confidentiality agreement and blow the whistle on his former employers. As they battle against corporate lawyers and frightened TV executives, the pair go through all the emotions of trust, mistrust, and trust again before finally getting to tell the story. At one point the tormented Wigand tells the journalist: 'I'm just a commodity to you, aren't I? I could be anything worth putting on between the commercials.' Bergman promises not to leave his source 'hanging out to dry' (Roth and Mann 1999). It is a telling exchange, raising ethical issues of motivation and responsibility.

Investigative journalists in movies are often unshaven characters – usually men – who meet mysterious whistleblowers in darkened car parks. They are chain-smoking obsessives who won't take 'no' for an answer; unorthodox loners who risk life and limb to establish 'the truth'. The reality is rather more mundane. Most **investigative journalism** would not make for dramatic footage – the meticulous cross-referencing of information strands, the days phoning people with similar names and trawling *FriendsReunited* until you hit upon the right one, and the hours poring over obscure documents or computer databases until your eyes scream for mercy. Compared with other forms of reporting, investigative journalism usually involves more risk, more time and more money (Palast 2002: 9). There is the occasional threat or even act of violence, of course. But, in the UK at least, legal or commercial **constraints** are more common risks than a sap on the head or an invitation to sleep with the fishes.

Although investigative journalism remains an integral part of journalism's image and sense of self-worth and professional standing, in reality it is a minority pursuit. Whenever the topic of investigative journalism is discussed, somebody can be relied upon

Investigative journalism

The concept of 'investigative journalism' is a problematic one. It smacks of 'pretensions to grandeur' (Hanna 2000: 1) and implicitly counterpoises a journalism that is investigative or inquiring with a journalism that is neither. However, the term retains currency among both practitioners and academics as denoting a particular type of journalistic inquiry, as defined by John Ullmann and Steve Honeyman:

> It is the reporting, through one's own work product and initiative, matters of importance which some persons or organisations wish to keep secret. The three basic elements are that the investigation be the work of the reporter, not a report of an investigation made by someone else; that the subject of the story involves something of reasonable importance to the reader or viewer; and that others are attempting to hide these matters from the public. *(Quoted in Northmore 2001: 188–9)*

Such a definition is not without its own problems, particularly its reliance on the formulation 'something of reasonable importance to the reader or viewer', which can be taken to mean anything from an obscure arms deal (for *Panorama* viewers) to the recreational drug-use of a Z-list celebrity (for *News of the World* readers). Nonetheless, it goes some way to help us understand what has been described as the 'self-motivation, the kind of experience and knowledge, the methodology and the set of skills' typical of 'investigative journalists' (Hanna 2000: 1).

For Stephen Dorril, the methodology of investigative journalism 'is characterised by in-depth and near-obsessional research, dogged determination, accumulated knowledge, team-effort (though some of our best ... have been loners), the crucial support of editors and the space to pursue stories not because of notions of the truth but because it might turn out to be interesting' (Dorril 2000). The extent to which investigative skills are, in essence, the same as those used by 'ordinary' journalists – but with added scepticism – varies according to which practitioner is consulted. However, it should also be considered that elements of investigation can come into otherwise simple reportage and that many journalists who conduct investigations also find themselves working on relatively straightforward news stories; investigative

to say that *all* journalism is supposed to be investigative. But much journalism, as it is practised, is reportage. It is descriptive. It is based on a reporter seeing or being told something and passing that on to an audience in the form of a story, as Martin Wainwright explains:

> I'm not like a detective, I'm more of a describer. Somebody rang me up the other day and said he had a scandal which involved everybody from the Prime Minister downwards, and you think 'Oh God . . . ' It's terribly difficult and you don't have very much time.

The head of news at Yorkshire Television's *Calendar* is explicit on this, describing her brief as producing human interest stories for ultra-busy people, adding: 'Our role is not to be investigative' (quoted in Ursell 2001: 191).

The public interest

Investigative journalism goes beyond description. For David Randall, investigative reporting differs substantially from other reporting because it involves *original* research into *wrongdoing*, because someone is trying to keep the information *secret*, and because the *stakes* tend to be higher (Randall 2000: 99–100). Although some investigations – many of those in the Sunday tabloids for example – expose nothing more than the personal predilections of some minor celeb, horny housewife or runaway vicar, the credo of investigative journalism is uncovering information that it is in the *public interest* to know.

But what *is* the public interest? The answer, according to the Press Complaints Commission, is: i) detecting or exposing crime or a serious misdemeanour; ii) protecting public health and safety; iii) preventing the public from being misled by some statement or action of an individual or organisation (www.pcc.org.uk). The Ethics Council of the National Union of Journalists has added the exposure of corruption, conflicts of interest, corporate greed or hypocritical behaviour by those in power (see Appendix One). The government-appointed Nolan Committee on Standards in Public Life declared in

> 'Remember, All the President's Men was so unusual they had to make a movie out of it.'
> – Greg Palast.

journalists and ordinary journalists not only inhabit the same universe, they may be the same people.

Constraints

Deborah Chambers wrote as recently as 2000 that investigative journalism in the UK had been 'flourishing in the last three decades of the twentieth century' (Chambers 2000: 89), prompting Stephen Dorril to retort that investigative journalism had enjoyed 'a brief bloom in the sixties, flowered for a short period in the seventies, badly wilted in the eighties and is now effectively dead' (Dorril 2000). Not dead but in decline, according to Mark Hanna, who blames structural changes within the media since the 1970s for 'shrivelling' investigative journalism at its roots; changes such as relentless cost-cutting, understaffing, speed-up and, on television, a ruthless drive for ratings (Hanna 2000: 2–7).

Working in such conditions effectively undermines the 'relative autonomy' enjoyed by journalists (Manning 2001: 105), an autonomy necessary if the time and space are to be made available for investigations. After all, investigative journalists might be seen as mavericks even by their colleagues, never mind their employers. As Tom Bower notes, investigations can frequently be unproductive, and 'even the rarity of success earns the investigative reporter only the irksome epithet of being obsessional or dangerous' (quoted in Spark 1999: 17). It is claimed that today's recruits to journalism 'are quickly schooled into understanding that investigative journalism is basically a myth and that their success is strongly related to their accuracy and skill in applying journalistic techniques and formulas' (Harrison 2000: 113). Constraints, including the law, are discussed further in Chapter 2.

Facts

Investigative reporting typically abandons the journalistic convention of allegation-and-denial, or attributed opinions, in favour of an attempt 'to establish facts which, if possible, decide the issue one way or the other' (Spark

1995 that 'a free press using fair techniques of investigative journalism is an indispensable asset to our democracy', contributing to 'the preservation of standards in public life' (quoted in Doig 1997: 210).

From a high point in the 1970s, investigative journalism in the UK is widely regarded as being on the wane (Northmore 2001: 183; Doig 1997: 189). However, as with all discussions about journalism, there is a long-established tendency to bestow 'golden age' status on events circa 20 years before such discussions take place. Before considering some examples of investigative reporting it is worth recording a cautionary note sounded by Martin Wainwright, who believes that investigative journalists may be tempted to ignore shades of grey: 'I'm always a bit suspicious of them, because often if you go into a story carefully you find there's another side to it, and it's not quite what it seems.'

> **'Get off your asses and knock on doors.'**
> – sign in the Washington newsroom of the LA Times.

Methods of investigation

Based on interviews with a wide range of practitioners, David Spark produced the following advice for fledgling investigators:

- Get to the **facts** at the heart of an issue – don't be content with spokesmen's comments.

- Explain difficult concepts – don't write around them.

- Don't just echo the views of your main source – find other sources with other views.

- Speak to as many relevant people as possible.

- Ask the simple and obvious questions which open out the subject.

- Don't take everything and everyone at their face value.

- Remember that everyone, every organisation and every event has a history which may have a bearing on what is happening now.

(Spark 1999: xii)

It sounds simple. That is the point. There is no need for the mystique that too often surrounds the subject. Veteran investigator Paul Foot believes there are dangers in treating investigative journalism as a separate genre carried out by 'grand' journalists:

1999: 1). However, 'facts' themselves are far from unproblematic. There does not exist some universally accepted bundle of facts, just waiting to be gathered, that will 'decide' most issues. Facts may be disputed all the way to the High Court or the prison cell. Even when the facts are accepted, their relevance – or the interpretation placed upon them – may not be. Investigative journalists may find themselves piling fact upon fact on shifting sands. Even so, the very pursuit of the facts – and the reporter's willingness to adopt the role of accuser – challenges the formal notions of 'balance' or 'impartiality' so important to much conventional reporting (Manning 2001: 70). Facts and truth are discussed further in Chapter 5.

Democracy

For Hugo de Burgh, the investigative journalist plays a vital democratic role as 'the tribune of the commoner, exerting on her or his behalf the right to know, to examine and to criticise' (de Burgh 2000: 315). It is a tempting image, particularly for those of us who have tried our hands at such stories. But how democratic is it really? Quite apart from legal and economic constraints, there are other limitations on the democratic claims of investigative journalism. *Who* decides what is worthy of investigation, and on what basis? Some stories are undoubtedly seen as more 'sexy' than others, some people are seen as more deserving of sympathy, and some people are easier to paint as villains. If there is the possibility of good pictures, film or audio material, then so much the better.

Of course, investigative journalism can achieve 'results' such as the jailing of Jonathan Aitken, but could that not be seen as perpetuating a myth that society is divided into a large number of 'good' people and a small number of 'bad' people? Where is the investigative journalism into *structural* forces in society? Largely notable for its absence. Instead, particularly on television, we tend to have personalised stories of goodies, baddies and heroic reporters. Hanna challenges us to consider whether, rather than exemplifying a democratic spirit, even the heyday of UK investigative journalism in reality offered an 'elitist and pompous' form of journalism (Hanna 2000: 16).

It's a complete fraud, the idea that there is race apart called investigative journalists. An ordinary reporter doing a perfectly ordinary story carries out these functions, the difference would be the enthusiasm and the scepticism with which you approach something.

Another difference might be the *time* you have available. Reporters required to produce up to a dozen stories a day will simply find it impossible if they question everything. On the other hand, journalists who invest their own time in working on their own stories can become known in the trade as 'self-starters'; if they are both lucky and skilled they may be able to earn themselves the rare luxury of being employed on a specifically investigative brief. That is how Paul Foot has been able to spend so much time at both the *Daily Mirror* and *Private Eye* 'piling fact on fact to present a picture of cock-up or conspiracy' (Foot 1999: 82).

Foot describes one of his most celebrated investigations, concerning the case of four men wrongly jailed for the murder of newspaper delivery boy Carl Bridgewater:

> I started writing about it in 1980. Ann Whelan, whose son was convicted, wrote to me at the *Mirror* a very moving letter. My initial feeling was 'What mother wouldn't say that her son was innocent?' So it was some time before I went up there. But I went up to Birmingham and met her and her family. I wasn't convinced to begin with because it was a horrible murder and there was *some* evidence against them, there was a confession. It took quite a lot of time before I became in any way convinced, but I did become absolutely convinced, and as I did so I wrote with more and more certainty. Ann found witnesses who said 'I told a pack of lies, I didn't realise how important it was'. But mostly it was just going over the evidence that had been presented in court against them, reading depositions, the judge's summing up and so on, talking to everyone involved. There were things showing they were somewhere else at the time, that somebody else had done the murder, it just went on and on. I must have written at least 30 articles in the *Mirror*. Eventually the men were released in 1997.

Apart from his forensic skill and the willingness to immerse himself in thousands of legal documents, what is immediately apparent from Foot's account is the *repetition* of stories over a long period of time:

> The *Mirror* subs would joke 'Here comes the man who supports the murder of newspaper boys', and occasionally the editor would say 'Oh Christ, you're not doing this again are you?' But the repetition is absolutely crucial because it encourages other sources to come forward.

Another experienced investigator, TV reporter Christopher Hird, describes his modus operandi as:

- Get everything we can anywhere in the public domain (libraries, Companies House and so on).
- Establish a chronology of events. We often see connections not seen before.
- Relentlessly look up everybody who might know something.

(Quoted in Spark 1999: 53)

These activities will often overlap. Checking the details of a company under investigation might give you some more names to contact; contacting those people might give you some more companies to check-out; doing that might throw up other connections; and so on. That's why Randall advises 'throw nothing away' – you never know when it might be useful (Randall 2000: 108). The phrase 'computer-assisted reporting' has entered some journalists' vocabularies in recent years, imported from the US. It involves the collection and manipulation of data from existing or specially created databases or spreadsheets, looking for patterns, trends, mistakes or missing information that might make stories. 'They have been there all the time, sitting in the data,' observes Mike Ward. 'It's just needed a journalist to ask the right questions, run the right sequence of numbers' (Ward 2002: 69).

As with all journalism, however, it should be borne in mind that connections may be as much coincidental as causal and that networks are not necessarily conspiracies. Despite the thrill of the chase, it is important to question your *own* expectations and assumptions during any investigation.

> '*All journalism should be investigative, from football to cookery.*'
> – John Pilger.

In addition to the above techniques, a relatively small portion of investigative journalism is carried out by *undercover* reporters pretending to be drug dealers, corrupt businessmen, arms dealers, or whatever. Some information is obtained by paying informants or private investigators. Some journalists have been known to keep unregistered mobile phones for talking to sensitive sources; they may also avoid leaving paper trails by ensuring they pay cash for meals and so on. Quite apart from any ethical considerations involved, such activities will not be considered here because they are not jobs for novice journalists.

Following a hunch

Let's now consider a story I investigated on the basis of a hunch. I'd like to say it was *my* hunch, but it wasn't. I was working a freelance shift on *Yorkshire On Sunday* when editor Mike Glover handed me a brief cutting he had taken from that morning's *Yorkshire Post*. It was a nothing story about a private health company going into liquidation after failing to pay a printing bill for publicity material. Mike's suspicions were aroused by the odd spacing of the paragraphs, suggesting to him that something might have been removed from the story at the last minute – possibly on legal advice. He asked me to dig around to see what I could find.

> 'In truth, the investigative journalist has always been more likely to inhabit the set of a television or film drama, or the covers of a racy novel, than the newsroom.'
> – Bob Franklin.

The result was a front-page exclusive – CLINIC HIT BY SCANDAL CLAIMS – and two full news pages inside – RIDDLE OF CLINIC BOSS: PATIENT'S THREE DAYS OF AGONY IN PRIVATE HOSPITAL (*Yorkshire On Sunday* February 19 1995). More stories followed, MPs demanded action, and finally the government reviewed its inspection procedures for private clinics. How did a hunch turn into a successful piece of investigative journalism? As Hird says, by getting hold of everything we could in the public domain, by tracing connections, and by tracking down as many as possible of those involved.

It meant repeated visits to Companies House, which has offices in London, Leeds, Manchester, Birmingham, Edinburgh and Cardiff as well as a website listed in Appendix Two. A vital source of information for journalists, Companies House holds records on 1.4 million 'live' companies and 2.6 million dissolved companies, including details of directors, major shareholders and company accounts. It was there I discovered that the company in liquidation was one of 49 businesses established by the same man. Most were involved in the private health industry, including pregnancy advisory operations, private abortion clinics and cosmetic surgery clinics. I found that, at the same time as one company was apparently unable to pay its printing bills, the firm running an abortion clinic made hundreds of thousands of pounds in profit. And I obtained addresses for the businessman and his wife, who was a fellow-director of some of the businesses.

With the names of several companies to go on, I searched local newspaper cuttings for related stories and found an account of an employment tribunal concerning the abortion clinic. That gave me a name of an ex-employee to follow-up, which in turn led to more names. As the story concerned abortion we contacted 'pro-choice' and 'pro-life' campaign groups who, from diametrically opposing stand-points, questioned the ethics of the same individuals running both a pregnancy 'advisory' service and the profitable abortion clinic that patients were referred to. One of the groups also referred to an earlier radio programme that had mentioned allegations of botched surgery. Following this up, and talking to friendly local solicitors, led to further cases. The solicitors were happy to pass on detailed information that raised serious concerns about procedures at the clinic. Further inquiries revealed that the local health authority – responsible for inspecting and licensing the clinic – had privately been alerted to staff concerns about standards.

All these leads gave me many individuals to contact by the usual methods of telephone books, directory enquiries, medical directories and the electoral register – hours and hours on the telephone, in the reference library, going back to Companies House, and driving around Yorkshire turning up unannounced on people's doorsteps. Some had moved home, meaning I had just a few seconds in which to persuade the new occupant to give a total stranger the forwarding address for the person who used to live in their house. The best advice I can offer for such occasions is to act confident but friendly, as if nothing in the world could be more normal.

When I found the right people, some were happy to tell their side of the story, some wanted to forget about it all, and others had to be assured of their anonymity before they would speak. There is no great trick in getting such people to talk, but a sympathetic and non-threatening tone certainly helps. Nick Davies adds the following advice on doorstepping:

> Don't park outside the person's house – if they are prompted to look out of the window they will make decisions about you before you introduce yourself . . . think why they might want to speak to you and put this message across . . . if it's raining don't wear a coat – you might garner some sympathy if you look like a drowned rat. *(Quoted in Hanna 2000: 15)*

Putting together what I was told on the doorstep and telephone with information in the public domain, plus the concerns of solicitors and others involved, meant there was sufficient evidence to put to the businessman at the centre of the story. We tried telephoning, we tried doorstepping, and we tried writing, all to no avail. No matter on this occasion. We had enough to go on. We obtained comments from the health authority, the General Medical Council, and an independent consultant gynaecologist – and we ran the story. That prompted other people to come forward, resulting in several follow-ups. We sent the published stories to politicians, whose reactions resulted in further articles and the aforementioned government review. All from a hunch.

Legwork and lateral thinking

As the above account shows, information already in the public domain can be vital if you know what you are looking for; so begin with the assumption that someone somewhere has *already* sourced the information you need (Northmore 2001:192). An 'amateur' investigator for a radical website, who relies largely on public records for his probes into the rich and powerful, told me:

> I've built up quite a good relationship with people in the local reference library. They can be really helpful, I think it makes their lives more interesting. You're getting annual reports, company accounts, all that kind of stuff, and spending weeks and weeks reading it, looking for connections. Also Companies House and other publicly available records like birth and marriage certificates. Then visiting buildings, going round talking to people, or trying to. I like to *go* to places to see them just to get a feel. It's not a mystery, it's just diligence and hard work.

It's all about combining 'legwork' with 'lateral thinking', according to Brian Whittle, whose freelance agency used both to good effect to break a number of stories about serial killer Dr Harold Shipman. After Shipman's trial, the agency's reporters revisited the small town in which he had embarked on his murderous medical career a quarter-of-a-century previously. They investigated deaths for which Shipman had not been charged, as Whittle explains:

> Before anybody else thought of it we obtained all the death certificates for the 22 people he'd signed while he was practising in Todmorden. Just looking at the death certificates told you that three people died in one day. We then went round all the addresses. A third of the houses no longer existed, and in another third the people had moved away and weren't contactable. But we did find relatives of the three people who died in one day, and we found relatives of the first male victim. This is old-fashioned reporting, it's knocking on doors, it's talking to people. If you turn up on the doorstep people will talk to you, if you ring them up it gives them the chance to put the phone down. If you want to find out about somebody you don't just knock on *their* door and the *next* door, you do the entire street. You do *both sides* of the street – two of you – and you do it again in the evening because people may be out in the daytime. Go to *every* address and ask 'What do you know about this person who lived here 25 years ago?' You don't know who you're going to find, maybe it's a son or whatever. Out of the 22, six or seven came out with absolutely key stuff. We were totally vindicated when

> 'Never believe anything until it is officially denied.'
> – *Claud Cockburn.*

the police started an investigation about a month later and sent various cases to the Crown Prosecution Service.

As well as uncovering new information about the UK's biggest mass murderer, the agency reporters' repeated visits also led them to a series of photographs of 'Dr Death' partying with his wife – all smiles and silly hats. The pictures probably didn't add much to the sum of human knowledge but, thanks to a 'world exclusive' deal with the *Sunday Mirror* in January 2001, they turned out to be lucrative for the agency as well as the owner of the photos. The technique of hitting the doorsteps early and often will be familiar to anyone who has worked as an agency reporter on the 'frontline' of domestic news.

> 'At the heart of being an investigative reporter is manipulating people to talk to you when they think they don't want to.'
> – Nick Davies.

That's entertainment

Most of the tasks outlined in this chapter are as applicable to broadcasting as to print, but investigative journalism on TV in particular has shifted its focus in recent years towards individual reporters such as Donal MacIntyre, Roger Cook and Paul Kenyon becoming stars in their own right. In a triumph of style over content, the journalist has too often become part of the spectacle. So, ignoring the idea that investigative journalism is supposed to tell us something we don't know, Donal MacIntyre memorably demonstrated that if you wander around Brixton looking vulnerable, holding a mobile phone out in front of you, eventually somebody will rob you.

David Hencke, a print journalist who has been known to dabble in television, has lost count of the number of times he has heard commissioning editors say 'we've got to have secret filming' or 'think there's any chance of some violence?'. He continues:

> They want this kind of material regardless of the content or even the need to do it. They're also in love with *MacIntyre Undercover*-style TV – the reporter as the hard man exposing the truth with no regard for his safety or sometimes even his life . . . By the end, as with a John Wayne movie, we can safely go to our beds, knowing that all the villains have had their just

deserts and that our hero has fought his way through, against the odds, and emerged victorious. *(Hencke 2001)*

More conventional investigative journalism, piling fact upon fact, can still be found on TV from time to time. A good example is the *Panorama* investigation *A Licence To Murder*, broadcast by the BBC in June 2002. Drawing on 13 years of research, reporter John Ware told the murky tale of alleged collusion between members of British intelligence services and loyalist death squads to kill suspected enemies of the state in Northern Ireland between 1985 and 1990. The essence of the story was pieced together through interviews with police officers and paramilitaries, backed up by access to secret documents and interviews with the victims' families. There was some secret filming and some reconstruction, of course, but it remained an exercise in journalism rather than drama; as such, it shed some light on the activities of the secret state *(Panorama* 2002).

A lengthy report on as 'boring' a subject as Northern Ireland is a rarity these days. Even in conventional TV current affairs and documentary there has been a blurring of the lines between journalism and entertainment, so we get a concentration on ratings-friendly subject matter such as sex, drugs and crime. Talking heads are deemed too old-hat for audiences in a multichannel age. Instead, we have a growing reliance on fast cuts, odd camera angles, brief soundbites, dramatic music, secret filming and often gratuitous reconstructions (usually, but not always, labelled as such). A good thing too, according to David Lloyd, head of current affairs at Channel 4. For Lloyd, UK television's self-indulgent 'leather jacket brigade' did nothing but produce monumentally dull programmes on obscure arms deals. Defending a shift to more popular topics and treatments, he says of the supposed heyday of investigative journalism: 'A lot of us spent much time at great cost investigating things that nobody was interested in and had no reason to be interested in' (quoted in Wells 2001c). Some of the ground vacated by traditional investigative journalism on TV has been occupied not by journalists but by comedians, particularly Mark Thomas, who has not been afraid to turn his attention to obscure arms deals. Journalism as entertainment is discussed further in Chapter 7.

What's it all for?

What is achieved by journalists taking on the role of investigators? Well, for a start, journalists exposing miscarriages of justice such as the Bridgewater Four, the Birmingham Six and the Guildford Four all resulted in innocent people walking free from prison, eventually. More recently, Don Hale took on the police, the local establishment and even his own employers to help free Stephen Downing from the prison cell in which he had spent 27 years maintaining his innocence of murder (Cohen 2002). Reflecting on the outcome of an investigation during which he suffered abuse, threats and violence, Don Hale says:

> This case has already raised a number of key issues within British law . . . It has also highlighted the need for constant vigilance to help prevent other similar claims of injustice. I am proud of my own small contribution to society. I took the trouble to stop and listen to a small voice in the dark. *(Hale 2002: 372)*

Sometimes journalists are more concerned with sending guilty people *to* prison than getting innocent people *out*, and Michael Crick's determined pursuit of Jeffrey Archer helped ensure that his Lordship ended up behind bars rather than as Mayor of London (Tench 2001). The *Guardian*'s dogged investigations into Jonathan Aitken in the 1990s resulted in the government minister being jailed for perjury, albeit only because the paper's team discovered a crucial piece of evidence at the very last minute of the court case (Spark 1999: 99).

Apart from the occasional release of an innocent prisoner or jailing of a rogue politician, what is it all *for*? Is investigative journalism really a force for **democracy** or merely a relatively minor subdivision of showbusiness? (de Burgh 2000: 315; Northmore 2001: 185). One of the most often-cited successes of investigative journalism is the *Sunday Times*' coverage of the Thalidomide babies in the 1970s. It was a success story in that it resulted in compensation for victims of the drug. But some of the journalists involved have since questioned what was actually achieved:

> It has taken me twenty years to face up to the fact that the *Sunday Times* Thalidomide campaign was not the great success it was made out to be . . . [When] some of us get together and look back at the fight on behalf of the children we end up discussing two crucial questions: Did we do it right? Would it have been better to have kept out of the whole affair? . . . To start with, some of the parents found the exposure in the press a painful experience . . . Next, there was discontent over the way the compensation was paid . . . Disturbing stories of greed and envy began to emerge. *(Knightley 1998: 155–78)*

Comedian Mark Thomas has managed a couple of results including the resignation of a government adviser (Hencke and Evans 1999). But repercussions on such a scale tend to be few and far between – and often an awfully long time coming. Paul Foot recalls that, at the time, it felt like few people noticed his early investigations in *Private Eye*, even those concerning the corrupt local government empire of John Poulson: 'Again and again real revelations sank like a stone' (Foot 1999: 82). Yet he is in no doubt that it is a socially worthwhile occupation:

> Apart from getting people out of prison who shouldn't be there, there are things like the cancer drugs that were killing people quicker. The publication in *Private Eye* of four or five of those articles and the whole project was exposed. And Frank Wheeler, the busman up in Scotland who kept asking why the government had stolen the pensions surplus of the National Bus Company when it was privatised. That was £300 million. He says the whole thing changed when I went up here and spent a couple of days with him and his wife and wrote a piece for the *Guardian*, and then several things for the *Eye*. That set of articles made a difference to those people in that they got their money back.

Be curious and sceptical

Investigative journalism is as much about approach as it is about subject matter. It is more of an attitude than it is a genre. And just as journalists working on investigations will use many of the techniques they would use on 'ordinary' stories – only more so – a more inquiring and investigative approach can also inform more mundane

> '*The main point is to be curious and sceptical . . . all the time.*'
> – Paul Foot.

reporting. How does Foot sum up the attributes necessary for a journalist to be an investigator?

> There are certain skills that you learn from experience, but the main point is to be curious and sceptical. You can't be an investigative journalist unless you are both curious and sceptical *all the time*. That, and the ability to ring people up and talk to them all the time, the ability to believe the most absurd things that people tell you – even when perhaps nine times out of ten they're talking absolute bollocks.

Don Hale admits to finding his Stephen Downing investigation 'totally addictive', adding that he became 'obsessed with following up new leads' to the detriment of his family life (Hale 2002: 321). David Hencke stresses the value of a bit of humility as you learn the basics of reporting:

> You can't come in as a high-flying reporter, you have to start with the parish fetes, the youth club and the magistrates court. I still make mistakes, but it's better to make the bog standard mistakes at a level where you can't cause too much damage. *(Quoted in Adams 2001a)*

In the end, though, for Foot it all boils down to the relationship between journalist and source:

> The source is more important than the story. The whistleblowers who break cover and say 'I'm not going to continue with this because I'm doing something wrong' – they are the goldmine. You do not sell them out.

Al Pacino couldn't have put it better.

Summary

Investigative journalism goes beyond description and attributed opinion to uncover information, typically about powerful individuals or organisations. Many investigative skills will be used by journalists every day. Stories are typically investigated by combining information already in the public domain with leaked information and/or by talking to as many as possible of the people involved. There are claims that investigative journalism has been in decline since its heyday in the 1970s, and that many investigations on television in particular are now more concerned with entertainment than information. Investigative reporting has been explained variously as an essential element of democracy, as a subdivision of showbusiness, as favouring a narrative of 'good versus evil' at the expense of questioning structural forces, as an elitist form of journalism of little interest to the public, and as the tribune of the common people.

Questions

How does investigative journalism differ from other journalism?

What are the main obstacles confronting journalists as investigators?

Why is investigative journalism said to be in decline?

Is investigative journalism essential or irrelevant to democracy?

Do investigative reporters create a myth of good versus evil?

Further reading

A personal account of investigative reporting is given in brief and entertaining fashion in Foot (1999). Spark (1999) offers an illuminating introduction to some of the techniques involved, based on a series of interviews with practitioners. His account of the downfall of Jonathan Aitken is instructive, although the book contains little analysis. Online methods of research are introduced in a useful chapter in Ward (2002). Contributors to de Burgh (2000) attempt, with varying degrees of success, to place investigative journalism within a wider context. It contains worthwhile material, notably D'Arcy (2000), but the case studies tend only to scratch the surface. Doig (1997) provides a brief historical account of investigative reporting in both print and television up to the mid-1990s, while Northmore (2001) discusses future directions. Palast (2002) includes several of his own investigative reports as well as details of the processes involved. Finally, Hale (2002) is a personal account of how the editor of 'a quiet little paper in a quiet little town' investigated a case that many people told him to drop.

Notes

Sources for soundbites: Palast 2002: 8; *LA Times* cited in Brennan 2003: 126; Pilger cited in Adams 2001a; Franklin 1997: 29–30; Cockburn cited in Foot 1999: 82; Davies cited in Hanna 2000: 15; Foot interviewed by the author.

Chapter Seven

The journalist as entertainer

Key terms

Entertainment

Dumbing down

Tabloidisation

Popular

Authority

Elitism

It was during a heatwave that some bright spark had the idea of testing the legend about it being 'hot enough to fry an egg on the pavement'. A posse was gathered and we rushed from the newsroom to put the theory to the test – but the egg steadfastly refused to fry. After half-an-hour we conceded defeat, scraped up the mess, and beat a retreat to the sound of jeers from drinkers outside the pub next door. It wasn't the best piece of investigative journalism I had ever been involved with. It was just a bit of fun – entertainment. Some stories are entertaining by virtue of their subject matter. Others can be rendered entertaining by being well written, by holding the attention of the audience, by the use of anecdotes or asides, or by injecting humour. One colleague used to speak of 'sprinkling topspin and stardust' onto a news story, brightening it up with that extra bit of colour or drama to make it more entertaining. After all, we call news items 'stories' because we adopt many of the conventions of the story-teller.

> **'We are in the entertainment business.'**
> – Rupert Murdoch.

Entertaining is not a new role for journalists. Hence the 19th century verse:

Tickle the public, make 'em grin,
The more you tickle, the more you'll win;
Teach the public, you'll never get rich,
You'll live like a beggar and die in a ditch.

(Quoted in Engel 1997: 17)

Even if we *do* want to 'teach the public', we won't get very far if nobody reads, watches or listens to our stories because they are too dull. Without an audience there can be no journalism, and we are not likely to gather much of an audience if we do not seek, at least in part, to entertain as well as inform. Difficulties can arise when we forget the distinction, as with some of the TV 'investigations' discussed in the previous chapter. And what of ITN's decision to replay images of hijacked planes hitting the World Trade Centre edited in time to music? That news item, broadcast the day after the September 11 attacks, was condemned by the Independent Television Commission as a tasteless offence to public feeling (Akbar 2001). But mood music frequently accompanies current affairs journalism on TV, including reconstructions of serious crime, and musical clips are common in radio packages.

Dumbing down

Debate about so-called 'dumbing down' extends far beyond journalism to include education, the arts and society in general. Of direct relevance to journalism is the claim that news is being transformed into 'newszak'; that is, 'news as a product designed and "processed" for a particular market and delivered in increasingly homogenous "snippets" which make only modest demands on the audience' (Franklin 1997: 5). Supporters of the dumbing down thesis bemoan the fact that news is being 'converted into entertainment' (Franklin 1997: 5). Chris Frost writes that journalists are facing increasing pressure to become entertainers by 'finding stories and features that will delight the audience rather than inform, titillate rather than educate' (Frost 2002: 5). For Pierre Bourdieu, this results in journalists being 'so afraid of being boring' that they increasingly favour:

- Confrontation rather than debate.
- Polemics or polarised views over rigorous argument.
- Promotion of conflict.
- Confrontation of individuals rather than their arguments.
- Discussion of political tactics rather than the substance of policies.
- Dehistoricised and fragmented versions of events.

(Bourdieu 1998: 3–7)

There is nothing new about the 'perennial' complaint that 'journalism just recently got worse', observes Samuel Winch. He argues that the boundary between news and entertainment is 'socially constructed' rather than based on essential elements (Winch 1997: 6 and 13). Martin Conboy agrees that it is far from a new phenomenon:

The suspicion of popular taste goes right the way back to the start of print technology – almanacs, chapbooks and printed ballads had been predominantly aimed at the lower end of the market – as soon, in fact, as print allows forms of expression which have escaped from the authorisation, approval and sense of good taste of the elite classes to have large circulation. *(Conboy 2002: 31)*

The popular press of today can be seen as drawing on the 19th century 'new journalism' that was 'marked

An agenda of crime, celebrity and miracle cures?

Someone who thinks things have gone too far in the direction of entertainment, or 'journalism as a performing art', is former BBC war correspondent Martin Bell (Bell 2002). His friendly fire against the BBC reinforces criticism by insiders that BBC news has become 'more Madonna than Macedonia' (Wells 2001b). But Bell's biggest guns are reserved for commercial television news:

> I can think of no time in my life when we needed to be better informed about the world beyond our shores, and no time when we have, in fact, been worse informed . . . The Palme d'Or for the **dumbing-down** of British television goes to ITN, which was once a proud name in journalism . . . In hock to the advertisers, ITN set the trend by its decision, early in the 1990s, to promote an agenda of crime, celebrity and miracle cures – and to downgrade foreign news to a couple of slots a week on Tuesdays and Thursdays, unless anything more sellable happened closer to home. The judgements were not editorial, but commercial. *(Bell 2002)*

> **'The history of the British press, since the emergence of popular journalism . . . has been a history of newspapers increasingly shifting editorial emphasis towards entertainment.'**
> – *Bob Franklin.*

In a similar vein, *Channel 4 News* anchor Jon Snow has accused ITV news of letting down the democratic process by abandoning serious news coverage in favour of more lifestyle and entertainment stories (Arlidge and Cole 2001). In an echo of their BBC counterparts, ITN reporters have complained about being urged to make news bulletins 'more Geri Halliwell than Gerry Adams' (Wells 2001a).

Nonsense, responds ITN chief executive Stewart Purvis, for whom ITV's main news bulletins continue to be what they were at their inception in the 1950s: 'the equivalent of a mid-market newspaper – **authority** with accessibility' (Purvis 2002). This view is backed, up to a point, by research into changing trends in TV news in the last quarter of the 20th century. Steven Barnett and Emily Seymour found that, despite a decline in political coverage and a shift towards a more tabloid domestic agenda, the overall picture was still 'a healthy balance of serious, light

by a definitive shift towards entertainment, a deliberate policy of appealing to the masses as part of a cultural and commercial proposition rather than as the more sedate organ of enlightenment and instruction' (Conboy 2002: 94).

Authority

Jon Dovey argues that journalism – in common with other media output – is now part of a culture in which individual subjective experience is fore-grounded at the expense of more general and authoritative 'truth claims' (Dovey 2000: 25). It is claimed that the 'we' of the bour-geois public sphere – which in any case was a rather narrow and male 'we' – has now collapsed into 'frag-mented individualised subjectivities' (Dovey 2000: 165). This can be translated into two contrasting ways of looking at media output:

Box 7.1

Box 7.1 Media output: traditional and popular views (Dovey 2000: 4)

TRADITIONAL	POPULAR
Authoritative	Reflexive
Film	Video
Public service	Reality TV
Observational documentary	Docu-soap
Investigation	Entertainment
Argument	Pleasure
TV news	TV chat
Working	Shopping
Elitist	Democratic
Boring	Fun

As we saw in Chapter 6, there is a tendency for traditional investigative journalism to be replaced, on TV at least, by more entertainment-driven formats. The rise of the docu-soap – a 'hybridised space that is at once fiction and fact' – is seen as reflecting 'a framework in

and international coverage'. However, the researchers warned that increasing commercial pressures would pose a serious threat to this balanced approach in the future (Barnett and Seymour 2000).

Broadcast news may have taken on board elements of the tabloid agenda, but the latter papers remain in a league of their own when it comes to the blurring of lines between news and entertainment through their coverage of sex, soaps and celebs. Consider page three of the *Sun* on Wednesday November 7 2001, a not untypical example. The page lead is an 'exclusive' about a pet rabbit who had scratched its owner's companions (HOP OFF! THUGS BUNNY SCARES AWAY ALL BOYFRIENDS RUTH HAS EVER HAD). There is also the traditional soft-porn photo, this one featuring a topless model in a soapy bath accompanied by two rubber ducks, in homage to the same paper's front-page splash of a few days earlier: QUEEN HAS RUBBER DUCK IN HER BATH. Of the four other items on the same page, one is a story about a TV chat show, another concerns a celeb's pregnancy, and two are news-in-brief items (nibs) about funny foreigners (*Sun* November 7 2001).

Broadsheet newspapers have not escaped charges of 'dumbing down', with critical commentators such as Bob Franklin arguing that there has been a process of tabloidisation affecting even the most serious newspapers (Franklin 1997: 7–10). Consider page eleven of the *Times* on Tuesday February 26 2002. Under a 'news' strapline, the page lead is a lengthy report on Kylie Minogue being voted 'best pop act' by readers of the *New Musical Express*, duly illustrated by a huge photo of Kylie and her cleavage (TRIUMPHANT KYLIE ADDS THE BRATS TO HER BRITS). The two other stories on the same page concern a record by the winner of TV talent show *Pop Idol* and the memoirs of dead rock star Kurt Cobain (*Times* February 26 2002). In common with other broadsheets, the *Times* has certainly changed since it unleashed a classical music critic on a Beatles record in the 1960s; the resulting article about the group's aeolian cadences and pandiatonic clusters baffled fans and Beatles alike.

But engagement with popular culture, leisure, life-style and entertainment does not mean that newspapers

> **'New journalism . . . has much to recommend it; it is full of ability, novelty, variety, sensation, sympathy, generous instincts; its one great fault is that it is feather-brained.'**
> – *Matthew Arnold, 1887.*

which "issues" and "social inquiry" are to be actively avoided in favour of entertainment and diversion' (Dovey 2000: 150 and 153).

Elitism

Critics of the dumbing down thesis argue that it is an elitist concept, far too simplistic to do justice to the complexity of today's journalism – or journalisms. Paul Manning points out that there needs to be some entertainment value in journalism because 'news audiences are unlikely to warm to a format that has the feel of a sociology seminar' (Manning 2001: 7). For Brian McNair, the recent proliferation of outlets and styles, along with the blurring of boundaries between elite and popular culture, mean that journalism is less deferential towards the powerful than in the past (McNair 2000: 59–60). He explains:

> [The] distinction between 'serious' and 'trivial' information is no longer one which can be taken as the basis for evaluating the public sphere . . . An earlier form of detached, deferential, more or less verbatim political reportage has gone from the print media . . . to be replaced by styles and agendas which, if they are occasionally entertaining, are at the same time more penetrating, more critical, more revealing and demystificatory of power than the polite, status-conscious journalisms of the past. And it is precisely the commercialising influence of the market which has allowed this to happen. *(McNair 2000: 60)*

Kees Brants argues that a mixture of 'entertainment and consciousness raising' could help to 're-establish the popular in politics', taking in not only 'the discursive and decision-making domain of politics but also the vast terrain of domestic life' (Brants 1998: 332–3). For Conboy, the debate about dumbing down and tabloidisation reflects anxiety about 'a slippage of control' on the part of those who have traditionally led public opinion (Conboy 2002: 181). But, given the multiplicity of media outlets now available to audiences, it could be that 'exposure to some kind of news is arguably better than no exposure at all' (Ursell 2001: 192).

necessarily *ignore* more traditionally weighty subject matter. Broadsheet editors such as Alan Rusbridger argue that their papers now have a much broader range of subject matter than in the past, incorporating the popular *alongside* the serious; and the fact that they also have many more pages means there has been no decline in the *quantity* of heavy news, foreign reports, political analysis or serious arts coverage (Rusbridger 2000).

At the *Yorkshire Evening Post*, David Helliwell recognises that he is in the entertainment business as well as the information business:

> First and foremost we're there to inform, but in this day and age you've got to do more than that because there's so much competition. There will always be pages in the paper where you are trying to be entertaining, to give people a read – features, the women's supplement, travel pages, reporters trying the latest high street fad, that sort of stuff. It's a balance, but our two big sellers are still local news and local sport.

Entertainment values

As we noted in Chapter 3, editors tend to look favourably on stories with the capacity to entertain or amuse. A national survey of 25,000 adults found that, while just over a third said they relied on newspapers to keep them informed, one in five admitted to reading a daily paper more for entertainment than for news (Powell 2001). They are unlikely to be disappointed. A study of the UK national press found that many news stories seemed to have been included not because they contained serious information for the reader but because of their entertainment value (Harcup and O'Neill 2001: 274). Patricia Holland writes, in the context of the *Sun* but with wider resonance, that the concepts of news and entertainment are becoming more entwined:

> The relentless push towards entertainment values has meant that the definition of what makes 'news' is itself constantly

> *'Readers are only really interested in people who are on television . . . And we like bottoms – because bottoms are fun.'*
> – Peter Hill, Daily Star editor.

> *'I would love to think that the type of documentary that didn't realise it had to entertain you as well as inform you is probably dead.'*
> – Jeremy Gibson, head of BBC features.

changing. The carefully established distinction between fact and opinion is now less easy to maintain. The need for accuracy has become dissolved into the excess of the headline, through a joke, an ironic exaggeration or an expression of outrage. *(Holland 1998: 31)*

A number of components go together to form the entertainment package that influences news selection in erstwhile 'serious' media as well as the tabloids. These entertainment values include: humour, showbiz, sex, animals, crime, and pictures.

Humour

Humorous stories are popular with newsdesks. When council workers took an unusually long time to mend a streetlamp it became national news not because of any particular significance, but because it echoed jokes about how many people it takes to change a lightbulb: FOUR MONTHS, 16 MEN AND £1,000 TO MEND LAMP (*Sun* September 16 2002). Sometimes the opportunity for a headline pun is enough to warrant a story's inclusion, as when Rolf Harris's accordion caught fire: FRY ME ACCORDION BROWN, SPORT (*Daily Mirror* August 5 2002). Or this piece of nonsense: A GAME OF CHEW SCARVES: ANDY NIBBLES SOUVENIR TO BRING HIS FOOTIE TEAM LUCK (*Sun* March 17 1999).

Showbiz

Stories about TV stars and other celebs are rife in the tabloids, but all UK national papers – with the exception of the *Financial Times* – carry large numbers of 'showbiz' stories. The *Independent*'s Paul Vallely believes it 'muddles world views' when journalists 'write about characters as though they were real rather than actors' (BBC 2002). Then there is the practice of introducing characters or plots from films and TV to enliven 'straight' news reports. Take this intro from a hard news story: 'Detectives hunting a brutal axe murderer are bringing in a *Cracker*-style psychologist to carry out a profile of the killer' (SEND FOR

CRACKER, *Yorkshire Evening Post* May 31 2001). Similarly, a story about working hours in the *Sunday Times* business section referred to northern bosses' attitudes as being 'more akin to that of *Coronation Street*'s Mike Baldwin', illustrated with a picture captioned: 'Northern boss: Mike Baldwin' (BOSSES WORK HARDER IN SOUTHEAST, *Sunday Times* February 24 2002).

Sex

If there is a sex angle to a story it is regarded as more entertaining and is therefore more likely to be used, with the sex angle emphasised even if it is marginal to the events described (Harcup and O'Neill 2001: 274). Court cases and employment tribunals with sex angles are more likely to be covered, all other things being equal, than are those without. A typical example is WREN HUMILIATED BY SUPERIOR'S SEX BANTER (*Daily Telegraph* March 23 1999).

Animals

Animals feature in many entertaining stories about unusual behaviour. Igwig the iguana, for example, made the front page of the *Times* when he was involved in a court case because his owner threw him at a police officer after being ejected from a pub (IGUANA IS CALLED TO THE BENCH, *Times* February 26 2002).

Crime

It is now more than half a century since George Orwell recorded the complaints of newspaper readers that 'you never seem to get a good murder nowadays' (Orwell 1946a: 10). But crime stories continue to fascinate journalists and readers alike. During the wall-to-wall coverage of the unfolding drama in the village of Soham in August 2002, when two girls disappeared and were eventually found dead, every national tabloid newspaper increased sales throughout the UK (ABC 2002). But David J Krajicek, for many years crime reporter for the *New York Daily News*, argues that the validity of news about

> **'The focus is on those things which are apt to arouse curiosity but require no analysis.'**
> – *Pierre Bourdieu.*

> **'We're in showbiz, aren't we?'**
> – *Richard Desmond, owner of Daily Express.*

> **'Journalism can be destroyed by forces other than the totalitarian state; it can also be destroyed by the entertainment state.'**
> – *James Carey.*

crime is compromised if it is told in such a way as to put entertainment before information and analysis:

[The] bulk of crime coverage amounts to drive-by journalism – a ton of anecdote and graphic detail about individual cases drawn from the police blotter but not an ounce of leavening context to help frame and explain crime. Too many of these reports begin and end with who did what to whom, embellished with the moans of a murder victim's mother or the sneer of an unrepentant killer in handcuffs. *(Krajicek 1998)*

Pictures

Many of the above stories will provide opportunities to include entertaining, amusing, dramatic, tragic or titillating pictures. *Sunday Express* editor John Junor once remarked that 'a beautiful young woman lifts even the dreariest page' (quoted in McKay 1999: 188), and his unreconstructed views live on in today's papers. Why else would events such as London Fashion Week receive such huge coverage every year? And how many newspapers would have written about Liz Hurley if the camera had never been invented?

Entertainment versus elitism?

Telling entertaining stories is part of the journalist's job, as is telling stories in entertaining ways. Lighter stories can be rewarding, as Yorkshire Television's Lindsay Eastwood explains:

I enjoy doing the 'And finally . . . ' stories because you can be creative. I've done a giant mushroom story, and a dog that was allergic to grass so they made it these special little red wellies. That was sweet. I did a lollipop man who'd won a 'best lollipop man' award and he did a rap, so we got him dancing with some kids. I did a baby boom in a Hull supermarket where everybody on the checkout had had a baby. We got them to do the Marge Simpson thing with the checkout going 'ping' when the baby was scanned in. And they've even taken a shot of my cleavage for National Cleavage Day. You can have a lot of fun on TV.

More serious news is also reported in ways designed to be entertaining. News is told in the form of stories that usually focus on individual people rather than abstract concepts. News stories are written in language that is accessible, active and sometimes colourful. And news stories may be presented visually and creatively to attract an audience. How journalists go about telling such stories is discussed further in Chapters 9, 10, 11 and 12.

Whenever journalists address 'popular' subjects, or report in ways intended to entertain, they run the risk of being accused of dumbing down – threatening civilisation as we know it. Almost 70 years ago FJ Mansfield recorded complaints about press sensationalism, distortion, invasion of privacy, and the reporting of sex 'beyond proper limits' (Mansfield 1936: 370). Ring any bells? David Goodhart rejects the dumbing down argument as **elitism** and nostalgia:

A combination of new media technology and social progress means, for good and ill, that common culture has gone forever. Welcome to what the critic Jason Cowley calls 'our crowded, fragmented, cultural market place'. *(Goodhart 1999)*

As this is the cultural market place in which journalists must sell their wares, it means that part of the journalist's job is to entertain as well as inform. The trick – for both journalist and audience – is to recognise the difference between the two. And to remember that sometimes the facts of a story, simply told, can be the most entertaining of all.

Summary

Journalists have long sought to entertain as well as to inform, to attract and retain an audience. This takes the form of selecting entertaining subject matter (humour, showbiz, sex, animals, crime, pictures) and of telling stories in entertaining ways. It has been claimed that the lines between information and entertainment have become blurred in recent years as part of the process known as 'dumbing down'. The dumbing down thesis has in turn been criticised as elitist. As the journalist's job will continue to involve elements of entertaining as well as informing, good practice requires both journalist and audience to recognise the distinction between the two.

Questions

Can journalism be both entertaining and informative at the same time?

Why do journalists tell news as stories?

Why do we read about crimes that have nothing to do with us?

Is there anything wrong with putting a musical soundtrack on broadcast news?

Is *any* news better than *no* news?

Further reading

For an enjoyable historical account of the press as popular entertainment, see Engel (1997). Conboy (2002) covers similar territory with a more analytical approach. Franklin (1997) offers an eloquent and still cogent critique of the tabloidisation of the print and broadcast media in the UK, countered in part by McNair's (2000) case that coverage of politics in particular has *not* been dumbed down. In exploring the 'carnivalesque excess' of reality TV, Dovey (2000) raises questions of authority and authorship within the context of the public sphere. Finally, Bourdieu's (1998) consideration of journalism concludes that the increasingly tabloid/human interest agenda of journalists serves to depoliticise citizens.

Notes

Sources for soundbites: Murdoch cited in O'Neill 1992: 30n; Franklin 1997: 72; Hill, cited in BJR 2002; Gibson cited in Dovey 2000: 137; Bourdieu 1998: 51; Carey cited in McQuail 2000: 159; Desmond cited in Ruddock 2001.

Chapter Eight
Interviewing

Key terms

Interviews

Questions

Conversation

Control

Performance

Doorstepping

Death knocks

Victims

Quotes

Selection

Pseudo-events

Pinned to the noticeboard in my newsroom is an excruciating apology that should serve as a warning to any journalist about to embark on an interview. It concerns a profile of a black woman who apparently revealed her support for the old South African system of racial segregation and discrimination. The apology is worth quoting in full:

> In an article headed BLACK AND BLUE, Page 6, *G2*, yesterday, we interviewed Patti Boulaye about her intention to stand for the Greater London Assembly, as a Conservative. The interview took place in Conservative Central Office. In the course of the article we quoted Ms Boulaye, a prominent black actress and singer, as saying: 'This is a time to support apartheid . . . I mean people say, "Why didn't you support it when it was in government?" Because it would have been the fashionable thing to do. This is a time to support apartheid because it's unfashionable.' What Ms Boulaye actually said was 'a party', meaning the Conservative Party. At no time during the interview was apartheid mentioned. The journalist concerned misheard Ms Boulaye's remarks but then asked no follow-up questions about what she thought she had heard. The offence was compounded by the picking out of part of these misheard remarks as a subsidiary heading in the middle of the text. The *Guardian* apologises profusely to Ms Boulaye for suggesting she made remarks which seemed to show she supported something totally abhorrent to her.
> *(Guardian, March 18 1999)*

The mishearing was unfortunate but the bigger mistake was the failure to follow it up during the interview. Such an apparently bizarre statement should have prompted further questions that would have revealed the misunderstanding. But at least that encounter actually took place, unlike a *Sun* interview with a widow whose husband was posthumously awarded the Victoria Cross for his actions in the Falklands war. Under the legend 'world exclusive', the article began: 'VC's widow Marcia McKay fought back her tears last night and said: "I'm so proud of Ian" . . . ' In fact, she had refused to speak to the paper. So the *Sun* stitched together quotes from old cuttings and a second-hand account from the soldier's bereaved mother, and presented it as an interview with the widow. The Press Council (forerunner of the Press Complaints Commission) ruled that the paper had

Pseudo-events

Daniel Boorstin categorises the media interview, alongside the press conference and the press release, as a 'pseudo-event'; that is, not so much a way of reporting the news, but of *making* the news. He records that 'the first full-fledged modern interview with a well-known figure' was an encounter with Brigham Young in Salt Lake City, published verbatim in the *New York Tribune* in 1859. Interviews were seen by some as invasions of privacy and by others as contrived events. One 19th century editor described interviewing as 'the most perfect contrivance yet devised to make journalism an offence, a thing of ill savour in all decent nostrils'. Despite such hostility, the interview gradually became established in the US, then Europe, as a legitimate way of gathering material for journalism (Boorstin 1963: 26-7). Not just *gathering* material but *creating* material, argues Boorstin:

> Nowadays a successful reporter must be the midwife – or more often the begetter – of his news. By the interview technique he incites a public figure to make statements which will sound like news. During the twentieth century this technique has grown into a devious apparatus which in skilful hands can shape national policy. *(Boorstin 1963: 34)*

Before interviewing became commonplace, notes Michael Schudson, 'President Lincoln often spoke with reporters informally but no reporter ever quoted him directly' (Schudson 2001: 156). Schudson argues that the growth of interviewing on both sides of the Atlantic helped journalists establish themselves as a separate group, brandishing notebooks and practising something called objective reporting:

> In the late 19th century and into the 20th century, leading journalists counselled against note-taking and journalists were encouraged to rely upon their own memories. But by the 1920s journalism textbooks dared to recommend 'the discriminate and intelligent use of notes'. The growing acceptance of note-taking suggests the acceptance and naturalisation of interviewing. This is not to say the interview was no longer controversial . . . There was still a sense that an 'interview' was a contrived event in which the journalist, in collusion with a person seeking publicity, invented rather than reported news. As late as 1926 the Associated Press prohibited its reporters from

perpetrated 'a deplorable, insensitive deception on the public' (Chippindale and Horrie 1992: 163–5).

The *Guardian* and the *Sun* are not the only newspapers to have given readers cause to doubt the veracity of interviews. Indeed, *all* interviews have been described as manufactured encounters or **pseudo-events**. Yet the interview – the asking of questions and the recording of answers in writing or on tape – is the basic ingredient of both news and features. As Cedric Pulford explains:

> Interviewing is the chief tool of active journalism. Without talking to people who can give us information or opinions, by phone or face to face, we can only print what others send us or recycle what has appeared somewhere else. *(Pulford 2001: 17)*

Preparation

The interview may be a brief encounter over the phone, a lengthy affair over lunch, a set-piece live broadcast, or even a few questions answered via fax or email. Whatever it is, you should have some idea *why* you are interviewing this particular person – for factual answers to one or two questions, opinions, quotes, emotions, description, scraps of colour, background, whatever.

Having decided *why* you are interviewing someone, *how* do you go about it? Many journalists stress the importance of meticulous planning to ensure they remain in control, working to set questions or even a 'script' determined by the particular angle being pursued (Aitchison 1988: 40–42). Planning anything that resembles a script may encourage a rather stiff and inflexible approach to an interview,

> *'The interview . . . is generally the joint product of some humbug of a hack politician and another humbug of a reporter.'*
> – The Nation, 1869.

but thinking of *some* questions in advance is certainly a good idea. You will often have time to conduct background research before the interview. You might spend a couple of hours reading cuttings about the subject, looking for basic information and useful insights, and possibly thinking of an angle nobody has yet come up with. You might search the internet, look in specialist magazines, consult reference books, and talk to colleagues or friends who know something about the subject. Of course, an interview may take an

writing interviews. But generally, reporting in the United States by that time meant interviewing . . . It [fitted] effortlessly into a journalism already fact-centred and news-centred rather than devoted primarily to political commentary or preoccupied with literary aspirations. *(Schudson 2001: 157)*

Pseudo-events are also discussed in Chapter 2.

Control

John Sergeant's account of his encounter with Tony Benn hinges on the question of *who* should have the right to control an interview. The relationship between interviewer and interviewee has been described by feature writer Fiammetta Rocco as an 'ambivalent coupling' (Rocco 1999: 49). Some of this ambivalence stems from the fact that, while today's journalistic style may be less deferential than that of half a century ago, the interviewee may be more media-literate and schooled in the arts of spin than were their predecessors.

Some celebrities try to impose tight control on interviews by setting conditions in return for (limited) access, as Gary Susman explains:

> There's always an army of publicists hovering over our shoulders, some from the studios, some employed by the stars, all making sure we don't ask anything impolite or embarrassing or anything that strays too far from the movie. The threats are never spoken but always implicitly – if you ask the star about his ex-wife, he'll walk out, and you'll have ruined the interview for yourself and your colleagues; or worse, you'll be blackballed from future junkets. *(Susman 2001)*

This 'increased PR interventionism' in interviews can result in 'journalistic passivity and compliance in a sanitised promotional drive', argues Eamonn Forde (2001: 38). At its most extreme, it leads to editors agreeing to give 'copy approval' to PR companies acting on behalf of highly-prized celebs. When the *Observer* was criticised for giving such approval to a singer's PR people, the deputy editor said the paper had signed the 'silly piece of paper' only because the interview was likely to be uncontroversial, adding:

unexpected turn, and that may be fine; but along the way you should make sure you cover the ground you need to.

The 'winning grace' of interviewing

There is plenty of often quite prescriptive advice available on interviewing techniques, but trial and error is the way most trainee journalists feel their way through their first interviews. Experiment with different approaches and see what works for you in different circumstances. Remember that it is rarely a good idea to pretend to have a completely different personality from your own, and there is no point in every fledgling hack trying to be Jeremy Paxman.

Journalists have to be comfortable speaking to all sorts of people from millionaires to the homeless. This remains as true today as when FJ Mansfield instructed trainees back in the 1930s:

> Personality counts for much. A reporter has to meet all classes of people, who are potential sources of news; to talk to Cabinet Ministers as well as costermongers, I am tempted to say on their own level, and to inspire in all the confidence essential to successful approach. The happy medium between the 'inferiority complex' and cocksure audacity, should be the aim – a reasonable self-assurance, born of a well-informed competence. The winning grace that will extract news equally from a Lord Lieutenant and a trade union secretary, is a great asset. A reporter touches life at all points and in his deportment should show respect for the feelings and opinions of others, no matter how much he may be out of sympathy with them. Journalism tends to breed cynicism and a hypercritical attitude, but good manners, and often diplomacy, forbid a display of contempt. *(Mansfield 1936: 87–8)*

Experienced interviewer Martin Wainwright believes that a journalist's main assets during interviews are being *curious* about people and allowing enough *time*:

> People can be diffident, so the interesting things sometimes come out only at the very end of an

> *'I always tell beginner journalists: "Look, all you have to do is be punctual, be polite, and ask questions".'*
> – Lynn Barber.

[Our] advice to anybody who signs anything like that is to utterly disregard it if it gets in the way of doing the piece that you want to do, even if that means retrospectively breaking an agreement with some tinpot PR agency. *(Quoted in Morgan 2002b)*

In that case, why sign it in the first place? Or why not at least give the article a 'health warning'?

The relationship between journalist and source is explored in more detail in Chapter 4 and Chapter 6. Control of the finished product is discussed in the section on quotes, below.

Victim

The victim is a familiar character in journalism. Most information on victims comes from interviews with victims themselves if they are still alive, or from interviews with the bereaved. Thoughtful journalists may pause from time to time to consider why reporters and, presumably, readers are so fascinated with details of victims' lives. 'Being the victim of crime is to lay oneself open to having one's privacy invaded,' argues Chris Frost, who adds:

> Journalists need always to remember that victims of crime are not there by choice and rarely through any fault of their own. If the report will make things worse for the victim, then the journalist should think carefully about how the report should be handled. *(Frost 2000: 146)*

And yet, do critics who flinch from the idea of 'death knocks' not want to know about the person who was found dead in their neighbourhood last night? Where do they think such information comes from if not by interviewing distressed relatives, friends, neighbours and workmates?

The idea of the victim is discussed in more detail in Chapter 9.

interview. That's true to an amazing extent. As a journalist you spend most of your life rushing, but it's still worth spending as long as you can with people. Also, people can open up more if you appear a bit naïve.

An example of somebody opening up came when Conservative party leader Iain Duncan Smith held a lunch to 'meet and greet the local hacks'. Sara Dixon, a reporter on the *Wanstead and Woodford Guardian*, took the opportunity to ask him about his first six months as party leader. In the course of discussing his own situation he remarked that Tony Blair's children had been used 'ruthlessly' to promote the Labour Prime Minister. The day after the local paper appeared, the Tory leader's views were being quoted throughout the national media. *Daily Telegraph* columnist Tom Utley wondered aloud if Duncan Smith had lowered his guard because he thought it had not mattered what he said to his 'local rag'. Utley had a point, conceded the local reporter who scooped the nationals, but it was also a question of interviewing *style*:

> A young Diet-Coke-drinking local reporter sitting opposite you in a Woodford restaurant is distinctly less threatening than a grilling on party policy under the glare of studio lights by Andrew Marr or Jonathan Dimbleby. But it is also a question of approach . . . [Without] the roundabout questions of how have the past six months been treating you Mr Duncan Smith, the contentious statement would never have been uttered. The comment about Blair and his children is not a thing that is extracted in pugnacious interviews, rather *it emerges out of conversations*. *(Dixon 2002; my emphasis)*

Conversation is the key to good interviewing. Even the briefest interview should involve the techniques of conversation: listening as well as talking, engaging with what is being said rather than just waiting for a gap to fill with your next question, making eye contact in face to face interviews, and encouraging the interviewee through sounds or gestures.

On the telephone

You cannot make eye contact over the telephone, and the vast majority of interviews for print journalism are conducted this way. But, although there is an

Quotes

A good quote is highly prized. According to Allan Bell, direct quotation serves three key purposes in journalism:

> First, a quote is valued as a particularly incontrovertible fact because it is the newsmaker's own words . . . A second function is to distance and disown, to absolve journalist and news outlet from endorsement of what the source said . . . The third function of direct quotation is to add to the story the flavour of the newsmaker's own words. *(Bell 1991: 207–9)*

But most of what is said in most interviews will not be quoted directly; rather, the bulk of information gleaned from sources will be used as background or turned into reported speech. Bell argues that this power to edit 'puts the journalist in *control* of focusing the story, able to combine information and wordings from scattered parts of an interview' (Bell 1991: 209; my emphasis).

Ethical concerns are raised about this role of the journalist in selecting the parts of an interview to quote, the parts to paraphrase, and the parts to discard, as Lynn Barber explains:

> The journalist has *all* the power when it comes to writing the piece: she chooses which quotes to use and which to omit, which to highlight and which to minimise. I use a lot of quotes compared with most other interviewers, but they probably still only amount to at most two pages out of a twenty– or thirty-page transcript. So obviously with this degree of selection, one has almost limitless opportunities for 'slanting' the interview, favourably or unfavourably. All I can say is that I don't aim to do that and I hope I don't. *(Barber 1999: 202; emphasis in original)*

impersonality about the phone, many journalists develop chatty relationships with regular contacts they may never have met in the flesh.

Tone of voice is obviously important, as is the manner in which you begin the call. When somebody answers the phone, you have no idea what they were in the middle of doing when you called – or whose call they might have been hoping for – so it is not usually a good idea to launch into a fusillade of questions the second they come on the line. Speaking clearly, politely and not too fast, explain who you are and why you are ringing them. Ask them for a few minutes of their time – be prepared to call back at a pre-arranged time if you are not on deadline – and try to sound bright, alert and friendly. It has been suggested that standing up while speaking on the phone exudes extra confidence, and that making facial and arm gestures can help inflect the voice with the appropriate tone (Keeble 2001a: 63). I've also heard advertising reps being urged to 'smile while you dial'. This might be the sort of advice to make most self-respecting hacks do the finger-down-the-throat routine, but it is endorsed by Sally Adams, who adds that 'probably the most important thing is to *like* talking on the phone' (Adams 2001b: 85; my emphasis).

Telephone interviews are almost always shorter than face to face ones, so you tend to get down to details pretty quickly. It is usually worth getting the interviewee talking by asking 'Could you talk me through what happened to you?', 'Describe what you saw,' or 'What is your reaction to . . . ?' Their replies should prompt further questions. This is all well and good when you have called somebody and your research is fresh in your mind. But it's not so clever when *they* call *you* back hours or days later, by which time you may have forgotten why you wanted to talk to them in the first place. That's one reason why most journalists prefer to keep ringing somebody rather than rely on a return call that, if it comes at all, will probably be at the least convenient moment.

A word of warning on telephone interviews. You need to be absolutely clear if the interviewee is being serious or is joking. Given that you have no visual clues you may have to ask 'Are you being serious?' Better to be thought of as lacking a sense of humour than to risk publishing a flippant or ironic remark as if it were a genuine opinion.

Email and fax

Telephone interviews may be impersonal but trying to establish a rapport in written communication via email or fax is even harder. Email and fax interviews are not to be recommended except when they are the only way of getting through to somebody. Email may be the best way of contacting a range of academic experts all over the world. Your message will be waiting for them when they log on in their different time zones and, if you have tried several, one of them may get back to you with some answers before your deadline. Email and fax are also used for questionnaire-style celeb interviews, featuring questions such as 'What is your favourite smell?' and 'How often do you have sex?' But, apart from the difficulty of establishing a rapport, you cannot be sure if the replies are really coming from the subject or a PR minion.

The upside is that fax and email have made it harder for people in power to hide from journalists by resorting to the age-old device of never being available. When Paul Foot rang people from his desk at the *Daily Mirror* they tended to take his calls because of the kudos associated with that title. But when he switched to *Private Eye* people often seemed to be 'in meetings' whenever he telephoned. A frustrating experience when investigating alleged wrongdoing, because you need to put allegations to those involved, as Foot explains:

> Getting information out of the people you're accusing is absolutely crucial to the whole operation. Just as email has changed our lives, the fax changed our lives. I got in the habit of faxing questions to people. Whereas if you rang them up they would never be available, once you've got the fax through, you're home. Because if you don't get an answer you can always say 'well I faxed them with these questions'. With the phone you might never get even to ask the question.

Face to face

When I interviewed veteran Labour politician Tony Benn in his Chesterfield office he brought out his own tape machine to record the conversation. He recorded all interviews partly to check later if he had been misquoted, and partly to warn journalists not to turn him over when writing up their stories. The only other interviewee I have seen make their own recording was miners' leader Arthur Scargill. Profile writer Lynn Barber expresses surprise that so few interview subjects make their own tapes to safeguard against being misquoted (Barber 1999: 201). But then, not every interviewee has been on the receiving end of as much hostile media coverage as Messrs Benn and Scargill.

Tony Benn, as fans of Ali G's early political encounters will recall, was the only subject to challenge the spoof interviewer's attitude problem rather than accept it as representative of 'yoof TV'. His refusal to accept that journalists should have total **control** of interviews even managed to unsettle seasoned campaigner John Sergeant, who recalls arriving at the MP's home to record an interview during the 1984–85 miners' strike:

> When he opened the door, I immediately noticed a small tape recorder, which he thrust forward, with its red light on, showing that it was recording. 'Hello,' he said; and I did not know whether to reply to him directly or speak into the tape recorder. I said hello to the machine. He then proceeded to give me a short lecture on the unfairness of the BBC's coverage of the miners' dispute. I took this in reasonably good heart, but *knowing that all my remarks were being recorded I said nothing which might be used against me.* (Sergeant 2001: 236–7; *my emphasis*)

A rare case of the tables being turned, with the journalist rather than the interviewee being careful what they said. That particular interview ended with the MP erasing the BBC's tape with a demagnetizing device, leaving the journalist 'struck dumb' (Sergeant 2001: 238).

Happily, most encounters are less prickly affairs. Just as well because, unless you are accusing the interviewee of wrongdoing, you need to establish a *rapport* between the two of you. First impressions are important, so don't be late, don't smell of booze, and do dress appropriately – not as if you are going to a wedding or a funeral, but smartly enough so that your state of dress will not be an issue for the interviewee. Non-verbal communication is important, so show interest by making eye contact without staring,

> **'I am always asking myself why is this lying bastard lying to me?'**
> – Jeremy Paxman.

nodding but not nodding off. Give verbal reassurance that the interviewee is not speaking into a vacuum – laugh at their jokes, sympathise with their troubles, and use phrases such as 'Really?', 'Yes', 'uhh-huhh' and so on to demonstrate that you are engaged. But don't overdo it.

Learn to listen, interrupting their flow only if they are digressing too much and you are on deadline. Interrupting a dramatic narrative to check a minor detail – 'How do you spell the name of the first boy eaten by the crocodile?' – can be irritating. Make a note and check at the end. But don't be afraid to interrupt to clarify something you don't understand or to get some specific examples. Keep your eyes as well as your ears open because you might discover a visual clue to the interviewee's character or a visual prompt for an unusual question. Clothes, hair, tattoos, piercings, pictures on the wall, books on the shelves, an unusual plant, the view from the window – all might spark off a question and lead to the discovery of a different angle.

Chat is more common at the end of an interview conducted in person than one conducted on the telephone, and sometimes this can result in further information or angles to follow up. Unless you don't mind risking any future relationship with the interviewee, you might think twice before quoting something said after a formal interview has finished without asking 'Do you mind if I use that?'. See discussion below of 'off-the-record' comments.

Broadcast interviews

Much of this chapter deals with interviews for print journalism. Many similar approaches will be used by online, TV and radio journalists but there are also many differences – notably the fact that you can use the speaker's *voice* as well as their words and that broadcast interviews often have more than an element of *performance* about them. Whereas the questioning is often invisible to the reader of a print interview, it is central to many broadcast interviews. None more so than when Jeremy Paxman asked Home Secretary Michael Howard the *same* question 14 times without getting an answer (*Newsnight at 20*, BBC2, January 29

2000). If that was a moral victory for the interviewer, another *Newsnight* interview turned into a personal disaster for Peter Snow. Miners' leader Arthur Scargill turned the tables on the experienced journalist who gave in to the fatal temptation to bluff.

Scargill: Have you read my full speech in Moscow?

Snow: Yes I have.

Scargill: Have you? I don't believe you, I'm sorry . . . Mr Snow, have you seen the full text, because every other broadcaster has told me that they haven't? Have you seen it, truthfully?

Snow: Can you, can you . . . ?

Scargill: No, I'm asking you a question then I'll answer your question. Have you seen the full text?

Snow: I have not seen any reference . . .

Scargill: I didn't ask you that. Have you seen the full text?

Snow: I have not seen any reference . . .

Scargill: Have you seen the full text?

Snow: Would you tell me Mr Scargill, would you tell me . . . ?

Scargill: I'm asking you a question.

Snow: I'm asking the questions, if I may say so.

Scargill: Well, not this time you're not. I'm asking you, have you seen the full text?

Snow: To be quite honest, I have not seen the full text.

Scargill: Right . . .

(Newsnight at 20, BBC2, 29 January 2000)

All this talk of victory and defeat emphasises the adversarial nature of many such interviews. But, apart from the set-piece studio slanging match or the doorstep challenge to a rogue, the aggressive approach is not usually to be recommended. You will win few prizes by treating a local charity fund-raiser to a Paxmanesque sneer and a demand to 'Come on, answer the question'.

> **'I've done hundreds of doorsteps, and I doubt if half-a-dozen have given anyone a story.'**
> – Jim Lewthwaite, Sun reporter.

Asking questions

The precise nature of the questions you ask will be determined initially by the purpose of the interview and the research you have done, but it is important that you *listen* to people's answers and adjust your line of questioning if necessary. It is usually a good idea to get the interviewee talking in an open way at the beginning, even if you intend to end up by accusing them of some wrongdoing. So, unless you specifically want a yes or no answer, try to avoid asking *closed* questions such as 'Did you see the accident?' To get them talking opt for more *open* questions such as 'What did you see?' People often stop after a sentence or two, looking for reassurance that this is what you want. Give it to them by asking 'And then?' or 'What happened next?'

Whatever the topic, you are likely to want to know the answers to the five Ws of journalism introduced in Chapter 1: Who? What? Where? When? Why? And, of course, How? You may have to keep working at it because, as Fiammetta Rocco notes: 'The story that a subject tells about himself is almost never the whole story. "Why?" is the question I ask most often' (Rocco 1999: 50). You will often have to do some lateral thinking while listening. *Who* is that person? *What* is their relationship to so-and-so? *Where* did they meet? *When* did they arrive? *Why* did they go there? *How* did they travel? The answer to any one such question might end up providing you with the most newsworthy angle to a story. But you might never know if you don't ask. Clarify any vague answers such as 'recently' or 'about'. Getting specific examples by asking 'Such as?' can sometimes bring a dull interview to unexpected life. And do not be afraid to say: 'I don't understand that, please explain.'

Unless you are broadcasting live, it is a good idea to ask towards the end: 'Is there anything else you'd like to add?' It is polite, it stops the interviewee feeling annoyed that they didn't get the chance to talk about their pet subject, and they might just say something far more important and interesting than anything that has gone before. Then, make sure you have checked spellings, especially names, and exchanged contact numbers. And don't forget to thank people for their help and time.

Off-the-record

An interviewee may tell a journalist that something is 'off-the-record', meaning 'Don't attribute this information to me'. That does not mean that you cannot include the information in an unattributed form. Check exactly what information they are referring to. They may have good reason – perhaps they might lose their job for criticising their employer in public – or they may be feeling paranoid with little justification. As the interview progresses they may begin to trust you more, so you could try suggesting that something said off-the-record might be restored to on-the-record. But if you break your word, having agreed to something being off-the-record, then you will have betrayed a source.

Confusion arises if somebody *assumes* that a journalist will treat something as off-the-record without making it explicit, as when a politician put his hand over a journalist's tape recorder when he passed on some gossip about the Prime Minister's wife during an interview about the health service. His comment was included in the subsequent article, causing outrage in Downing Street. A *Press Gazette* leader column noted at the time:

> [Lord Winston's] naivety serves to remind us that interviewees and journalists can have very different beliefs about what constitutes off-the-record. Most of the public would regard Winston's covering of the mic as placing the Cherie item out of play. Most journalists would not: *something is off-the-record only when interviewee and journalist so agree. (Press Gazette January 21 2000; my emphasis)*

Such agreement cannot be imposed unilaterally by the interviewee, and it certainly cannot be made retrospective by adding: 'Of course, everything I have said must be off-the-record.' In such circumstances the journalist *may* choose to agree, but it remains a *choice*.

People may say things that, with hindsight, they wish they had kept to themselves. A journalist who combines a conversational tone with a keen news sense will sometimes be 'lucky' enough to catch an interviewee in just such a mood. Press Association reporter Jane Merrick recalls making a routine telephone call to the press office of a petrol company at the beginning of the fuel protests that paralysed the UK in September 2000:

> It was during the protesters' first blockade of an oil refinery. In London the company's line was that petrol supplies won't be affected. When I called the PR guy in the North-West I got lucky because he was really annoyed and he said: 'Don't these people realise we're going to run out of fuel by Sunday night?' I said, like, 'Really?' And he said 'Yeah, and it's really peeing me off.' I said 'OK, fine', put the phone down and ran the story 'Warning of fuel shortage by Sunday'.

The warning became a national talking point and the panic-buying of petrol increased as a result. Merrick continues:

> This guy got into so much trouble. He phoned me on the Monday and said: 'It wasn't off-the-record because I didn't say it was off-the-record, but I shouldn't have said that to you because our line was that it was fine.' When clearly it wasn't fine.

Doorsteps and death knocks

Some interviews are fraught with difficulties ranging from the boredom of hanging around for hours waiting for somebody to emerge to the possibility of a punch in the face. The 'doorstep' and the 'death knock' bring out differing emotions in journalists and interviewees alike.

Doorstepping is a peculiarly British tradition, argues Matthew Engel. And a peculiarly ineffective one, it seems:

> Photographers and reporters descend on the home of a person touched by scandal or tragedy . . . and wait, in the hope of a picture of one of the actors in the drama or, far less probably, a comment. It is a tiresome and, for the reporters, almost always a pointless chore, unless they are actually paying to buy the story. *(Engel 1997: 279)*

Not so, according to Nick Davies. He has no time for reporters who bully people, camp outside their homes and peer through their windows, but he argues that arriving unannounced on people's doorsteps remains an integral part of the journalist's armoury: 'That's how you get good stories. It is the most exciting and most skilful part of our job' (quoted in Stevens 2001).

When it comes to death knocks – calling on a bereaved family to ask for information, quotes and a picture – few journalists actually enjoy the task, although some adopt a macho pose and boast of their experiences. Both the Press Complaints Commission and the National Union of Journalists advise reporters to be cautious about intruding on people's grief, and families may be actively hostile to journalists' enquiries at such a difficult time. Some people genuinely welcome the chance to talk about the death of somebody close to them, even to a stranger with a notebook, while others may answer questions to avoid inaccuracies appearing in the media, or simply because they do not think of refusing.

Reporter Sue White describes her technique for death knocks:

> Normally it would be quiet and I'd knock on the door. It would open a crack and someone would answer . . . I'd say 'Hello, I'm Sue White from the *Birmingham Evening Mail*. We've heard from the police about the dreadful accident last night. Could I come in and have a word with you about it?' Almost everyone would say 'All right' . . . It's important to be very, very courteous and understanding . . . I'd be taken in and sat in the lounge. It would be very quiet, they'd be stunned. I felt if I talked openly, in as friendly and sympathetic a way as possible – one person to another, making it clear I just wanted to confirm some facts – people would give me that information. I was usually right. *(Quoted in Adams 2001b: 142–3)*

To the non-journalist it might sound callous, even manipulative. But when we hear there has been a murder or a terrible accident, we *expect* the media to tell us about the **victim** – their name, how old they were, and something about their character and interests. This information does not appear in the media by magic and full details are rarely supplied by the police or other third parties. Such stories are usually obtained by journalists knocking on the doors of relatives, neighbours and friends.

Bereaved relatives are not the only people approached by journalists at times of trauma. Jane Merrick was working for a regional news agency when news came through that the former Beatle George Harrison had been attacked. She recalls:

The name of the man arrested had got through the rumour mill so we contacted all the names in the book and I got to his mum first. I introduced myself as a journalist and she asked me what had happened. I said 'It's OK, I'll come out and speak to you.' She said 'Tell me what's happened, is he OK?' I said 'He's absolutely fine but I need to come and see you in person'. Then she got very defensive and said she would put the phone down if I didn't tell her what was going on. So I said 'There's been a bit of an incident that Michael has been involved in, but he's absolutely fine'. She put two and two together and shouted to her husband 'Oh my God, Michael's stabbed a Beatle!' And then she put the phone down. In the end I had to go out there. Eventually she invited everyone in, but by then we weren't the only ones.

Reflecting on the experience, Merrick says:

I felt terrible because you can't say straight out 'Your son has stabbed someone', and I was quite surprised that the police hadn't contacted her. It was a really difficult way to tell her, and I tried to soften it as much as possible, but you can't just be really mysterious and say 'I need to come and speak to you'. With hindsight, I should just have established that she was the mother, and then turned up at the door to speak to her.

Brian Whittle favours the in person approach because it means people cannot put the phone down on you. They can, however, shut the door and tell you to go away. Experienced doorstepper Chris Bucktin, of the *News of the World*, reckons that 'you know in the first 45 seconds whether you've got your yea or nay' (quoted in Stevens 2001). The Press Complaints Commission tells journalists that, except in cases in the public interest, they 'must not persist in telephoning, questioning, pursuing or photographing individuals having been asked to desist' (PCC Code of Practice 4 (ii)). It still goes on, but not as much as it did. As agency reporter Denis Cassidy says: 'If you are told to leave, nowadays, then you leave' (quoted in Stevens 2001).

> 'If I said that, I was misquoted.'
> – Lord Hanson.

Quoting

As well as a means of obtaining information, interviews provide journalists with direct quotes. **Quotes** are a vital ingredient of journalism, adding authority, drama and powerful or colloquial expression to an account. Opinions differ on the editing of quotes, although all agree that little purpose is served by including excessive repetition of phrases such as 'like', 'know what I mean?', or 'um' – unless you are doing it to make a point about the speaker. The National Council for the Training of Journalists expects a quote to be a verbatim account of the speaker's words, and David Randall questions the point of quotation marks if what is inside them is not 'a word for word, syllable by syllable, accurate report of their actual words' (Randall 2000: 187). But journalists frequently 'tidy up' quotes. If they did not, it would be a remarkable coincidence that sources interviewed by tabloid journalists seem to speak in short, sharp sentences, while those quoted by broadsheet reporters speak in more complex sentence structures – even when they are the same people.

News agency editor Brian Whittle defends the practice of 'going over' quotes:

> I think you can put words in people's mouths in the sense that most people are not particularly literate. That's perfectly acceptable if you know what you're doing, but only experience can tell you that. We go over people's quotes. Don't misunderstand me on this, we're pretty careful about it.

Jane Merrick found different policies at work when she moved from another regional news agency to the Press Association:

> At the agency we could paraphrase people almost and still put it in quotes because it would be neater, whereas at PA it's the *exact* words. Now I have two dictaphones as a back-up and tape everyone as well as take shorthand notes, to cover my own back really.

Wynford Hicks and Tim Holmes urge a similar caution:

> [You] can always summarise quotes in indirect speech if tidying up causes difficulty – but you must never do the reverse: indirect speech can never be used as the raw material for a concocted quote. In subbing quotes . . . the key word is accuracy: the exact meaning of the original must be preserved. In condensing and clarifying a quote . . . you must never change the emphasis. So if somebody makes a statement that is qualified in some way, you remove the qualification at your peril. *(Hicks and Holmes 2002: 65)*

The ethical line between tidying and changing can be a fine one. It can sometimes disappear entirely, especially if a reporter edits somebody's comments when making notes, then slightly strengthens them when writing up, before passing the story on to a sub who might tidy the quotes a bit more. The published result might be unrecognisable to the 'speaker', not just in words but in meaning. The golden rule when selecting or shortening quotes, and pruning out repetitions or irrelevancies, is to retain not just the speaker's *voice* but the speaker's *sense*. Otherwise, why bother quoting at all?

Summary

Journalists interview sources – on the telephone, in person, or occasionally by fax/email – to obtain information, facts, opinions, analysis, description, emotion, colour, background, and direct quotes. The interview has been described as an ambivalent encounter in which the interviewee controls what information they disclose but, with the exception of live broadcasts, the interviewer retains control of how the interview is passed on to the audience. Interviews can themselves create news and in this sense can be seen as 'pseudo-events'. Ethical issues associated with interviewing include questions of intrusion into grief, control of access, selection of material, copy approval, and the alteration of direct quotes.

Questions

Why do journalists interview people?

Why do people agree to be interviewed by journalists?

How can journalists prepare for interviews?

Who has most power, the interviewer or the interviewee?

Can it be right to edit people's quotes?

Further reading

Despite the rather prescriptive tone there are many good tips and instructive anecdotes to be found in Adams (2001b); it also includes some interesting material on body language, but don't take all the pop psychology as gospel. Keeble (2001a), Randall (2000) and Frost (2002) all have sections on interviewing. For more detailed exploration of the various techniques and rules of broadcast interviewing, see Boyd (2001). Beaman (2000) offers a practical guide to radio interviewing.

Notes

Sources for soundbites: *Nation* cited in Boorstin 1963: 27; Barber 1999: 200; Paxman cited in Flett 2001; Lewthwaite cited in Engel 1997: 279; Hanson cited in Boyd 2001: 117.

Chapter Nine
Writing News

Key terms

Stories

Kiss and tell

Inverted pyramid

Chronology

Attribution

Myths

Text

Polysemic

Dialogic

Early in the 21st century a group of scientists claimed to have come up with a computer program capable of taking 'raw' facts from the wires and rearranging the text into punchy news stories. The only drawback was that Arthur, as the program was known, seemed to lack the human ability of telling fact from fiction (Millar 2001).

Replacing journalists with robots may be a dream of the 'bean counters' in charge – no attitude problems, no ethical qualms, no expenses claims – but the idea isn't as new as it seems. Back in 1965 journalist Michael Frayn invented just such a news machine in his novel *The Tin Men*:

> Assistants bent over the component parts of the [Newspaper] Department's united experiment, the demonstration that in theory a digital computer could be programmed to produce a perfectly satisfactory daily newspaper with all the variety and news sense of the old hand-made article. With silent, infinite tedium, they worked their way through stacks of newspaper cuttings, identifying the pattern of stories, and analysing the stories into standard variables and invariables. At other benches other assistants copied the variables and invariables down on to cards, and sorted the cards into filing cabinets, coded so that in theory a computer could pick its way from card to card in logical order and assemble a news item from them.
> *(Frayn 1995: 37)*

So a story such as a child being sent home from school because of unsuitable clothing would have just three variables: the particular clothing objected to, whether the child also smoked, and whether the child was humiliated in front of the whole school. Verdict: 'V. Satis. Basic plot entirely invariable . . . Frequency of publication: once every nine days.' (Frayn 1995: 38.) Throw in the odd haircut or piece of body-piercing, and you've got a hardy-perennial story as common today as 40 years ago.

We have already seen, in Chapter 3, that news can be predictable and repetitive. This is partly because little happens that hasn't happened somewhere before. But it is also because much news tends to be written, or constructed, in the predictable, almost formulaic way satirised by Frayn. Journalists often say about a particular story that 'it writes itself'; it is such a good story that, having established the intro or the top line, the rest flows almost effortlessly from the notebook

Stories

Allan Bell argues that journalists do not so much write articles as *stories*:

> Journalists are professional story-tellers of our age. The fairy tale starts: 'Once upon a time.' The news story begins: 'Fifteen people were injured today when a bus plunged . . .' *(Bell 1991: 147)*

Traditional stories start at the beginning and continue to some sort of resolution at the end. But news stories start with the end and often end in the middle. As Bell notes, the central action of news stories is told in a non-chronological order, 'with result presented first followed by a complex recycling through various time zones' (Bell 1991: 155). And the story is not usually 'rounded off' or resolved, but finishes in 'mid-air' (Bell 1991: 154). This is not simply because news values dictate that the least important material be left to the end, but also because many stories are ongoing. The version of events given in the newspaper is merely a snapshot taken at deadline time, and a typical news story 'moves backwards and forwards in time' (Bell 1991: 153). According to Dan Berkowitz, journalists develop 'a mental catalogue of news story themes, including how the "plot" will actually unravel and who the key actors are likely to be' (quoted in Cottle 2000: 438).

Myths

Simon Cottle argues that story-telling has long been used by society to 'tell and re-tell its basic myths to itself', thereby reaffirming society as (after Anderson) an 'imagined community':

> Approached thus, news becomes a symbolic system in which the informational content of particular 'stories' becomes less important than the rehearsal of mythic 'truths' embodied within the story form itself. *(Cottle 2000: 438)*

Jack Lule argues that journalists repeatedly write the news in terms of myth; that is, stories that draw on 'archetypal figures and forms to offer exemplary models for human life' (Lule 2001: 15). Not *every* news story is written in such terms, but many are. Why? Because, for Lule, stories already exist before they are written:

to the finished product. An experienced journalist may be able to rush from a courtroom or a news conference and, seconds later, be dictating a perfectly constructed news story over the phone without pausing to write it first. It looks like magic to the beginner who has to pore over every word, but it can be learned with practice and it is made possible by the fact that journalists already have potential **stories** in their heads. It is even said that many news stories are rewrites of ancient **myths** in contemporary settings.

The language of news

There are some obvious differences in the writing styles of different types of newspaper, and the UK national press is divided into 'three clear, if not uniform, variants which address different constituencies' – broadsheets, mid-market titles, and popular tabloids (Bromley and Cushion 2002: 173). Style often differs in the amount of colour, and the number of adjectives, allowed into news copy. For example, when Jane Merrick worked for a regional agency selling mostly to the tabloids, her copy would be sprinkled with words such as 'brave', 'pretty' and 'tragic'. When she switched to the Press Association the style was to remove all such adjectives.

But, although journalists working for different outlets may differ in their news values and their stylistic flourishes, they mostly share a common language – a basic grammar of journalism. Study the language of news stories in broadsheets, tabloids or the provincial press and you will find that most news is written in the past tense, reporting on something that has happened or been said. (This contrasts with broadcast news, in which the present tense is the norm.) You will find that reporters' sentences are mostly active rather than passive, with somebody *doing* something rather than having something done *to* them. And you will find that concise writing is the norm – journalists never circumambulate the domiciles when they could simply go round the houses. So news sentences are made up of active and concise language. They also tend to be short. They must have a subject

> *'Always grab the reader by the throat in the first paragraph, sink your thumbs into his windpipe in the second, and hold him against the wall until the tag line.'*
> – Paul O'Neill.

Journalists approach events with stories already in mind. They employ common understandings. They borrow from shared narratives. They draw upon familiar story forms. They come to the news story *with* stories. Sometimes the story changes as the journalist gathers more information. But the story doesn't change into something completely new and never before seen. The story changes into . . . another story.
(Lule 2001: 29; emphasis and ellipsis in original)

He identifies seven enduring myths that are told and retold by journalists through 'new' news stories. They are:

- The victim – transforming death into sacrifice.
- The scapegoat – what happens to those who challenge or ignore social beliefs.
- The hero – the humble birth, the quest, the triumph and the return.
- The good mother – models of goodness.
- The trickster – crude, stupid, governed by animal instincts.
- The other world – the contrast between 'our' way of life and the 'other'.
- The flood – the humbling power of nature.

(Lule 2001: 22–5)

Consider the crime news that makes up such a large proportion of our print and broadcast news, particularly at a local and regional level. As we have seen in Chapter 4, most crime news is supplied by the police. Journalists can predict there will be a reasonably steady supply of crime news and how many of various types of crime are likely to occur on their patch. A murder will be a shock in a rural village but 'expected' to occur in an inner-city area (though it may still come as a shock to those who live in nearby streets). It does not take long for recruits to journalism to absorb how particular crimes tend to be covered. Murder victims, for example, might be innocent ('wouldn't hurt a fly'), heroic ('have-a-go-hero') or tainted ('gunned down in a drugs turf war'), and this approach helps determine how much effort is expended on painting a sympathetic

and a verb, although the subject may be implied. Paragraphs, too, are much shorter than in other forms of writing, often just one sentence long. Journalists are taught to use short pars because when stories are set in newspaper columns long pars look like indigestible and off-putting chunks of text. Shorter pars are also thought more likely to keep the attention of readers, although some variety in longer stories is probably a good idea. Wynford Hicks offers the following advice:

> In news a par that goes beyond three sentences . . . is likely to be too long; never quote two people in the same par: always start a new one for the second quote; never tack a new subject on to the end of a par. *(Hicks 1998: 43)*

Structure: 'KISS and tell'

Most news stories follow the 'KISS and tell' formula – KISS standing either for 'keep it short and simple', or 'keep it simple, stupid'. I know of journalists on a local freesheet who are instructed to 'keep it simple, as if you are writing for your granny'. Complexity, abstract notions, ambiguity and unanswered questions tend to be frowned upon and subbed out of news copy. As is anything seen as personal comment by the reporter.

The National Council for the Training of Journalists (NCTJ) sets out what it expects when it comes to writing news:

> The trainee will be able to select the content and style required for a variety of news stories or features; to recognise, obtain and select the relevant and newsworthy facts from either written or verbal sources; to write a clear, vigorous and balanced news story in a form that will attract and interest the reader . . . *(NCTJ 2002: 11)*

More detailed requirements include that:

- Stories reflect the brief given to the journalist;
- Content is comprehensive and balanced;
- The intro contains the main point of the story and is clearly developed, with the most important information coming early in the story, followed by a coherent, logical and readable structure;
- Personal comment is avoided;

picture of their lives by means of comments from family, friends and neighbours, duly illustrated by snaps from the family album.

Lule studied coverage of an American tourist who was killed when hijackers seized a cruise ship and he concluded that, 'by elevating the victim into a hero through the great grief of those left behind', journalists consciously or unconsciously 'give meaning to the meaningless and . . . explain that which cannot be explained' (Lule 2001: 58–9). So the story of the victim is told again and again in the news:

> Names and places change but the story remains essentially the same: an innocent victim – guilty only of coincidence, bad timing, the unfortunate fate of being in the wrong place at the wrong time – is somehow killed in a hijacking, airline crash, fire, robbery, flood, or explosion. Then, through the words of the widow or others left behind, the news elevates and transforms the victim into a hero, a person whose life story is gathered and told, whose passing is marked and mourned. *(Lule 2001: 54)*

He adds that telling news as myth usually helps to 'manufacture consent' towards the existing social order. In other words, news-as-myth usually supports the status quo. However, such ideological power is not predetermined because 'news is messy and complicated' and is 'a site of personal, social, and political struggle from its conception by a reporter to its understanding by a reader'. Therefore, mythic stories might potentially be used to offer alternative perspectives on society (Lule 2001: 192).

Inverted pyramid

The very concept of the 'inverted pyramid' and the order in which more or less 'important' information is placed raises the question of who decides what is more or less important. Daniel Hallin argues that *where* information appears in a story, and *how* it is inflected, can have an ideological effect by emphasising some views and marginalising others. To illustrate the point, he suggests that reporting of the Vietnam war saw a 'reverse inverted pyramid' in operation, whereby the nearer the information was to the truth, the further down the news story it would be placed (cited in Schudson 1991: 148–9).

- Facts are well marshalled and logically presented;
- Copy is free of innuendo and ambiguity, and words are chosen with precision;
- Copy is in house style;
- Quotes are accurate and in context.

(NCTJ 2002: 11–14)

In other words, don't write news like this:

A police officer working for the police force in the north part of the country was accused of doing something he shouldn't have been doing. The officer, said to have been in the force since he joined a while back, was described by other officers as one of the boys in blue. Last year sometime another bobby was involved in a similar investigation somewhere else, but apparently claimed it wasn't him. Workers have been told by someone pretty high up in the government that what they're hoping for isn't what they're going to get. Speculation was growing as to what the outcome might be. According to experts, who know quite a bit, it could go one way or the other, depending on what happens. A spokesman for the workers, speaking on behalf of his colleagues at work, said he wanted the government to listen to what he had to say: 'I want the government to listen to what I have to say.' *(BBC Radio 1, Mark Radcliffe Show, October 13 1999)*

> **'Who the hell's gonna read the second paragraph?'**
> – The Front Page.

What's wrong with copy like the above, from the aptly-named Vague Newsdesk, is just about everything. It fails to tell us anything, because it fails to answer the five Ws that, along with an H, are the starting point of most journalism: Who? What? Where? When? Why? And: How? Contrast with:

Lady Godiva [WHO] rode [WHAT] naked [HOW] through the streets of Coventry [WHERE] yesterday [WHEN] in a bid to cut taxes [WHY]. *(Hicks 1999: 15)*

News should be specific, not general; clear, not vague. Telling the five Ws is one way of achieving this. In most cases you shouldn't try to answer *all* those questions in the intro – it will be too wordy and clumsy – but news intros are likely to give us the answers to two or three of the five Ws. The others should normally follow fairly quickly afterwards.

Attribution

Bell argues that one of the primary questions of journalism is 'Who says?' (Bell 1991: 190). He suggests that, as so much news is based on *somebody saying something*, a pertinent question for journalists and readers is to ask what credentials the source has:

> Attribution serves an important function in the telling of news stories. It reminds the audience that this is an account which originated with certain persons and organisations. It is not an unchallengeable gospel, but one fruit of human perception and production among other conceivably alternative accounts. In theory a news story should be regarded as embedded under a stack of attributions, each consisting of source, time and place. *(Bell 1991: 190)*

Attribution of sources is important to the notion of journalistic 'balance', writes Keeble:

> Reporters use sources to distance themselves from the issues explored. Rather than express their views on a subject, reporters use sources to present a range of views over which they can appear to remain objective and neutral. The title or descriptive phrase accompanying the quoted person clarifies the bias. But this is the bias of the source, not the reporter. *(Keeble 2001a: 44)*

Text

Much ink has been spilled in recent years in analysing media texts from a perspective that says the text is not simply the collection words on the page – or pictures on the screen – but 'the meaningful outcome of the *encounter* between content and reader' (McQuail 2000: 349; my emphasis). In other words, the work of the journalist only becomes a *text* when it is read by somebody. And, given that we bring our own knowledge, experience, expectations and prejudices into play when we read a news report, the same piece of work may have multiple meanings (be *polysemic*). Of interest here is the work of Mikhail Bakhtin, who spoke of language as *dialogic*; that is, everything we say or write is in some

Traditionally, trainee journalists have been taught to think of the structure of a news story as a triangle, a pyramid or, more commonly, an **'inverted pyramid'**. However it is visualised, the idea is that the most important information should be at the top, followed by elaboration and detail, ending up with the least important information at the bottom (Hicks 1999: 16). If space is short, the material at the bottom can be removed by subs, and what's left should stand alone and still make sense. So a 500-word article could swiftly be transformed into a newspaper nib (news in brief), a five-par story for the web, a three-par story for Teletext, or even a 21-word item for a text-phone. Combined with the five Ws, the pyramid – or inverted pyramid – is a good way of starting to think about constructing relatively simple news stories. The most striking or important information goes at the top – usually several of the Who? What? Where? When? Why? How? – and the rest follows in diminishing order of importance.

> '*In news, order is everything but chronology is nothing.*'
> – Allan Bell.

The intro

The intro is crucial because it sets the tone for what follows. A poorly written intro might confuse, mislead or simply bore the reader – a well written intro will encourage the reader to stay with you on the strength of the information and angle you have started with. Lynette Sheridan Burns explains the importance of the intro in this way:

> News writing always starts with the most important fact. When you report on a football game, you do not start with the kick-off, you begin with the final score. So it is with news. If someone were to blow up the building across the street from where you work today, when you got home you would not start the story by saying, 'Today seemed like an ordinary sort of day, little did I know how it would turn out.' You would say, 'Someone blew up the building across the street!' In other forms of journalism it is fine for your story to have a beginning, a middle and an end. News stories, in contrast, blurt out something and then explain themselves . . . (*Sheridan Burns 2002: 112*)

sense both *responding* to things that have already been said and *anticipating* future responses:

> The living utterance, having taken meaning and shape at a particular historical moment in a socially specific environment, cannot fail to brush up against thousands of living dialogic threads . . . After all, the utterance arises out of this dialogue as a continuation of it and as a rejoinder to it . . . [Every] word is directed toward an answer and cannot escape the profound influence of the answering word that it anticipates . . .
> (Bakhtin 1935: 76)

Where does the journalist figure in all this? Cultural analysis of texts sometimes gives the impression that the work of the journalist is irrelevant to the production of meaning by the audience. But just because a text is *capable* of being interpreted in many ways does not mean it necessarily *will* be, and 'many media genres are understood by most of their receivers most of the time in predictable ways' (McQuail 2000: 485). According to Colin Sparks:

> To acknowledge that any text is polysemic is not the same thing as to say that it is capable of *any* interpretation whatsoever. Put more concretely, the sense which people can make of newspapers depends at least in part in *what the journalists have actually written in them in the first place*. (Sparks 1992: 37; my emphasis)

As McQuail notes: 'There is a power of the text that it is foolish to ignore' (McQuail 2000: 485).

Study news intros in any paper, any day, and you will see a variety of techniques at work. In the literature of journalism training, these are often given fancy names like the 'clothesline' or the 'delayed drop'. But, as with so much in journalism, there is no hard and fast rule saying that a particular kind of story should have a particular kind of intro. The familiar question 'what works?' is best answered through observation and trying it out yourself.

> 'Lots of facts, plainly stated and grouped with drama and maybe a dash of sentiment – no more. That's the journalistic cocktail.'
> – James Milne.

Let's take a common newspaper story – the tragedy. There is the straightforward unadorned factual style:

A yachtsman died and a fisherman was feared dead in gales yesterday. (SAILOR, 80, DIES IN GALE, *Daily Mirror, October 21 2002*)

Another example from the same day's paper:

Two strawberry pickers were crushed to death after falling into a machine, it was revealed yesterday. (TWO KILLED AT FARM, *Rosa Prince, Daily Mirror, October 21 2002*)

Neither intro gets bogged down in too much detail and each tells us in essence what happened and to whom – not with a name but a handy label.

Sometimes one element of a story will be particularly striking and the journalist's nose for news should make sure it appears in the intro, as in this example:

An anguished girl of 13 hanged herself while waiting for the result of a pregnancy test that proved negative. (BABY FEAR GIRL OF 13 IS FOUND HANGED, *Geoff Marsh, Daily Express, October 24 2002*)

Or this:

A father of four died of a brain tumour after a hospital sent him home, insisting he was drunk. ('DRUNK' PATIENT DIES OF A BRAIN TUMOUR, *Martyn Sharpe, Sun, July 20 2002*)

Even the *absence* of information might provide a lead, as in:

Mystery surrounded the death of a heavily pregnant teenager whose body was found today at the foot of a tower block in the Black Country. (FLATS DEATH RIDDLE, *Simon Hardy, Birmingham Evening Mail, September 17 2002*)

It might be something about the subject's *life* rather than the manner of their *death* that provides the angle, as in:

A ten-pin bowling champion who dedicated her life to helping youngsters, has died suddenly. (BOWLING CHAMP DIES, *Yorkshire Evening Post, October 24 2002*)

Or the focus might be on the bereaved:

A grief-stricken mother today told of her shock when her teenage son suddenly collapsed and died after complaining of a swollen throat. (MOTHER'S GRIEF OVER DEATH OF SCOTT, 19, *Kim McRae, Bradford Telegraph and Argus, November 27 2001*)

Some intros manage to combine the victim with grieving loved ones and the act of discovery, as in this example:

A property tycoon and his wife found the body of their 'sweet and gentle oddball' son lying in a pool of blood at his home. (PROPERTY TYCOON FINDS 'GENTLE' SON KILLED AT HOME, *Laura Peak, Times, October 25 2002*)

The above intros, and countless other variations, tend to focus on one or two elements. They give us what the journalist has decided is the best news line, and they do it quickly and clearly. Occasionally you will find an intro that breaks with such conventions of news writing. Here is one example that seems to work, maybe because the story was so big that most readers could be assumed to have heard the basic facts by the time they read the following day's front pages:

Although he could not see right inside, the customs officer knew something was terribly wrong the moment he opened the heavy swing doors. The container on the white Mercedes lorry was a refrigeration unit, yet the air that belched out was warm and smelled putrid. In the half light, he saw two Chinese men sprawled in front of him, gasping for breath. Behind him in the gloom, the officer saw what a colleague described as a scene 'out of a nightmare'. Fifty-eight bodies lay haphazardly on the metal floor in between seven crates of tomatoes. (GRIM FIND OF 58 BODIES IN LORRY EXPOSES SMUGGLERS' EVIL TRADE, *Nick Hopkins, Jeevan Vasagar, Paul Kelso, Andrew Osborn, Guardian, June 20 2000*)

Although the style is not conventionally newsy, even this intro begins its narrative not at the start of the lorry's journey but at the moment the bodies are about to be discovered – the most important fact of the story.

Sometimes a journalist will delay the obvious news angle for a more imaginative approach, as in this example about a community campaign for a zebra crossing:

> Woe betide anyone who crosses Jade Hudspith when she grows up. For the Bramley schoolgirl has already shown her mettle at the tender age of nine by collecting no less than 100 names on her petition for a zebra crossing outside Sandford Primary in busy Broad Lane. (JADE ON WARPATH FOR ZEBRA CROSSING, Sophie Hazan, *Yorkshire Evening Post*, October 30 2002)

Apart from the misuse of the word 'less' (it should be 'fewer'), it shows that an imaginative intro can lift even a relatively straightforward story.

The rest

If the pyramid is a good starting point for thinking about intros and basic news stories, it can come to seem inadequate for more complex and/or lengthy stories, particularly those based on many different sources. David Randall talks of constructing such stories through 'building blocks' which should be linked logically to each other (Randall 2000: 175). Richard Keeble prefers the concept of stories having a *series* of inverted pyramids:

> News stories, whether of five or thirty-five pars, are formed through the linking of thematic sections. The reader progresses through them in order of importance, except on those few occasions when the punch line is delayed for dramatic reasons. The journalist's news sense comes into operation not only for the intro but throughout the story. Who is the most important person to quote? Who is the next most important person? What details should be

> **'Words are facts. Check them (spelling and meaning) as you would any other.'**
> – Keith Waterhouse.

> **'It will be taken for granted that "this town was thrown into great excitement" over a sensational occurrence. Tell the facts in the story and let the town recover from hysterics as best it can.'**
> – Daily Tribune style guide, Sioux City.

highlighted and which left to the end or eliminated? How much background information is required and where is it best included? All these questions are answered according to a set of news values held by the reporter. (Keeble 2001a: 108)

Let's take two examples from the news items cited above.

The *Daily Mirror* story about the dead yachtsman is tightly-written, consisting of 71 words in five one-sentence paragraphs, giving an average sentence length of just over 14 words. After the intro we have a par giving us the location of the accident and the age of the man, then a third par telling us that his body was found by a Navy helicopter. This is followed by two pars giving us details of the separate search for a missing fisherman. Any cutting from the bottom upwards would still leave a readable story. Fairly simple stuff.

The *Times* story about the property tycoon's 'odd-ball' son is longer and more complex as it brings in a variety of sources – yet it is still written in a concise news style. It consists of 602 words in 34 sentences and 19 paragraphs, giving an average sentence length of just under 18 words – not *that* different from the tabloid story above. After the intro we are quickly given names, time, location and the information that somebody is being questioned by police. The basic story having been told, we are then given detail, colour, context, attribution and quotes. There are descriptions of the victim based on interviews with neighbours, background on the location, the results of the post mortem examination, and quotes from the police about the death and appealing for information. The continuing police presence at the house is then linked to the fact that the bereaved parents are being comforted by police family liaison officers, which leads in turn to quotes from a statement issued by the family. The story ends with some extra biographical details about the father.

This device of telling the basic story, and then telling it again in more detail, is common in news. In most cases chronology goes out the window when it comes to writing news. But it is important that, in a desire to include all the most important information, you do not end up writing a story that reads like a *list of points*. Ideas, sentences, paragraphs should be linked and follow on in some kind of logical sequence, or series of sequences. Facts, description, context, reported speech and direct quotes must all be *woven* into the text, to achieve a whole. Pick up any newspaper and study the structure of news stories and you will see how neat are the links, how smooth are the transitions, and how additional information is slipped in without disrupting the flow.

> 'Newspapers are not literature. But then nor is most literature.'
> – David Randall.

Note, too, the use of quotes and **attribution**. Direct quotes can add authority, drama, immediacy or emotion to an account as well as giving the reader a sense of the quoted person's voice and personality. Direct quotes will normally be outnumbered by reported speech and/or the attribution of facts and opinions to sources. Together, they tell the reader 'who says so'. Keeble says that clear attribution is particularly important when covering 'allegations and counter-allegations' (Keeble 2001a: 103). Yet some journalists fail to give adequate attribution in stories for fear of what Randall terms 'a certain loss of journalistic virility'. He argues: 'The reader should never have to ask, "How does the paper know this?"' (Randall 2000: 179) As a reporter with the Press Association, Jane Merrick has observed this differing attitude at first hand:

> There is always attribution in our intros, to prove to our customers that it's properly sourced. We have to say 'police said today . . . ' or 'an inquest heard today . . . ' Newspapers then get rid of the attribution in their intros.

But good journalism retains the attribution somewhere in the story.

Writing plea move drama

When writing a story for any news organisation you should always retain the idea that your **text** is to be read – and understood – by others. As Keith Waterhouse notes, we rarely hear people at bus-stops using words such as 'bid' or 'probe', or phrases such as 'love-tug mum' or 'blaze superstore'. And we do not hear them saying things like 'Did I tell you about young Fred being rapped after he slammed his boss? He thinks he's going to be axed.' Waterhouse comments:

> Words that have never managed to get into the mainstream of the language are suspect as a means of popular communication. They are, and remain, labels. They do not convey precise meanings. The reader looks at the label, opens the tin – and finds a tin of labels. *(Waterhouse 1993: 230)*

Journalists should beware what Michael Frayn satirised as Unit Headline Language (UHL): words so ambiguous they could be put together in almost any order:

> . . . 457 people were shown the headlines
> ROW HOPE MOVE FLOP
> LEAK DASH SHOCK
> HATE BAN BID PROBE
> Asked if they thought they understood the headlines, 86.4 per cent said yes, but of these 97.3 per cent were unable to offer any explanation of what it was they had understood. With UHL, in other words, a computer could turn out a paper whose language was both soothingly familiar and yet calmingly incomprehensible. *(Frayn 1995: 68)*

If you find yourself writing in Unit Headline Language – or in the style of Vague News – stop immediately. Put yourself in the place of the reader and see if *you* can understand what you've written. The chances are that nobody else will bother.

Summary

News is written in active and concise language with an emphasis on short sentences and short paragraphs. News is structured with the most newsworthy information first. News is told in the form of stories but these stories are not normally recounted in chronological order. Journalists may have storylines already in mind when approaching events and this may affect how those stories are constructed. It has been suggested that many news stories are the re-telling of ancient myths in contemporary settings. Readers may interpret news stories in different ways but their interpretations will be based, at least in part, on what the journalist has written.

Questions

Why are most news stories not told in chronological order?

Why are news articles called 'stories'?

Can a story 'write itself'?

To whom are different newspapers addressed?

To what extent is the news full of unfamiliar names but familiar characters?

Further reading

Randall (2000) has a wealth of good advice on writing news, as do Hicks (1999) and Keeble (2001a). Reah (1998) offers an introduction to the textual study of newspaper articles, while Bell (1991) subjects news stories and newspaper language to detailed linguistic analysis. Conboy (2002) draws on the work of Bakhtin to explore the 'carnivalesque' nature of the popular press. Lule's (2001) thought-provoking work on news as myth is also recommended as providing an alternative perspective to both practitioner and linguistic accounts of news construction.

Notes

Sources for soundbites: O'Neill cited in Randall 2000: 162; *Front Page*, Hecht and MacArthur 1974; Bell 1991: 172; Milne cited in Mansfield 1936: 221; Waterhouse 1993: 249; Daily Tribune cited in Mansfield 1936: 246; Randall 2000: 141.

Chapter Ten

Writing features

Key terms

Feature writing

Intro

Facts

Quotes

Description

Anecdotes

Opinions

Analysis

Payoff

Linking words

Columns

Backgrounders

Profiles

Subjective experience

Reflexivity

The clock reads 4.27am. Outside, a pale sun begins to emerge from behind my neighbours' red-tiled roofs. Inside, the coffee has long gone cold. But I don't care. Six months' hard labour have just come to an end with a glorious click on the 'save' button, and I am happy with what I've written. I pause the Lee Perry CD and switch off the computer. As the whine of the PC fan fades into silence, I head downstairs to the fridge. I've earned a beer. One chapter of this book completed . . . only 12 to go.

Unlike news stories, the intro to a feature can beat about the bush, go round the houses, and take a leisurely, scenic route to its destination. As long as the reader goes along for the ride too.

Look again at the first paragraph above, the intro to this chapter. Note the incidental detail, the range of sentence lengths (from 26 words down to just four), and the use of contrast between the effort expended on one chapter and the fact that there are another dozen to write. Note also the use of the present tense and the presence of the writer, both of which are common in feature writing but rare in news. There is little 'news' in that paragraph. Its purpose is not so much to impart information as to draw in the reader. It may not be the best piece of writing you've ever read, but the fact that you are still reading this suggests it may have served its purpose.

How features differ from news

On newspapers, the word **features** usually covers all editorial content apart from news, sports news, and reports of sporting fixtures. That includes reviews, horoscopes, TV listings, advice columns, gardening tips and so on, as well as news backgrounders, analytical articles, thinkpieces, profiles and celebrity interviews. In broadcasting, as Andrew Boyd notes, the term feature often means a human interest or 'soft news' story:

> The hard news formula calls for the meat of the story in the first line . . . The feature style, which leads the audience into the story rather than presenting them with the facts in the first line, is used more freely wherever greater emphasis is placed on entertainment and a lighter touch than on straightforward and sometimes impersonal, hard news. *(Boyd 2001: 73)*

Features

The distinction between news and features is widely accepted. However, a different perspective is offered by David Randall, who argues that too many journalists 'see the reporter as an earnest collector of "facts" and the feature *writer* as someone who wanders around thinking of fine phrases which save them the trouble of doing much research' (Randall 2000: 193; emphasis in original). He continues:

> The truth is that trying to make distinctions between news and features does not get us very far. In fact, it is positively dangerous. It produces narrow thinking which can restrict coverage of news to conventional subjects and puts writing it into the unimaginative straitjacket of a formula. With features, it encourages the insidious idea that normal standards of precision and thorough research don't apply and that they can be a kind of low-fact product . . . The opposite, of course, is the case. Most news pages could benefit from a greater sense of adventure and a more flexible approach to stories. Similarly, most features sections cry out for sharper research and less indulgent writing. There is no great divide between news and features. *Best to think of it all as reporting. (Randall 2000: 193–4; my emphasis)*

Yet the market appears to value celebrity columnists higher than the reporters who get their hands dirty finding things out, as Francis Wheen complains:

> [The] getting and giving of information now seem to be a minor function of the press, as newspapers become 'lifestyle packages' stuffed with It girls and solipsists who witter on profitably about their love lives or their shopping habits . . . [The] status of the reporter – as against the lifestyle gusher, or the sad sap who rewrites PR handouts about minor pop stars for a showbiz column – has been dangerously downgraded. *(Wheen 2002: xii-xiii)*

Subject

Why is it that features can be about virtually any subject, when news is more restricted? Features need not necessarily conform to the notions of 'newsworthiness' discussed in Chapter 3, but how much *agency* do

Features should not be thought of as synonymous with entertainment, though. Features also deal with serious topical issues at greater length, and in greater depth, than is possible in simple news reports (Boyd 2001: 127).

Irish journalist Nell McCafferty touched on some of the differences between what we think of as news and what we think of as features when she introduced a collection of her columns in the following terms:

> It is the modest ambition of every journalist to write a front page story – the big one at the top left hand side, with large headlines, that tells the world the main event of the day. The front page story tells what happened, where, when, and gives the explanation usually of the person in charge. If you want to know how the rest of us feel about it, you turn to the inside pages. I discovered, early on, that I'd never be able to write a front page story. I'd be inclined to argue with the person in charge, and feel obliged to give the other version in brackets. I discovered this particularly on Bloody Sunday in Derry, when I was lying on the street while people around me got shot dead. I saw everything while the other reporter was at the back. He, rightly, wrote the front page story, because somebody had to establish the name of the officer in charge, interview him, and provide all the deadly details. Had it been up to me to phone the officer, the row would still be going on and the story would never have been written. My version appeared on the inside pages. I wrote about how the rest of us felt, lying on the ground.
>
> (McCafferty 1984: 14)

Writing a front page splash remains the ambition of many aspiring journalists, but having a personal column – complete with picture byline – seems to be an increasingly common goal. Columnists have certainly proliferated as newspapers have got fatter and as print has conceded some of its traditional 'breaking news' role to electronic media. Some columnists are engaged for their knowledge and insight and others because they can turn out an entertaining sentence or two. It is usually their task to be controversial, to get the newspaper talked about. But there are limits, if the case of John MacLeod is

journalists have in choosing subjects and style? Certain subjects will be either 'in' or 'out' at certain publications, and journalists quickly absorb expectations of what is required of them, sharing a set of 'formulas, practices, normative values and journalistic mythology passed down to successive generations' (Harrison 2000: 108).

Some subjects are selected for feature treatment 'solely to attract certain advertisers' (Randall 2000: 21). This is particularly the case in the growing number of magazine-influenced newspaper supplements – covering subjects as diverse as fashion, media, education, computers, gardening, cars, travel, and food – where editorial features act as bait to attract readers to the advertisements that provide the sections with their economic *raison-d'être*. For Bob Franklin, broadsheet newspapers are aping the tabloids in more than just the production of advertiser-friendly feature copy; broadsheet features pages display an increasing reliance on opinion over fact, often about subjects he dismisses as 'cripplingly banal' (Franklin 1997: 7–10). Writing in a US context, Hanno Hardt argues that such a business-friendly system of 'patronage' is anti-democratic:

> Emerging from the practices of contemporary advertising and public relations efforts is a journalism of a new type which promotes the construction of corporate realities at the expense of a common-sense desire for a fair and truthful representation of everyday life . . . It is one of the dangers of the anticipated or realised business mentality of the media that content – which represents an expression of freedom – will be defined by those who seek to serve the public as *consumers* rather than by society as *participant* and source of democratic power. (Hardt 2000: 218–9; my emphasis)

> '*Read over your compositions, and where ever you meet with a passage which you think is particularly fine, strike it out.*'
> – Dr Samuel Johnson.

The presence of the journalist

The personal pronoun 'I' is absent from 'normal printed texts', according to Roger Fowler (1991: 64). But it appears in many features. Jon Dovey notes that 'confessional modes of expression' have proliferated in journalism and beyond from the 1990s onwards (Dovey 2000: 1). Letting the journalist appear as an *actor* in the drama

anything to go by. He was sacked by the *Herald* in Glasgow because his piece on the death of two school-girls in Soham was deemed a bit *too* controversial (Morgan 2002a).

Whether they represent strong opinion, expert analysis, an individual profile or a piece of descriptive writing, good features require both content *and* style. They have a beginning, a middle and an end – usually in that order. Not to be confused with Philip Larkin's phrase about a beginning, a *muddle* and an end (cited in Adams 1999: 50). Features should also have a theme, an idea, something to say; though readers of some of our newspapers and magazines might be forgiven for thinking that content has gone out of fashion. Style is everything for some, as parodied in the radio programme *Sunday Format*:

> **'Nothing wrong with opinions . . . But they need some sort of anchorage in fact.'**
> – Francis Wheen.

CONTENTS PAGE. In this week's Sunday Format. RELATIVE VALUES: a famous celebrity and a relative discuss how much they think the other is worth, page 5. BOOKS BY MY NAMESAKE: former All Saint Shaznay Lewis discusses *The Lion, the Witch and the Wardobe*, page 3. ME AND MY DUVET: Salman Rushdie, page 49 . . . MY NAME SOUNDS LIKE YOUR NAME: pop singer Geri Halliwell talks to former drugs tsar Keith Helliwell about fame, the Spice Girls, and comparative arrest rates between different police authorities, pages 42 to 59 . . . Do teeth matter in a modern romance? . . . How we haven't yet met yet . . . Celebrity legover . . . Ten fruits that are now . . . Ten occupations that are in . . . Ten Downing Street . . . Ten things that are bigger than a cat . . . Ten new buzzwords . . . Ten occupations that are out . . . Ten ways to improve yourself . . . Ten things that could kill you . . . (*BBC Radio Four, Sunday Format, September 18 and 25 2001*)

Harsh but fair. Many features are indeed rather formulaic affairs, as agency editor Brian Whittle points out:

> If you look at women's mags, the stories have got to be TOT – triumph over tragedy. There's got to be a happy ending, otherwise they won't run them. It's unbelievable, they're so formulaic, they're homogenised. They are the Mills and Boons of today.

may be driven by a desire to tell stories in more interesting ways, but for Dovey it also reflects a changing cultural climate:

> [We] are witnessing the evolution of a new 'regime of truth' based upon the foregrounding of individual subjective experience at the expense of more general truth claims . . . Subjectivity, the personal, the intimate, becomes the only remaining response to a chaotic, senseless, out of control world in which the kind of objectivity demanded by grand narratives is no longer possible. *(Dovey 2000: 25–6)*

This account raises (at least) two questions. First, how new *is* this foregrounding of the journalist? Not very, according to Lynn Barber:

> [This] supposedly new postmodern development of the picaresque interview actually has very long antecedents. Rudyard Kipling's 1889 interview with Mark Twain starts with a good ten paragraphs about the difficulty of finding Mark Twain's house, complete with the statutory cab-driver who doesn't know the way. *(Barber 1999: 199)*

Second, if newspaper features and much documentary TV *have* shifted towards reflexivity in recent years, will this eventually challenge the 'regime of truth' represented by the traditional, impersonal method of telling the *news*? Such issues are touched on in Chapter 5.

Anecdote

Behr's argument that an anecdote can illustrate a 'general truth' raises the question of what exactly *is* a general truth? In any event, couldn't an anecdote just as easily illustrate a generally-held falsehood?

But that is only part of the story. Across the spectrum of the press, there are also features that illuminate, features that have the power to make us laugh out loud or cry into our cornflakes, features that impart information or question our assumptions, that make us look at things in different ways, that shine a torch into some darkened corner. And features that are simply good writing.

The best way to learn about features is to *read* lots of features, to *write* lots of features, and to get other people to *read* your features. Like all journalism, features should be produced for the *reader*, not the *writer*.

> *'In these times of media saturation and its subsequent neurosis – information anxiety – columnists in their idiosyncratic ways wade through the mire of information about the world we live in.'*
> – Suzanne Moore.

Where do features come from?

Virtually anything can be the **subject** of a feature, and sources for feature ideas are similar to the news sources discussed in Chapter 4. With features, however, there is a tendency for more ideas to come from personal experience. For example, Leah Wild wrote a double-page feature about her battle with bureaucracy to get a toilet seat suitable for her disabled daughter, to which a sub added the rather unimaginative headline: THE STORY OF MY DISABLED DAUGHTER'S TOILET SEAT (*Guardian*, March 7 2002). If a lot of your twenty-something mates are still hanging around the parental home, you might think of writing a feature on the choices and problems confronting this generation. You might abandon the car and start cycling to work, prompting a feature on how lorry drivers seem to be out to kill you. You might be on a postgraduate journalism training course, so you could think of submitting an account of your experiences to the media pages of one of the national papers or to the trade rag *Press Gazette*. (That one's already been done, by the way, but you get the idea.)

Just as news feeds on itself, features are often prompted by other features and by news. For example, a tabloid front page splash (WORLD'S TALLEST BLOKE LIVES IN NEASDEN, *Sun*, February 18 2002) becomes food for a more 'thoughtful' broadsheet feature (TOUGH AT THE TOP, *Guardian*, February 21 2002).

Although the latter is ostensibly a serious discussion of health issues prompted by the claim that 'the tallest die young', it is illustrated with one of the pictures used by the *Sun*, showing 7ft 7in Hussain Bisad towering over a pillar box. Six weeks later Hussain's story became a 30-minute radio feature, *It's My Story* (BBC Radio Four, April 8 2002).

A common cycle is that a news story is followed up with more news stories, then background features, and by the third or fourth day it becomes a peg for columnists to hang their personal opinions on. Those opinions may provoke further articles, all rounded off by a 'why oh why?' piece in one of the Sunday papers. Sometimes it reaches farcical proportions, as when film star Kate Winslet mentioned in an interview with *Radio Times* that she wanted to lose some weight after giving birth. This prompted a feeding frenzy by tabloids and broadsheets alike, who ran feature after feature on obesity, dieting, Hollywood waifs, eating disorders, and working out, topped off with a columnist's complaint that Kate Winslet should stop going on about her weight. As *Private Eye* commented at the time, it was 'a perfect example of the reverse-alchemy whereby one nugget of news can be transformed into several tons of base metal' (*Private Eye* 2001).

Let's suppose you've got a better idea than the above. And that you've done your research along the lines suggested in Chapters 4, 5 and 6. Before you lay a finger on your keyboard, Sally Adams suggests that you consider the results of your research and ask yourself:

What's

- The most startling fact you've discovered?
- The best anecdote unearthed?
- The most astonishing quote?
- The most surprising event?
- The item with the greatest 'Hey, did you know that . . . ?' factor?

(Adams 1999: 74)

When you've done that, you should have a fair idea of the angle you want to take, so it's time to start writing.

Beginning

The feature intro, sometimes known as the lead, is hard to pin down because there are so many different styles. The main purpose of the intro is to make the reader want to read on, so the key question is: what works?

Sometimes it might be a *general statement*, as in this exploration of the case of a Texan woman who killed her five children:

Mental illness has never been much of a mitigating factor in the great retributive machine that is the US criminal justice system. *(Andrew Gumbel, Independent, March 14 2002)*

Gumbel goes on to detail two other cases before getting around to asking 'why would anyone imagine that the heartbreaking case of Andrea Pia Yates would be any different?' It seems like he is taking a long time to give us the 'meat' of the story, but we do not read these opening sentences in isolation. They are put in context by the 'page furniture' so important to features; in this case the stark headline IN GOD'S NAME superimposed on a picture of the mother, accompanied by the explanatory standfirst:

Andrea Yates was a respectable wife and mother, raising a God-fearing family. Then, one fine morning last summer, she drowned her five children. Why? Only now can the full, dreadful story be told. *(Andrew Gumbel, Independent, March 14 2002)*

Presentation is important to the ways in which journalism is consumed, and features depend more than hard news on being 'sold' to the reader 'by means of a complex of headlines, pictures, blurb, standfirst . . . caption and significant quotation' drawing out 'the mood and underlying substance' of the feature (Hodgson 1993: 247–8).

Some features begin by getting to the point directly with a *bold statement*, as in this discussion of smacking:

The parents I really despise can be spotted all over the place. You will have seen them – they are the ones in supermarkets or shopping centres who suddenly address their child in the sort of vicious tones you wouldn't even use on a disobedient dog. *(Jayne Dawson, Yorkshire Evening Post, April 3 2002)*

It demands attention because of the strength of feeling, notably 'despise' rather than any of the softer alternatives. The wording involves us – 'you' – as assumed witnesses to such behaviour, able to tut-tut along with the writer.

News writing tends to concentrate on giving answers rather than asking questions, but features are more open to the unresolved question. Occasionally you might even begin a feature with a *question*:

What on earth is going on at the National Theatre? We certainly know what is not going on. Previously announced productions of Alice and Wonderland and The Playboy of the Western World have been postponed indefinitely . . . *(Michael Billington, Guardian, October 10 2000)*

Note the double meaning of the phrase 'going on'. Billington's intro gives us a pretty clear steer that the feature is going to discuss recent events at the National Theatre, and if we want to find out what's been going on then we will read on.

At other times, though, writers take a more oblique route, hoping to draw in the reader with a piece of *descriptive* writing:

Nik Entwistle unwraps the first of his newly delivered white leather sofas. He strokes a cushion tentatively, slides his hand into the crevice between arm and back as if searching for a missing coin and finally allows himself a shy smile. 'S'great,' he says. 'S'really diff'rent. Modern. Minimal. Goes with the flat.' Less than two years ago, Nik was still a student at Leeds Metropolitan University, living in digs on the edge of town. Now, aged 23, he is something whizzy in information technology and the proud owner of a light-filled, one-bedroom apartment, newly converted from a former textile factory in Leeds city centre. *(Susannah Herbert, Daily Telegraph, February 19 2000)*

Or the more stark:

Drissa takes off his T-shirt. His numerous wounds are deep and open – down to the bone. If it weren't for the maggots that have nested in his skin, he would surely have succumbed to gangrene. Drissa was a slave on an Ivory Coast cocoa plantation. Forced to work for 18 hours a day on little or no food, and locked in a small room with his fellow captives at night, he was regularly, systematically, brutally beaten. It is scarcely credible that such cruelty and disregard for human life should be employed in the production of a chocolate bar. *(Fiona Morrow, Independent, September 27 2000)*

The intro about Nik Entwistle contains many details, descriptions, quotes and the wonderfully vague phrase 'something whizzy in information technology', none of which would make it anywhere near a news story. In contrast, it is possible to imagine the material in the Drissa intro being rewritten as a news story along the lines of: 'Slaves on a cocoa plantation are systematically beaten and denied food, according to . . .' But the feature intro is effective because of its focus on the individual, because of the rhythm of the writing ('. . . regularly, systematically, brutally beaten . . .'), and because of the delayed contrast between the horrors described and the realisation that the purpose of this brutality is the production of a mere chocolate bar.

A frequently used device is to include **the presence of the journalist** in the story, as in this example:

> It was a simple assignment: go and interview the editor of *Who's Who*. I duly bunged in a request to Messrs A & C Black, the publishers. 'I'm afraid not,' the firm's spokeswoman, Charlotte Burrows, informed me sternly. 'All the editors have to remain anonymous, to protect them.' Protect them from what? 'From people wanting to be in *Who's Who*.' *(Francis Wheen, Sunday Telegraph, March 17 1996)*

This interface between journalist and subject is a popular one with feature writers, not just to attract the reader but also to set the tone for what follows. From the above paragraph, for example, we are left in little doubt that Wheen feels the publishers need to be brought down a peg or two. A rather different mood to the following intro, from a sympathetic profile of New York Mayor Rudolph Guiliani:

> Rudy is late. He has gone to see his tailor about a suit to wear for tea with the Queen. But I don't care how long I have to wait. Rudy the Rude is now Rudy the Rock. *(Alice Thomsen, Daily Telegraph, February 12 2002)*

> 'Most features sections cry out for sharper research and less indulgent writing.'
> – David Randall.

One brief paragraph at the head of a lengthy interview, but we are already introduced to the idea of the former Mayor's informality ('Rudy'), the fact that he went from zero to hero ('the Rock') in the wake of September 11, and the cultural relevance of his visit to the UK ('for tea with the Queen'). These themes are then developed throughout the feature.

Sometimes a bit of *dramatic licence* is employed, as in this example from a profile of a crime writer:

> Harry Patterson, aka thriller writer Jack Higgins, is a man of cast iron habits. I find him sitting at his usual table in his favourite Italian restaurant, his perennial glass of champagne in hand. On the table in front of him lie the tinted glasses of unvarying design that make him look like a hit man. *(Cassandra Jardine, Daily Telegraph, February 25 2000)*

Or this intriguing opening with the echo of a thousand westerns:

> A silence descended on the little grassy racing track behind the car park of the Jolly Friar pub in the former pit village of Blidworth, on the border between Nottingham and South Yorkshire, when Mark Pettitt appeared. It was an uncomfortable silence, the kind you get in cowboy films when the gunman walks into the small town. For Mark Pettitt is currently the most unpopular man in whippet racing. *(Paul Vallely, Independent, August 11 2000)*

Unlike the who, what, where, when and why of the hard news story, the feature intro sometimes leaves the reader with little clue as to the subject about to be addressed. Consider this *anecdotal* and colloquial example:

> Standing in a night club in Banja Luka in the Republic of Serbska, I'm starting to feel a wee bit nervous. We've bunked out of Nato's vast metal factory base with five pissed squaddies for a Friday night on the town, and the locals have got wise to the fact that we're Brits, mainly because the squaddies are wearing Sheffield United shirts. Three terrifying Serb boneheads are gathering nearby, getting just that bit too close for comfort. No one is talking to us. We stand out like sore thumbs. *(Stephen Armstrong, Guardian, September 25 2000)*

It turns out to be a feature about a music radio station in former Yugoslavia, run by the British Army to win the 'hearts and minds' of the young.

Freed from the constraints of hard news, feature writers sometimes make use of a more poetic style. Take this extended *metaphor* that, combined with description, anecdote and the presence of the journalist, introduces an analysis of problems at Coca-Cola:

There is a slight problem with the front door at Coca-Cola's European headquarters. It is gleaming and wide, like a movable wall of glass, with the outline of a row of giant Coke bottles gleaming across, but it will not open properly. The lock seems to be broken; visitors must knock to gain the attention of reception. The glass, though, is very thick, and the headquarters is in the middle of a noisy shopping centre, in the middle of perhaps the busiest roundabout in west London. The receptionists take quite a while to look up, clack across the lobby, and unfasten the door. There is time to take in the lobby's blaze of logos and bright red walls, as if the building were a vast Coca-Cola vending machine, with a malfunction. *(Andy Beckett, Guardian, October 2 2000)*

> *'I thought, "Well, I've got a showbiz column, I can slag you off in it."'*
> – Eva Simpson, Daily Mirror '3am girl'

The key phrase comes in the last three words, and the feature goes on to explore whether Coca-Cola is indeed malfunctioning as a global corporation.

A slightly less elaborate example of *imagery* at work comes from a local newspaper feature about inner-city areas in a so-called 'boom' city:

> On a clear day people in parts of Beeston and Holbeck can see the cranes towering over Leeds city centre at yet another multi-million pound development.
>
> For many in the communities north of the Aire, the cranes helping to build the latest upmarket apartments or plush offices are symbols of hope and opportunity.
>
> But for some in poverty-stricken Beeston and Holbeck, they are a depressing reminder of a successful local economy that is largely passing them by. *(David Marsh, Yorkshire Evening Post, March 20 2002)*

Occasionally a short, sharp *quote* might be used to introduce a feature:

> 'Wotcher Ricky!' cry the stallholders as I pursue Ricky Gervais through Slough's busy market. *(Steve Jelbert, Independent, September 30 2002)*

Feature intros, as we have seen, often focus on something quite *specific*, something human, some tiny detail – painting the little rather than the big picture. Of course, it can all go horribly wrong, as in this profile of satirist Chris Morris:

A few days ago, as Phil Collins, the man who once memorably made boatloads of money with an actionably mawkish song about the homeless called 'Another Day In Paradise', then threatened to leave the country if we didn't vote Tory, was beginning to seethe at Chris Morris's latest trick, his nemesis was walking out of Oxford Circus tube station into a blattering rain. *(Euan Ferguson, Observer, July 22 2001)*

There are some nice turns of phrase in that swollen 63-word sentence – 'actionably mawkish' and 'blattering rain' – but the focus is confused and there are too many sub-sub-sub-clauses. Back in the day, when journalists dictated their words of wisdom down the phone, they would often be asked by a deeply unimpressed copytaker: 'Is there much more of this?' A useful reminder that we do not write for ourselves.

Middle

If the beginning is the single most important element in feature *writing* – because it doesn't matter how good the rest is if readers never venture beyond a dull intro – then the middle is the *point* of it all. Even the best intro in the world can't salvage a feature with nothing to say, with no substance.

The content and structure of a feature will vary depending on the subject matter, the style of the publication, the perceived interests of the readers, the intentions of the writer, and on the time and energy available for research. Unlike hard news stories, features rarely 'write themselves'; they must be worked at so they do not come across as a series of unrelated points or as a meandering but aimless stroll around a topic. So there must be some logic to the order in which subjects are introduced, shifts of emphasis are made, and the tone of writing is altered. It is an internal logic rather than a formula and will differ from feature to feature, from journalist to journalist.

A feature will utilise some or all of the following, often overlapping with each other:

- Facts.
- Quotes.

- Description.
- Anecdotes.
- Opinions.
- Analysis.

Facts

All features need facts. Apart from straightforward opinion pieces and the most personalised 'lifestyle' columns, that means research. The process of gathering facts for features is essentially the same as for news – interviewing people, searching databases, reading reports, witnessing events, and so on – with the main difference being that features tend to be written over a longer period of time and tend to contain more words. So there is often the time to consult a wider range of sources and the space to include more of the information gathered during your research. Andy Beckett's feature on Coca-Cola, for example, is full of facts gleaned from a variety of sources including cuttings, websites, and books, as well as a range of interviews with actors and 'experts' alike; dates, prices, percentages and ingredients are all introduced to support the analysis, description and anecdote that structure the feature. When you have a lot of facts to include, you may wish to make your feature more digestible by including the facts at appropriate points in the text rather than in off-putting chunks; alternatively, you can separate some facts into a 'factbox'.

Quotes

As with news stories, direct quotes can add authority, drama and powerful expression to an account. In the Texas mother feature discussed above, the first quote is a long time coming, after the writer has already given us a lot of the story in his own words. When it arrives it is worth the wait, being a controversial opinion simply expressed by a credible source:

> 'It seems we are still back in the days of the Salem witch trials,' one of Yates's lawyers, George Parnham, commented after the verdict was returned on Tuesday afternoon. *(Andrew Gumbel, Independent, March 14 2002)*

More direct speech will normally be included in profiles of individuals, because the subject's voice, their use of language, can be as important to the story as what they are saying. Hence we are treated to Rudolph Guiliani as a self-effacing and vulnerable hero, in his own words:

> 'It's weird getting used to being loved . . . My scowl has turned into a smile. I'm becoming soft . . . Sometimes, I would have to slip into the bathroom and cry.' *(Alice Thomsen, Daily Telegraph, February 12 2002)*

Description

There's an old journalistic maxim: 'Show, don't tell.' In other words, use description to express what you see, and let readers make up their own minds what to think about it. We have already seen many examples of description in the intros quoted above. David Randall offers the following guidance:

> Description brings the story alive, takes readers to where you have been and evokes atmosphere . . . So long as you remember that description goes into a story to aid readers' understanding and not provide you with an opportunity to display your latest vocabulary, it will be an aid to clarity and not an obstacle to it . . . Avoid vague, judgmental adjectives and descriptions. To say that an office is 'imposing' tells you something, but not very much. Far better to say that it is so big that you could park two cars in there, that it has plush red carpet, a new black desk with brass fittings and that the windows command a view of the capital. That gives a far better idea. Apply this thinking to people, too . . . Descriptive writing is about finding ways of *bringing something to life*, not the random sprinkling of adjectives through a piece. *(Randall 2000: 182–3; my emphasis)*

Anecdotes

Anecdotes play a far greater role in features than in news stories, where they are often squeezed out by tight word limits and an emphasis on the facts. As well as sometimes being funny or moving, anecdotes can help to explain how the actors in a story felt or reacted, tell us something about the human condition, and create a big picture by painting small pictures in sufficient detail. Foreign correspondent Edward Behr says that even the most 'trivial, nonsensical **anecdote** can be made to illustrate a general truth' and may reveal more than the 'careful marshalling of facts' (Behr 1992: x). While interviewing school careers advisers for a background feature on a strike, I took a note of the sort of incident that wouldn't have made it into a hard news story but which helped to bring a worthy but potentially dull feature to life:

> Staff first realised something was brewing in the summer, when their leased yucca plants were unceremoniously removed and office supplies of pens and paper suddenly dried up. 'One of our managers was telling us there was no financial crisis just as a yucca was wheeled out behind her,' recalls Lisa Cooper. *(Tony Harcup, Guardian, October 10 1995)*

In a stroke of genius, a sub came up with the headline FIRST THEY CAME FOR THE YUCCAS, a reference to Pastor Niemoller's famous lament: 'First they came for the Jews . . . '.

Opinions

Some features make the opinions of the writer clear, others do not – it depends on the style, the subject, the publication, and on whether the writer *has* an opinion. But there is usually more opinion in features than in news, from a greater variety of sources. Rather than the traditional 'both sides of a story' adopted in much news, features often allow room for more subtle or 'nuanced' differences of opinion to emerge. And it is not unknown for the stated opinion of the writer to have changed by the time the feature ends.

Analysis

Again, not all features are analytical, but they have more scope for analysis than do tightly-written news stories with a more immediate focus. Beckett's Coca-Cola feature includes a range of analyses of the company's performance, based on its historical position, on its product diversification, and on its brand image. Apart from the writer's own analysis of what is going on, he invites Coke's UK chief and a range of independent experts to put forward their own explanations. In the Texas mother feature, the case is analysed by reference to how a similar case would have been handled in the UK, with a British lawyer explaining that Yates would probably have been cleared on the grounds of temporary insanity, if she had been tried at all. More likely, she would have been sent to a psychiatric hospital until she was declared fit enough to be discharged. The purpose of such analysis

in features is to take journalism beyond reportage and description with a view to helping us not just know *what* is going on, but to *understand* it a little more.

The end

As with the intro, the feature ending – known as the 'payoff' because it rewards the reader for sticking with you – can come in all shapes and sizes. Whereas news stories often end on the least important information, allowing them to be cut from the bottom upwards, features tend to have a more rounded ending. This might mean a summary of what has gone before, a return to the scene of the intro, or a new twist to leave the reader pondering.

Gumbel's story of the mother who drowned her children ends by referring to the unrepentant state prosecutor, leading to the payoff:

> Her conviction is clearly another feather in his cap. Whether it advances the cause of civilisation, however, is another matter. *(Andrew Gumbel, Independent, March 14 2002)*

The writer tells us an individual tale in sometimes gory detail, but the subject of the feature is not actually Andrea Yates at all. Rather, it is the US justice system.

The Rudolph Guiliani profile discussed above ends with the former Mayor's own words:

> 'You know what I'm looking forward to most in London, apart from meeting the Queen? Prime Minister's questions. I'd do anything to be on it. I don't even understand half the issues, but it's so dramatic. You have to focus, focus, focus.' He laughs. 'Maybe I should go into politics in England.' *(Alice Thomsen, Daily Telegraph, February 12 2002)*

A return, then, to the topic of his visit to England that was signalled in the intro – with the twist that a hero-worshipped US politician actually admires the much-derided British institution of PMQs. The suggestion in the final sentence is not to be taken seriously ('he laughs'), but it helps make the subject of the feature comfortably familiar for UK readers.

A bigger twist, as well as a return to the opening scene, is offered in the payoff to Armstrong's feature about the British Army running a radio station as part of Nato's SFOR force in Bosnia:

Back in the club, you could believe there is some hope. The squaddies have split and they're all in the middle of the dance floor, hands in the air as the DJ builds a storming set. There are Croats and Serbs and Bosnians here and people may be slagging off SFOR but they're buying the squaddies rounds of Amstel. The guy on the podium with the lurid green glo-sticks steps down and chats to me about music, always music, and doesn't want to know when I get on to politics, so that just for one, naïve, 1988 Summer Of Love moment you actually do think that music could make a difference. Or maybe that's just the beer talking. *(Stephen Armstrong, Guardian, September 25 2000)*

So we are back in the opening scene but everyone is more relaxed, and we have heard an upbeat story about music promoting peace, love and understanding. Then the final sentence arrives to raise a question mark about the meaning of everything we have just read. Similarly, Beckett's lengthy piece on Coke's problems in Europe is put into perspective by the payoff quote from an analyst:

'If Coca-Cola get people in China and India to drink one more a year, they needn't give a toss about people like us.' *(Andy Beckett, Guardian, October 2 2000)*

We may well be better informed than at the start of the feature, but let's not kid ourselves that we know everything.

Putting it all together

Whereas news stories for print are normally written in the past tense, features tend to be written in the present tense. The only hard-and-fast rule on the tense of a feature is to be consistent throughout. However, variety is important when it comes to the length of sentences, as too many long sentences can become a stodgy read, and too many short ones can have a jerky effect.

In a good feature the transition between different sections and different ideas should be smooth. Like a duck in the water, you will have to work hard to produce a smooth effect on the surface. The reader should not have to break sweat to find out what you are getting at. Linking words and phrases are essential in good writing. Do not simply give the reader a succession of points apparently unrelated to each other, and do not leave quotes flapping in the breeze. Strive to link one idea with the next, one paragraph with the previous one.

Linking words and phrases can be as simple as 'and' and 'but'. Again, variety is important. This chapter, for example, includes the following links, among others:

Outside . . . Inside . . . But . . . As long as . . . above . . . Note . . . Note also . . . That includes . . . though . . . their task . . . He was . . . They have . . . indeed . . . But that . . . also . . . And . . . however . . . Although . . . Those opinions . . . This prompted . . . it was . . . Or the more stark . . . Or this . . . It turns out . . . as we have seen . . . Again . . . As with . . . A return, then . . . A bigger twist . . . So . . . Now . . . I'm back . . . Or

It is a useful exercise to take a feature from a newspaper or a magazine and go through it highlighting the linking words or phrases.

Now it's 4.51am. I'm back at my desk, beer in hand. Think I'll just turn the PC on and check that chapter one more time. See if I can think of a more striking intro. Or maybe a better payoff.

Summary

A feature may give background information and analysis on a topical issue; may profile a person, place or organisation; may convey controversial opinion; and may be entertaining in style and/or content. Virtually anything can be the subject for a feature, although subject matter will be selected according to the perceived interests of readers and advertisers. Features tend to be longer than news stories and tend to use more sources. There are many styles of feature writing and features do not conform to the 'inverted pyramid' formula of most news reporting. Journalists working on features have greater freedom to experiment with style, and the journalist is often included in the story. The 'confessional' mode of feature writing has been increasingly prevalent in recent years, and it is argued that this reflects wider social changes which challenge 'general truth claims' in society.

Questions

What are features *for*?

How do features differ from news?

Are some subjects more suited to features than news?

Why do national newspapers pay star columnists more than reporters?

Why is 'I' more common in features than in news?

Further reading

Adams (1999) and Keeble (2001a) deconstruct various feature articles in the process of offering much useful advice on feature writing. Although critical of the strict division between news and features, Randall's (2000) emphasis on reporting is welcome and his pointers towards good writing are invaluable. For an introduction to the process of writing reviews, see Gilbert (1999). Dovey (2000) is a useful starting point for discussion of reflexivity within journalism and beyond.

Notes

Sources for soundbites: Johnson cited in Hicks 1999: 124; Wheen 2002: xiii; Moore cited in Keeble 2001a: 217; Simpson cited in Stevens 2002; Randall 2000: 194.

Chapter Eleven

Style for journalists

Key terms

Newspaper style

Style guide

Plain style

Consistency

Language

Voice

Imagined audience

Ideology

All news organisations have a concept of house style; that is, the **language** in which stories should be written. Why? According to Wynford Hicks and Tim Holmes:

> The argument for consistency is very simple. Variation that has no purpose is distracting. By keeping a consistent style in matters of detail a publication encourages readers to concentrate on *what* its writers are saying. *(Hicks and Holmes 2002: 19; emphasis in original)*

To this end, many newsrooms have their own style books, some have electronic style guides, while others rely on new recruits picking up unwritten rules from more experienced colleagues. A style guide contains rules, reminders and points of clarification – but there is no consensus on many of these points and style evolves over time:

> There are unmistakable trends in house style: in grammar, loose, colloquial usage is more accepted than it was; there is less punctuation, ie there are fewer capital letters, full stops for abbreviations, apostrophes, accents etc; in spelling, shorter forms are increasingly common and the . . . -ize ending has lost ground to -ise . . . *(Hicks and Holmes 2002: 21)*

Arguments over style can get pretty heated. The use of a dash instead of 'proper punctuation' prompted an *Independent* journalist to write to his union journal and rail against such slapdash standards drifting from the tabloids to some broadsheets. Readers were informed in no uncertain terms that the author of an offending piece on style was unfit even to be sent for the teas (Johnston 2002). When it comes to style, it seems, the number of opinions is matched only by the vehemence with which each one is expressed.

The sample style guide below is an edited version of one developed for use by my postgraduate journalism trainees and undergraduate journalism students, drawing on common – but by no means universal – practice within the UK press (Harcup 2001).

Style

Like all such style guides, the one presented in this chapter contains a mixture of common practice, pointers towards correct use of English, points of clarification, and attempts at attaining consistency. The aim is to 'eliminate undesired idiosyncrasies' in copy (Bell 1991: 83). However, it no doubt contains its fair share of 'personal idiosyncrasy and whimsy' (Cameron 1996: 323).

The underlying ethos of most such guides, as of Chapter 9 on writing news, is the plain, terse style of writing advocated by George Orwell:

> A scrupulous writer, in every sentence that he writes, will ask himself at least four questions, thus: What am I trying to say? What words will express it? What image or idiom will make it clearer? Is this image fresh enough to have an effect? And he will probably ask himself two more: Could I put it more shortly? Have I said anything that is unavoidably ugly? *(Orwell 1946b: 151–2)*

> **'Never use a long word where a short one will do.'**
> – George Orwell.

Orwell went on to list six rules to be relied upon 'when instinct fails':

- Never use a metaphor, simile or other figure of speech which you are used to seeing in print.
- Never use a long word where a short one will do.
- If it is possible to cut out a word, always cut it out.
- Never use the passive where you can use the active.
- Never use a foreign phrase, a scientific word or a jargon word if you can think of an everyday English equivalent.
- Break any of these rules sooner than say anything outright barbarous.

(Orwell 1946b: 156)

While aiming to eliminate inconsistency within a title, a style guide also identifies those 'minor style choices by which one news outlet's finished product is different from another's' (Bell 1991: 82). As Deborah Cameron points out, style guides produce distinctive voices for different titles by submitting the voices of individual journalists (columnists usually excepted) to 'the corporate norms of the newspaper' and by 'differentiating one newspaper from others'. Such rules may reflect the usage of the target audience or even the audience's 'aspirations', as when the *Today* paper banned words such as mum, dad, kids and toilet. In this sense, style 'is one of the things *brand image* is made of' (Cameron 1996: 320–24; my emphasis).

It has been argued that the issue of style goes beyond questions of presentation to have an ideological effect. 'Formats are never neutral in their ideological implications', says Paul Manning, who argues that the journalist's concern to meet restrictive requirements can result in 'less discursive news treatments and fewer opportunities for a wider range of news sources to inject critical or oppositional voices' (Manning 2001: 60). Mark Pursehouse notes, for example, that the mode of address of the *Sun* is 'heterosexual, male, white, conservative, capitalist, nationalist' (cited in Stevenson 2002: 101). For Cameron, style guides themselves are ideological:

> Though they are framed as purely functional or aesthetic judgements, and the commonest criteria offered are 'apolitical' ones such as clarity, brevity, consistency, liveliness and vigour, as well as linguistic 'correctness' and (occasionally) 'purity', on examination it turns out that these stylistic values are not timeless and neutral, but have a history and a politics. They play a role in constructing a relationship with a specific imagined audience, and also in sustaining a particular ideology of news reporting. *(Cameron 1996: 316)*

Yet journalism can break with consensus in both style and ideology. When Nell McCafferty covered the Dublin criminal courts for the *Irish Times* she abandoned the conventional rules of court reporting and journalistic style, as she explained in the introduction to a collection of her descriptive and often plaintive articles:

> Because these people have suffered more than enough by appearing in court in the first place, I never used their real names and addresses. I have named the Justices who decided their fate. Hopefully, this collection of articles will put them in the dock for a change. *(McCafferty 1981: 2)*

Language

Journalists are often dismissive of academics' attention to the language used in newspaper and other reports, but the choice of language is 'inseparable' from issues of 'truth' and 'what really happened', argue Robert Hodge and Gunther Kress:

> It is common for linguistically-oriented critics to attend too much to language, and to overvalue the importance of what is contained in words, especially words in written texts; but the opposite can also be the case. All the major ideological struggles will necessarily be waged in words, through texts that circulate in various ways by virtue of various technologies, in forms of language that bear the traces of these struggles in innumerable ways. *(Hodge and Kress 1993: 161)*

For Cameron, the plain language celebrated by Orwell – and embraced by most UK news media to this day – also has ideological implications:

> The plain and transparent style recommended by Orwell is particularly well suited to the prevailing ideology of modern news reporting as simply 'holding up a mirror to the world', and it is not coincidental that this style is most strictly adhered to in news rather than feature items. The use of a plain, terse, concrete language in news items – a language that deliberately aims not to draw attention to itself as language – is a code, not unlike the code of realism in fiction, and what it conventionally signifies is unmediated access to the objective facts of a story. It implicitly conveys to us, in a way a less self-effacing kind of language could not hope to do, that what we are reading is not really a representation at all: it is the simple truth . . . [It] is the linguistic analogue of the camera never lies, and should be treated with similar suspicion. *(Cameron 1996: 327)*

> *'Tight writing is one of the greatest journalistic virtues.'*
> *– Cedric Pulford.*

Style guide

A

a or an before h? If the h is silent, as in hour, use an; otherwise use a, as in *a* hero.

abbreviations Abbreviations such as *can't* or *that's* are increasingly common in today's newspapers but are still frowned on by the NCTJ unless they are in direct quotes. Shortened versions of words such as doctor (Dr) or Labour (Lab) do not need full stops, nor do initials such as GP, BBC or MP (which should be upper case with no spaces). Explain all but the most famous either by spelling out: National Union of Students (NUS); or by description: the transport union RMT. If the initials have become known as a word they form an *acronym*.

accommodation Double cc and double mm.

acronyms A word formed by using the initial letters of other words, as in Nato. Explain all but the most famous like this: train drivers' union Aslef; or Acas, the arbitration service.

Act Upper case in the full name of an act, as in the Official Secrets Act.

addresses Most addresses in news articles give the street, not the number. But if giving the full address for contact details, write it as follows: 999 Letsby Avenue, Leeds LS18 5HD.

adrenalin Not adrenaline.

advice, advise Advice (noun) is what you ask for. Advise (verb) is what you might do to somebody else.

adviser Not advisor.

affect Not to be confused with *effect*. To affect is to change. Such a change may have effects.

ageing Not aging.

ages David Connolly is 26 years old. You may also write: David Connolly, 26, or 26-year-old David Connolly.

Aids Not AIDS.

A-levels Hyphen and lower case l.

> '*Every word must be understood by the ordinary reader, every sentence must be clear at one glance, and every story must say something about people.*'
> – Harold Evans.

all right Two words.

Alzheimer's disease Upper case A, lower case d, and note the apostrophe.

amongst Prefer *among*.

ampersand (&) Use in company names when the company does: Marks & Spencer. Otherwise avoid.

and You may begin sentences with the word *and*. But not every sentence, please.

apostrophes Use an apostrophe to show that something has been left out of a word (eg *don't*, short for *do not*) and to mark the possessive (eg *John's foot*). Plural nouns such as children and people take a singular apostrophe (eg *children's games, people's princess*).

armed forces Lower case.

Army Upper case A if referring to *the* (ie British) Army. Army ranks should be abbreviated as follows: Lieutenant General (Lt Gen); Major General (Maj Gen); Brigadier (Brig); Colonel (Col); Lieutenant Colonel (Lt Col); Major (Maj); Captain (Capt); Lieutenant (Lt); 2nd Lieutenant (2nd Lt); Regimental Sergeant Major (RSM); Warrant Officer (WO); Company Sergeant Major (CSM); Sergeant (Sgt); Corporal (Cpl); Lance Corporal (L Cpl); Private (Pte). Do not abbreviate Field Marshall or General.

asylum seeker Two words, no hyphen.

authoress Prefer author for male or female.

B

B&Q No spaces.

backbenches One word, as in backbencher.

bail, bale Somebody might be on police *bail*, and a cricket player will be familiar with *bails*. But a boat could be *baled* out, and a pilot could *bale* out of an aeroplane.

Bank of England Upper case B and E. Subsequently the Bank.

bank holiday Lower case.

banknote One word.

barbecue Not Bar-B-Q, BBQ or barbie.

Barclays Bank Upper case Bs, no apostrophe.

bare, bear Often confused. *Bare* means unclothed, unadorned, just sufficient, and to reveal; *bear* means to carry, to produce or give birth, and a furry animal.

begs the question Best avoided because even the 'experts' can't agree on what it means.

biannual Means twice a year. Not to be confused with *biennial*, every two years. Probably best avoided.

Bible Upper case. But biblical is lower case.

billion One thousand millions. Write the word in full (£1.4 billion).

birthplace One word.

boffins Do not use for scientists or researchers unless you are being ironic; even then, must you?

Boxing day Upper case B, lower case d.

breach Means to break through or to break a promise or rule. Not to be confused with *breech*, which is either part of a gun or something to do with short trousers.

breastfeeding One word.

brownfield One word.

brussels sprouts Lower case, no apostrophe.

BSE Bovine spongiform encephalopathy, but not normally any need to spell out. You may refer to it as 'mad cow disease'.

Budget Upper case B if this is *the* Budget set by the Chancellor of the Exchequer, otherwise lower case.

but You may begin sentences with the word *but*. But not too many.

byelection One word.

bylaw One word.

bypass One word.

C

cabinet, shadow cabinet Lower case.

caesarean section Lower case.

canvas, canvass Tents are made of *canvas*, whereas politicians may *canvass* for support.

capitals UK newspapers now use upper case letters far more sparingly than they did even just a few years ago. Clarity and consistency can sometimes be at odds with each other, in which case clarity should be allowed to win.

cappuccino Lower case.

Caribbean One r and two bbs.

cashmere A fabric, not to be confused with *Kashmir* in the Indian subcontinent.

CD-rom Note the upper case *CD* and the hyphen.

cemetery Not cemetry or cematery.

censor Means to suppress and should not be confused with *censure*, meaning to criticise harshly.

centre Not center.

century Lower case, with numbers, as in 9th century or 21st century.

chairman, chairwoman Use chairman if it's a man, chairwoman if it's a woman, and chair if it is simply a position (eg The committee's first job will be to elect a chair). Lower case.

Chancellor of the Exchequer Upper case C and E. Subsequent mentions: the Chancellor.

Channel tunnel Upper case C, lower case t.

cheddar, cheshire cheese Lower case.

Chief Constable Upper case Cs.

Christian Upper case C, though unchristian is lower case.

Christmas day Upper case C, lower case d.

churches Full name, upper case, eg Sacred Heart Roman Catholic Church; then Sacred Heart or just the church.

citizens advice bureau Lower case, no hyphen.

city centre Two words, no hyphen.

CJD Creutzfeldt-Jakob disease, but not normally any need to spell out. You may refer to it as 'the human form of BSE'.

Clichés Some say 'avoid clichés like the plague', but opinions vary. Keeble (2001a: 117), for example, advises reporters to avoid saying that so-and-so is 'fighting for her life' when a hospital reports her condition as 'critical', on the grounds that it is a cliché. Maybe it is, but so is 'critical', and at least 'fighting for her life' gets closer to the drama of the situation. Clichés are hard to avoid completely, they change over time, and just occasionally they might be used ironically. If you are tempted to use a cliché in your copy, stop and ask yourself if it really is the best way of expressing what you want to say. Particularly tired words and phrases include:

a bridge too far;

acid test;

as so-and-so looks on (in picture captions);

back to square one;

between a rock and a hard place;

bitter end;

bombshell;

bubbly character;

budding (in stories about young people);

burning issue;

chickens coming home to roost;

cold comfort;

curate's egg;

cyberspace;

drop-dead gorgeous;

fairytale ending;

first the good news;

flash in the pan;

flushed with success (in stories about toilets);

goes without saying;

horns of a dilemma;

interesting to note;

. . . is the new black;

. . . is the new rock'n'roll;

kick-start;

last but not least;

leave no stone unturned;

level playing field;

mega;

morning after the night before;

pillar of the community;

political correctness gone mad;

purrfect (in stories about cats);

rich tapestry;

ripe old age of . . . ;

speculation was rife;

storm in a D-cup (in stories about bras or breasts);

take the bull by the horns;

the devil is in the detail;

torrid time;

tucking into festive fare (in picture captions);

untimely death;

up in arms;

wake up and smell the coffee.

collar bone Two words, no hyphen.

comedienne Prefer comedian for male or female.

company names Use spellings, upper or lower case

letters, and apostrophes as the companies do themselves.

conman, conwoman Both one word.

connection Not connexion.

Conservative party Upper case C, lower case p. *Conservatives* and *Tories* are also acceptable. The Conservative party is singular; Conservatives are plural.

Continent Upper case C only if you are referring to *the* Continent, ie mainland Europe.

convince You convince someone of the fact; you do not convince someone to do something, you *persuade* them.

cooperate, cooperative No hyphen.

Coroner's Court Bradford Coroner's Court, with upper case and apostrophe. But lower case if general, eg 'The cause of death will be decided in the coroner's court'.

council leader Lower case.

councillors Lower case for councillors in general, but upper case and abbreviate for individuals, eg *Coun Neil Taggart*. Not Cllr.

councils Upper case on first use – Leeds City Council – then the council if it is the only one referred to in the story. The council *is* rather than the council *are*. Committees, panels and boards should all be in lower case

couple Plural, so the couple *are* planning a holiday, not *is*.

Crown Prosecution Service Upper case first letters. May subsequently be abbreviated to CPS.

curate's egg *See clichés.* If you are tempted to use it, please be aware that it does not mean a bit good and a bit bad – an egg that is 'good in parts' is still rotten.

D

dashes Two dashes may be used – as in this example – to mark a parenthesis. One dash may also be used to introduce an explanation, to add emphasis, or to mark a surprise. But avoid littering your copy with too many dashes.

dates June 21, or June 21 2002. Not June 21st or June 21, 2002.

day-to-day Hyphenated.

D-day Just the one upper case D, plus a hyphen.

decades 1980s, 1990s, 2000s, with no apostrophe. Swinging 60s is acceptable if used ironically (and sparingly).

decimate Means to kill or remove a tenth of the population – not to defeat utterly.

defuse Means to render harmless or to reduce tension. Often confused with *diffuse*, meaning spread about.

disabled people Not the disabled or the handicapped.

discreet Means circumspect and should not be confused with *discrete*, meaning separate.

disinterested Means impartial, but is often confused with *uninterested,* meaning bored or not interested.

Doctor Abbreviate to Dr without a full stop.

dotcom Dotcom companies, not .com or dot.com.

dots Use three dots (ellipsis) to indicate that something has been omitted when quoting a document; also if you want to indicate that more could be said on the subject, eg 'But that's another story . . . '.

double-decker bus Not double-deck.

dreamed Not dreamt.

drink driving Not drunk driving. Court reports should include the measurements and the relevant legal limit: 80 milligrams of alcohol in 100 millilitres of blood; 35 micrograms of alcohol in 100 millilitres of breath; or 107 milligrams of alcohol in 100 millilitres of urine.

E

earring No hyphen.

Earth The planet takes an upper case E.

east Lower case e if it is a description (east Leeds) or a direction (head east), but upper case E if it is the name of a region or a county (the North-East).

E.coli Upper case E, lower case c, with a full stop and no space.

e-commerce Hyphenated, lower case.

> '*A piece of writing can drone or it can splutter or it can mumble or it can sing. Aim for the singing kind – writing that has life, rhythm, harmony, style – and you will never lose your reader.*'
> – Keith Waterhouse.

ecstasy Lower case. Write 'Es' only if you are quoting somebody.

Edinburgh Not borough. *See also Middlesbrough and Scarborough.*

eg Means for example. Lower case, no full stops.

email No hyphen.

enclose Not inclose.

enormity Monstrous wickedness. Do not use to mean very big.

euro Lower case for the currency.

exclamation marks Known in the trade as 'screamers', these are found by the dozen in the work of amateur journalists and the editors of parish newsletters. They should generally be avoided except in titles, when quoting somebody shouting at the top of their voice, or when someone genuinely exclaims ('Ouch!'). They should certainly not be used to signal that something is supposed to be funny! Ha ha ha!!!!

exhaustive Means comprehensive, but is often confused with *exhausted*, meaning tired.

expense Not expence.

eyewitness One word, but what's wrong with witness?

F

fairytale One word

fast food Two words, no hyphen.

fewer Means smaller in number, eg fewer hours of sunshine, fewer people. Should not be confused with *less*, which means less in quantity, eg less sunshine, less money.

fireman Prefer firefighter.

first aid Lower case.

first, second Not firstly, secondly.

flaunt Means to show off or display something, but is often confused with *flout*, meaning to disobey contemptuously.

focused Not focussed.

foot and mouth disease Lower case, no hyphens.

fulsome Means excessive or insincere, so *fulsome praise* means excessive praise rather than generous praise. Often misused.

G

GCSE, GCSEs Upper case, no full stops, and the plural takes a lower case s.

general election Lower case.

gentlemen's agreement Not gentleman's agreement. But *verbal agreement* would be less sexist.

getaway One word (as in getaway car).

God Upper case.

government Lower case.

government departments Use upper case like this: Department for Culture, Media and Sport; Department of Health. Use lower case for descriptions, as in transport department.

graffiti Two ffs, one t.

green belt Two words, lower case, no hyphen.

greenfield One word.

Greens Upper case for the Green party, lower case for the green movement.

green paper Lower case.

gunman One word.

Gypsy Upper case. Not Gipsy.

H

half Half-a-dozen, half-past, half-price, halfway, two-and-a-half.

hardcore One word.

headteacher One word.

heaven / hell Both lower case.

height Give people's heights in feet and inches (6ft 1in), but other heights (eg buildings) in metres (12.25m) or centimetres (25cm).

hello Not hallo or hullo.

heyday Not hayday or heydey.

hiccup Not hiccough.

hi-tech Hyphenated.

high street Lower case if referring to general shopping but upper case if it is the name of an actual street.

hijack One word.

his, hers No apostrophe

hitman One word.

housewife Can't you find a better description?

humour Not humor.

hyphens Many words begin life as two words, become hyphenated, and eventually become one word – but rushing in too soon can create confusion. Check individual entries and in other cases be guided by current newspaper practice, by pronunciation, and by the need for clarity.

> 'What the Times and the Economist ban today, they may approve tomorrow.'
> – *Wynford Hicks.*

I

ie Means that is to say. Lower case, no full stops.

in order to An over-used phrase usually best avoided.

income support, income tax Lower case.

infinitives Avoid split infinitives when they may confuse or sound inelegant. But, as Raymond Chandler told one of his editors: 'When I split an infinitive, God damn it, I split it so it will stay split.' (Chandler 1984: 77)

inner-city Hyphenated.

inquests A coroner *records* a verdict. A coroner's jury *returns* a verdict.

inquiry, inquiries Not enquiry, enquiries.

internet Lower case.

ise Not ize, eg organise.

its, it's There is no apostrophe in the phrase *its death*, meaning the dog's death, just as there is no apostrophe in the phrase *her death*. The apostrophe is introduced when *it's* is short for *it is*. It's that simple.

J

jack russell Lower case for the dog (but upper case for the wicketkeeper).

jail Not gaol.

jibe Not gibe.

jobcentre, jobseeker's allowance Lower case.

judges Full name and title for the first mention, eg *Judge Roger Scott*; then *Judge Scott* or *the judge*. High Court judges are known as Justice, as in *Mr Justice Henriques*; then *the judge* or the full version – not Judge Henriques. Recorders (part-time judges) are known as *the recorder Mrs Mary Smith*. Full-time magistrates who used to be known as stipendiary magistrates are now 'district judges (magistrates courts)'.

junior Abbreviate to Jr without a full stop.

K

kick-off Hyphenated.

kilogram, kilometre, kilowatt Abbreviate as kg, km, kw.

knockout One word.

Koran Upper case.

L

Labour party Upper case L, lower case p. Subsequent mentions: Labour. Both are singular.

labour Not labor.

lamp-post Hyphenated.

landmine One word.

lay, lie He was *laying* the table while she was *lying* on the bed.

layby One word.

lead, led Arsenal *lead* the table now, but Newcastle *led* at the start of the season.

less Means less in quantity, eg less sunshine, less money. Should not be confused with *fewer*, which means smaller in number, eg fewer hours of sunshine, fewer people.

liaison Not liason.

Liberal Democrats Upper case L and D. She is a Liberal Democrat (singular). She is a member of the Liberal Democrats (plural). May also be abbreviated to Lib Dems.

licence You need to buy a TV licence (noun). You will then be *licensed* (verb) to own a TV.

linchpin Not lynchpin.

lists Introduce a list with a colon: separate elements with semicolons; end with a full stop.

literally I'll literally explode if I see another example of this word being used inappropriately.

Lloyds Bank No apostrophe.

loathe A verb meaning to hate, not to be confused with loth, meaning reluctant.

Lord's Note the apostrophe in the name of the cricket ground.

lottery Lower case.

lovable Not loveable.

M

McDonald's Upper case M and D, plus an apostrophe.

mankind Use only if you intend to exclude females, otherwise use humankind, humanity, or people.

Marks & Spencer Subsequently M&S.

Mayor Upper case when referring to a particular person (eg 'London Mayor Ken Livingstone'), but lower case when referring to the job of mayor in general.

measurements For long distances, use miles; for people's heights, use feet and inches; for people's weights, use stones and pounds; for drinks, use pints; otherwise, use metric measurements. In time we will no doubt switch fully to metric measurements as advocated in an informative guide produced by the UK Metric Association (2002).

media Plural ('the media *are*'), not singular ('the media *is*').

medieval Not mediaeval

memento Not momento.

mentally handicapped Do not use. Prefer 'person with learning disabilities'.

mentally ill Refer to 'mentally ill people' rather than 'the mentally ill'.

mic Abbreviation for microphone. Not mike.

midday One word, no hyphen.

Middlesbrough Not borough. *See also Edinburgh and Scarborough.*

midweek One word.

mileage Not milage.

million One thousand thousands. Write in full (£1.4 million).

miniskirt One word.

ministers Lower case, as in international development minister Hilary Benn.

minuscule Not miniscule.

misuse One word, no hyphen.

Morrisons Not Morrison's.

Mosques Full name, upper case, eg Drummond Road Mosque. Then: the mosque.

mph Lower case, no full stops, as in 20mph.

MPs No apostrophe.

Miss, Mr, Mrs, Ms Courtesy titles are usually used for subsequent mentions in news reports, so John Smith becomes Mr Smith after the first time unless he is a defendant in a court case – in which case he becomes plain Smith.

Muslim Not Moslem.

N

names Always check the spelling and use both first and family name on first mention. Do not use initials except in those rare circumstances where somebody famous is known by their initials (eg OJ Simpson), in which case there are no full stops.

national lottery Lower case.

nationwide One word.

Nazism Not Naziism.

nearby One word.

nightclub One word.

no one Two words.

north Lower case n if it is a description (north Leeds) or a direction (head north), but upper case N if it is the name of a county or a region (North Yorkshire, the North-East).

north-south divide Lower case, one hyphen.

numbers One to nine inclusive should be spelled out; 10 to 999,999 should be given in numbers, with commas to mark thousands; then 2 million, 4.5 billion. Exceptions: speeds will be expressed in numbers, eg 5mph; temperatures take numbers, eg 30C (85F); sports scores will have numbers, eg 2–1; but numbers at the beginning of a sentence will always be spelled out, eg 'Seventeen England fans were arrested last night . . . '

O

off-licence Hyphenated.

Ofsted Just an upper case O.

oh! Not O!

OK Not okay.

O-levels Note the lower case l and the hyphen.

online One word.

P

parliament Lower case.

passerby One word. Plural: passersby.

pensioner Not OAP.

per Prefer *£10,000 a year* to *per year* or *per annum.*

per cent Not % or pc.

persuade *See convince.*

phone No apostrophe.

phone numbers Like this: 0113–2837100.

place names Use an atlas, a gazetteer or an A-Z to check spellings. Never guess.

play-off Two words, hyphenated.

plc Lower case.

poetess Prefer poet.

police West Yorkshire Police, then the police. Also lower case for the police in general. Note that police is plural, while police force is singular, so 'police *are* investigating . . . ' but 'the force *is* short of money'. Police ranks should be abbreviated as follows: Chief Superintendent (Chief Supt); Superintendent (Supt); Chief Inspector (Chief Insp); Inspector (Insp); Detective Inspector (Det Insp); Detective Sergeant (Det Sgt); Sergeant (Sgt); Detective Constable (DC); Constable (PC). Do not use WPC. Do not abbreviate Chief Constable, Deputy Chief Constable or Assistant

Chief Constable – write it in full at first, then Mr or Ms.

postgraduate One word.

postmodern One word, lower case.

post mortem Lower case, two words, no hyphen; and you should always write *post mortem examination*.

Prime Minister Upper case P and M.

principal The first in rank or importance, who may or may not have *principles*.

prodigal Means recklessly wasteful, not just someone who returns.

programme Not program, unless computer program.

prostitutes Not vice-girls.

protester Not protestor.

Q

queuing Not queueing.

quotes Use double quote marks unless there is a quote within a quote, which should have single quote marks. If a quote runs over more than one paragraph, open each paragraph with quote marks but close them only once, at the end of the full quote. Punctuation marks come inside quote marks when a full sentence is quoted but outside if a phrase or partial sentence is quoted.

R

refute Means to disprove, not to deny.

reported speech Should be reported in the past tense.

restaurateur Not restauranteur.

reviews Always give full details of title, venue, when the run ends and so on, including certificates for films.

ring-road Lower case, hyphenated. Also: inner ring-road and outer ring-road.

robbery Means theft using force or the threat of force, and should not be confused with theft or burglary.

rock'n'roll One word with two apostrophes.

Rolls-Royce Upper case, hyphenated.

Royal Air Force Upper case, then the RAF. RAF ranks are abbreviated as follows: Group Captain (Group Capt); Wing Commander (Wing Cmdr); Squadron Leader (Sqn Ldr); Flight Lieutenant (Flight Lt); Warrant Officer (WO); Flight Sergeant (Flight Sgt); Sergeant (Sgt); Corporal (Cpl); Leading Aircraftman (LAC). Do not abbreviate Marshal of the Royal Air Force, Air Chief Marshal, Air Vice Marshal, Flying Officer, or Pilot Officer.

Royal Navy Upper case, then the Navy. Naval ranks are abbreviated as follows: Lieutenant Commander (Lt Cmdr); Lieutenant (Lt); Sub Lieutenant (Sub Lt); Commissioned Warrant Officer (CWO); Warrant Officer (WO); Chief Petty Officer (CPO); Petty Officer (PO); Leading Seaman (LS); Able Seaman (AS); Ordinary Seaman (OS). Do not abbreviate Admiral, Vice Admiral, Rear Admiral, Commodore, Captain, Commander or Midshipman.

S

Safeway Not Safeway's.

Sainsbury's Not Sainsbury.

Scarborough *See also Edinburgh and Middlesbrough.*

schizophrenia An illness – do not use to mean 'in two minds'.

school names As in Bracken Edge primary school.

scrapheap One word.

seasons As in autumn, winter and so on, lower case.

Secretaries of State Cap up titles, as in *Home Secretary David Blunkett* and *Foreign Secretary Jack Straw*.

senior Abbreviate to Sr without a full stop.

September 11 Not 11th or 9/11.

shear, sheer It will be *sheer* luck if you manage to *shear* the wool off that sheep.

Siamese twins Prefer conjoined twins.

sit, sat He was *sitting* on the left until the teacher *sat* him in the middle. You may write that he sat on the left; do not write that he *was* sat on the left, unless by a third party.

soccer Banned. Write *football* instead.

> 'All the major ideological struggles will necessarily be waged in words.'
> – Robert Hodge and Gunther Kress.

south Lower case s if it is a description (south Leeds) or a direction (head south), but upper case S if it is the name of a region or a county (the South-West or South Yorkshire).

spelled Not spelt.

spokesman, spokeswoman The former if it is a man, the latter if it is a woman, and spokesperson if it is neither (eg a faxed statement).

standing, stood She was *standing* at the back until the photographer *stood* her at the front. You may write that she stood at the back; do not write that she *was* stood at the back, unless by a third party.

stationary, stationery With an *a* it means not moving, with an *e* it means writing materials (think 'e for envelope').

streetwise One word.

swearwords Swearwords can offend many people for little purpose. Swearwords should almost never be used outside direct quotes, and even then anything stronger than 'bloody' needs a powerful justification. Stop and think before using. Do not use asterisks.

T

targeted Not targetted.

taskforce One word.

temperatures Give celsius with fahrenheit in brackets: 7C (45F).

Tesco Not Tesco's.

that or which? That defines, which informs. This is the style guide *that* is given to students at my university. Students at my university, *which* is in Yorkshire, are given this style guide.

theirs No apostrophe.

times Use am and pm, not hundred hours. Do not write 12 noon or 12 midnight – noon and midnight will suffice.

tonne Prefer to ton, but be aware that they are different. A tonne (1t) is 1,000kg or 2,204.62lb; a ton is 2,240lb.

trademarks(tm) Take great care with these, and use an alternative unless you mean the specific product in question. So, if you mean ballpoint pen, don't write Biro.

trillion A thousand billion; that is, a million million.

tsar Not czar.

T-shirt Not tee-shirt.

U

under way Two words.

unique Something is either unique or it is not. It cannot be very unique.

universities Like this: Leeds Metropolitan University; University of Bradford.

V

Valentine's day Upper case V, lower case d, and note the apostrophe.

VAT Upper case, no need to spell out.

versus Use a lower case v for Warrington Wolves v Leeds Rhinos. Not vs.

#

Wall's Note the apostrophe.

Wal-Mart Note the hyphen.

wander, wonder You may *wander* from place to place while others *wonder* why you don't settle down.

war Lower case, eg Gulf war, apart from the First World War and Second World War.

web, website, world wide web All lower case.

weights For now we still give people's weights in stones and pounds (12st 3lb) but other weights in tonnes (17t), kilograms (36kg), grams (75g) or milligrams (12mg).

welfare state Lower case.

west Lower case w if it is a description (west Leeds) or a direction (head west), but upper case W if it is the name of a region or a county (the North-West, West Yorkshire).

whatsoever One word.

wheelchair-bound Do not use. Prefer *wheelchair user* or *in a wheelchair*.

whereabouts Are plural.

whilst Prefer *while*.

whiskey, whisky *Whiskey* is for Irish and *whisky* for Scotch.

white paper Lower case.

withhold Not withold.

workmen Prefer workers.

World Trade Centre Not Center.

wrongdoing One word.

X

x-ray Lower case, hyphenated.

Y

yo-yo Lower case, hyphenated.

yorkshire pudding, yorkshire terrier Lower case.

yours No apostrophe.

Z

zero Plural zeros, not zeroes.

zigzag One word, no hyphen.

Summary

All news organisations have rules governing style, whether or not such rules are codified in written guides. Their purpose goes beyond minimising mistakes in spelling, grammar and vocabulary to ensuring consistency *within* titles and differentiation *between* titles. The most common style in UK journalism is based on the 'plain style' advocated by George Orwell. It has been claimed that style is not neutral and that stylistic choices and presentational formats can have ideological implications by reducing openings for critical voices. The rejection of such rules can be seen as stylistically and ideologically challenging or transgressive. The plain style of news reporting draws attention away from itself as language, leading to suggestions that it purports to be unmediated truth rather than a representation.

Questions

What is the point of house style?

Where does house style come from?

Have you noticed changes in style over time?

Are words never neutral?

Do style guides privilege some social groups over others?

Further reading

The classic text on newspaper style is by Harold Evans (2000), the iconic ex-editor of the *Sunday Times*. Although slightly dated even in its revised edition, it remains full of good advice on essentials such as active writing and wasteful words. For a useful chapter on broadcasting style see Boyd (2001), while Hicks (1998 and 1999) offers good general advice. Waterhouse (1993 and 1994) is always worth reading on the subject of writing. The *Guardian* style guide can be viewed online at www.guardian.co.uk/styleguide, both the *Times* (Austin 2003) and *Economist* (2000) guides are available to buy as books and the BBC radio journalism style guide (and bulletin scripts) can be accessed at www.bbc.co.uk/radionewsroom. House style is discussed in Hicks and Holmes (2002) which also includes a brief style guide containing some interesting differences and similarities with the one used in this chapter. Fowler (1983) is a handy companion for any journalist, along with a decent dictionary. For critical reflection on the language of journalism, the best places to start are Fowler (1991) and Bell (1991). Cameron's illuminating paper subjects style guides to the kind of academic scrutiny usually reserved for newspaper texts themselves (Cameron 1996).

Notes

Sources for soundbites: Orwell 1946b, 156: Pulford 2001: 52; Evans 2000: 15; Waterhouse 1994: 143; Hicks in Hicks and Holmes 2002: 21; Hodge and Kress 1993: 161.

Chapter Twelve

Beyond print: broadcasting and online journalism

Key terms

Broadcast journalism

Television

Radio

24-hour news

Internet

Blogging

Interactivity

Horizontal communication

There are few things local politicians like more than having their speeches reported, so there was a gleeful sight awaiting the councillors who broke for coffee during the Association of Metropolitan Authorities annual gathering. They emerged from the conference hall in Sheffield to be greeted by a screen showing an enlarged version of the *Municipal Journal* website. On the site were a series of news stories from the conference, quoting from debates that had taken place just a few minutes earlier. They read their words of wisdom on the screen, nodded sagely, and proceeded to coffee with their sense of self-worth duly enhanced.

The year was 1996 and *Municipal Journal*, a weekly magazine covering local government, had hired me to report on proceedings for its fledgling website. When it came to selecting potential stories, the magazine's normal news values would apply – but the stories were to be brief and had to be written virtually instantly. Each time I bashed out a few pars on a laptop, a colleague would do some technical jiggery-pockery, and moments later the story was on the web for all the world to see. How new and exciting it all seemed at the time, echoing the arrival, a century earlier, of that 'illimitable, incomprehensible, exquisite medium' called radio (*Quarterly Review* 1898, quoted in Briggs and Burke 2002: 155).

Different branches of journalism do not exist in isolation. Each form of journalism informs others, and journalists are increasingly having to think across traditional divides and delivery mechanisms, as Martin Wainwright explains:

> There's a feeling that people get their immediate news from radio, television and internet, so the *Guardian*, rather to my sadness, has become a bit stodgy with very long analytical articles. One good way out of that is we have the *NewsUnlimited* website. We have audio which is just like radio, so at the Great Heck rail crash I did a couple of audio reports, saying 'I'm standing here in front of the train'. I love doing stuff for them.

Just as traditional print organisations may now have websites featuring audio and video, so broadcasting journalists may be expected to contribute written text to the websites of TV and radio stations. Many of the

> '*The world goes on at a smarter pace than it did when I was a young fellow . . . It's this steam you see.*'
> – George Eliot, The Mill on the Floss, 1860.

Broadcast journalism

Journalism on radio and television shares with print journalism the basic techniques of news gathering and story telling, although the importance of sound and pictures for broadcast journalism can affect both *which* stories are selected and *how* stories are covered. Paul Chantler and Sim Harris argue that radio is 'the best medium to stimulate the imagination' because 'pictures on radio are not limited by the size of the screen; they are any size you wish' (Chantler and Harris 1997: 5). Just as pictures (in the head) are important for radio, so sound is vital for television, especially the sound of people's own voices (Holland 2000: 79). Stories with the potential of good pictures and/or sound stand a far higher chance of being covered by broadcast journalists than those without either; and reporters covering 'important but dull' stories without good visuals/audio may try out imaginative ways of *creating* them through stunts or extended metaphors.

Broadcast journalism tends to have a more immediate *feel* than does print journalism, reporting things that are happening *now* rather than things that happened earlier (even when this is an illusion). According to a classic study of the television industry, broadcast journalism is far from the 'random reaction to random events' that it sometimes appears:

> On the contrary, it is a highly regulated and routine process of manufacturing a cultural product on an electronic production line. In stages of planning, gathering, selection and production broadcast news is moulded by the demands of composing order and organisation within a daily cycle. The news is made, and like any other product it carries the marks of the technical and organisational structure from which it emerges. (Golding and Elliott, quoted in Manning 2001: 51)

Notwithstanding the powerful image of an 'electronic production line', individual journalists can still affect content to some extent through their own contacts, skills and attitudes (Manning 2001: 53).

Recent years have seen the emergence of 24-hour rolling news programmes on both radio and TV. According to Andrew Boyd:

core skills of *reporting* may be similar but there are some significantly different relationships involving sound, vision, time and space.

Telling it in pictures

Pictures may have become of more importance to newspapers and magazines in the last few decades but that is nothing compared to the centrality of pictures in television. In radio too, although there the pictures are in the heads of the listeners. When Lindsay Eastwood left newspapers for **broadcast journalism** she was struck by this central importance of pictures for television reporting. Other differences included the difficulty of persuading people to appear on screen, the amount of time it took to do everything, and the fact that her own clothes and hair suddenly assumed new importance. As somebody who had covered parish council meetings for her local newspaper as a 16-year-old on work experience, she also noticed that an awful lot of regional TV news involved following up stories that had already appeared elsewhere, mostly in newspapers.

As the Bradford reporter for Yorkshire Television's *Calendar*, Lindsay Eastwood's day begins by listening to local radio and scanning all the morning newspapers for stories on her patch that might translate to television. 'It's pictures that you're looking for all the time,' she says. This process results in several suggestions for stories that might be covered ('prospects'), alongside diary jobs, stories allocated by the newsdesk, and any stories that might break during the day.

> 'Each new mass medium has been hailed for its educational and cultural benefits, as well as feared for its disturbing influence.'
> – Denis McQuail.

One of the frustrating things about TV is that you do follow other media. I'm on my own in Bradford and I cover Keighley and Skipton as well. Think how many newspaper reporters are in that area, so how can I compete with that? Also, people are more likely to ring the local paper with a story, and that's where the exclusives come from. We don't get that amount of calls from people.

Like all good journalists, she doesn't wait for stories to come to her but makes the time to go off-diary and develop her own contacts:

The 24-hour news format has since developed a number of distinct styles: the magazine approach, which presents a variety of programmes and personalities throughout the day; and the news cycle, which repeats and updates an extended news bulletin, and lasts usually between twenty minutes and an hour. *(Boyd 2001: 130)*

Concern has been expressed about the tendency for such news to 'over-emphasise the live and dramatic' and to deliver over-simplified 'nuggets' (Harrison 2000: 209). In reality, 24-hour news quickly becomes repetitive. Despite its continuous nature, it still relies on selection and mediation by journalists. Yet there is now so much news being pumped into newsrooms electronically that there are fears that some broadcast journalists may forget where news actually comes from in the first place:

> We must guard against one of the biggest dangers of all, especially with the increasing use of new technology. There could be a tendency to think of news as that which simply appears on the screen or the printer. Never forget that real news is what you go out and find through your own efforts. *(Chantler and Harris 1997: 164)*

Questions about the quality of information and interpretation provided to citizens are also raised by a shift towards what Jackie Harrison characterises as a 'faster, racier style of news presentation':

> [What] appears to be a tinkering with production techniques and format style by news organisations eventually has an effect on news content and the amount of information available, and ultimately on the relationship of terrestrial television news to the public sphere ... *(Harrison 2000: 29 and 42)*

The regulatory regime under which broadcast journalists in the UK work is discussed in Chapter 2. Broadcast journalism style is discussed further in Chapter 7.

Internet

Online journalists differ from other journalists in the ways they relate to their respective audiences, according to a survey by Mark Deuze and Christina Dimoudi.

I'm working on an exclusive at the moment, a tip-off from somebody I have to protect so I have to find somebody willing to go on camera and say what I want them to say. It's highly controversial so it's not likely that I'm going to get that, so all I'm going to have really is me reporting what my source has said, and then try to confront the villain for their response. Whereas if I was on a newspaper now I could just do it, I'd get the response, and I'd have a front page story. On a newspaper you get a tip-off, you make a phone call, you chat to people, you go see them and it's there in your notepad and you just churn it out. But here it's trying to persuade people they want to go on camera. Everything takes so long, and it's very frustrating.

Frustrating is a word that Lindsay Eastwood uses frequently when discussing the differences between print and television. But that is only one side of the story. She recognises that there are other stories on which broadcasting comes into its own:

Where we obviously excel is breaking news, because you're there when it happens. You get it on first whereas a newspaper is the day after. That's where you get your kicks. That's the main thing to be proud of if you're working for TV, and radio is even more immediate. Television is good at showing things as they are, like fires, devastation, or when John Prescott punched that guy [during the 2001 general election campaign]. Fires and destruction make good TV. Also, you can show how people talk. In a newspaper you have a quote but you don't get the personality of the person. I love doing vox pops because you get a range of people and you can see and hear what they're like.

> **'[Radio] should bring into the greatest possible number of homes . . . all that is best in every department of human knowledge, endeavour and achievement.'**
> – John Reith, first director general of the BBC.

The Bradford riots in the summer of 2001 count as one of her most satisfying stories because all the above criteria were met. The riots were breaking news, and few things are more visually dramatic than petrol bombs being hurled through the air by masked youths. Being on the spot meant that broadcast journalists could report events as they happened and use the authentic voices of people on the streets.

The riots stick in my mind because I was out there filming in the thick of it. That was an unbelievable

Based on a study in the Netherlands, the authors conclude:

> [The] bottom-up concept of 'the public' suggests that this group of journalists is much more aware of an active role for the people they serve than their offline colleagues. This is an interesting result, as it ties in with the discourse of new-media technologies in which they are perceived to empower people and further democratise the relationships between consumers and producers of content (be it news or information). It also connects to online media logic as a concept which includes the notions of *the audience as an active agent* in redefining the workings of journalism.
> *(Deuze and Dimoudi 2002: 97; my emphasis)*

We might ask how active internet users really are, when four out of five subscribers to AOL apparently never venture beyond AOL sites to explore the rest of the web (McChesney 2000: 166). And what are the implications for the 'public sphere' if interactivity is mostly used for internet shopping or to pre-select certain news topics and exclude others? But, for Jim Hall, the passing of control from journalists to users/consumers holds out the promise that 'the roles that journalism assigned to itself in the mid-nineteenth century . . . as gatekeeper, agenda-setter and news filter, are all placed at risk when its primary sources become readily available to its audiences' (Hall 2001: 53).

Much theorising on the subject of the internet goes along with Hall in arguing that *everything* has changed, while others counter that *nothing* fundamental has changed. As Nick Stevenson points out, on the one hand we have the 'communicative possibilities that are suggested by horizontally rather than vertically organised information structures'; on the other hand, it is argued that new technologies are part of 'the accumulation of capital, commodification and the disappearance of public space' (Stevenson 2002: 184). This polarity is rejected by Manuel Castells, who argues that although the 'information society' may be a product of post-industrial capitalism, the internet is also used to build networks among oppositional social movements (Stevenson 2002: 192–5). For Castells, the economy has become organised 'around global networks of capital, management, and

experience really. Very scary. We ended up in a car behind the rioters. We thought they were people going to watch but they were people going to join the riot. So we were driving in the same direction as them and we gradually realised we were getting into a situation where it would be impossible to turn around and get away. We spotted these guys with scarves over their faces, carrying hammers and a crowbar and we thought 'we'd better get out of here'. We were trying to cover up our equipment and we managed to drive off and got behind police lines. There were bricks coming over. We were trying to find a spot to film because obviously behind police lines you can't see the rioters in front, so we were trying to get on high places on either side of the road. But we were also trying to watch our backs. Then there were rowdy people coming round the side of us. I interviewed some. You want to be interviewing the young folk that are involved, saying 'why are you doing it?'. I did feel a bit of hostility a couple of times, but nothing too in-your-face. There were a lot of university students involved so they were quite articulate about why they were doing it.

> *'[Television is] just another appliance . . . a toaster with pictures.'*
> – Mark Fowler, US Federal Communication Commission.

Reporters can get embroiled in the excitement, as she notes:

We should have been dodging bricks, but the adrenalin gets you and you're just caught up in the moment. But as a reporter you're responsible for the health and safety of the crew, and you can't ask them to do what they don't want to do.

In fact, some TV crews *did* film from in front rather than behind police lines, resulting in even more dramatic footage from a different perspective, but at much greater physical risk.

Blurring boundaries

Just as Lindsay Eastwood and her broadcasting colleagues scan the newspapers for stories, so print journalists monitor TV and radio, and most large newsrooms will have a television set permanently tuned to a text news service. Print and broadcasting both feed off the internet, and vice versa. David Walker

information, whose access to technological know-how is at the roots of productivity and competitiveness' (Castells 1996: 471). Yet, within the belly of this beast, 'the historical law that where there is domination there is resistance continues to apply', on the internet as much as anywhere else (Castells 1998: 351). Thus, 'communes of resistance' – from the Zapatistas to the feminist movement – use the internet to further 'people's horizontal communication' and to challenge society's dominant voices (Castells 1997: 358).

Where does this leave journalism? For Jim Hall, it means that journalists should be offering 'commentary, fact-checking and inflection' on material in the public domain, acting as map-makers to help people make sense of everything that's out there on the internet: 'The maps contextualise and mediate the sources that they point to but *the interpretation of sources becomes the responsibility of the readers themselves*' (Hall 2001: 54; my emphasis.)

See Appendix Two for some websites of interest.

writes that, in his experience, stories often 'do not exist' for BBC newsdesks unless they have already appeared in print (Walker 2000: 239). Local radio stations have long had a cannibalistic relationship with local papers and all elements of the media now feed off each other in an increasingly orgiastic frenzy. The **internet** means the process is both quicker and more international in scope.

Now journalists have instant access to source material, analysis and opinion from near and far to help with hard and soft news alike. It's not only that the same stories do the rounds of different media, but the boundaries between different media platforms themselves are blurring. Just as traditional newspapers have websites featuring audio and video, so broadcasting operations such as the BBC and ITN have websites featuring background articles, maps, photo galleries and other contextual information. Previously ephemeral journalism such as a radio report can remain archived and accessible on the web, giving it the quality of what has been termed 'printed radio' (Brown 2000: 181). Website users have the power to go where they please 'from information chunk to audio file, to database, to graphic, to text summary, to video, to archive', and then either back again or off to an external site to consult primary sources and original documentation (Ward 2002: 121). The trends of the last few years suggest that, increasingly, journalists will deliver material *across* different media platforms; potentially, at least, this could blur the boundaries between the distinctive worlds of print, radio, TV and online journalists.

The 'empowering' of internet users also blurs the boundaries between journalist and audience, it has been argued. Writing about the phenomenon of 'blogging' – creating a personal online journal, in real-time, with links and responses – print journalist Andrew Sullivan describes it as 'peer-to-peer journalism' more like a 24-hour broadcast than 'a fixed piece of written journalism'. When his 'readers' began responding not only with opinions but with information, he felt the blog's advantage over traditional

> '*I try to use words that people relate to – I try to keep it conversational but direct.*'
> – Andrew Marr on TV reporting.

> '*Of course the world wide web is full of lunatics and lies; but it's not technology that is responsible for this, but simply human failings like sloppy journalism and ignorance.*'
> – Andrew Brown.

one-way journalism was that it could 'marshal the knowledge and resources of thousands, rather than the few' (Sullivan 2002).

The potential for electronic communications to be used to challenge the powerful was further demonstrated in 2003 when the UK government's dodgy dossier on Iraq was exposed as being based, not on the work of the intelligence services, but on a thesis by a postgraduate student. This cut-and-paste plagiarism was spotted by researchers in Sweden who emailed a UK academic whose students in turn forwarded it to journalists (Hinsliff et al 2003). Within days of the dossier being published it had been exposed in the press. Thanks to another advance of the electronic age, the official explanation remains archived for all to see on the government's website (www.numberten.gov.uk/output/Page1701.asp).

Telling it interactively

Radio journalists commonly refer on air to emails from listeners and sometimes put questions to interviewees prompted by emails sent *during* interviews. Turning interactivity almost full circle, *Channel 4 News* journalists send out 'personal' daily emails to those viewers who have signed-up to the service, commenting on the news of the day and telling them what to expect on that night's programme. A typical example sent by Krishnan Guru-Murthy began:

Hello, Krishnan here with your briefing from the Channel 4 News room. DEBATING IRAQ. I'm not normally a conspiracy theorist, but you know something's up when nobody wants to talk to you about it. Tonight we reveal the results of our poll into whether Britain wants to go to war against Saddam Hussein – and more than half of you, apparently, don't. This as the US bats off another offer from Iraq – this time inviting Congressmen and their experts to come and find those alleged weapons of mass destruction. Another move in the slow diplomatic game. Yet tonight the government will field no interviewees to answer a few simple questions about our foreign policy – like is it Tony Blair's goal to change the regime in Iraq? And will he consult Parliament about it? Strangely neither will the Tories talk about it, on the day that David Davis takes charge while Ian and Theresa are on their hols. However, as the Church of England appears to be making a war on Iraq a moral and religious issue, we are joined by the Bishop of Oxford . . . (Email from snowmail@channel4.com August 5 2002)

However, as discussed in Chapter 2, not all interaction between journalist and audience is quite so chummy. Many of the more than 2,000 emails received by Seumas Milne within days of criticising US foreign policy came from people in the US and elsewhere who read his column on the web and who did not necessarily share the presumed values of traditional *Guardian* readers – as indicated by the emails threatening him with mutilation and torture (Mayes 2001a).

But input from readers is vital for Trevor Gibbons, who works on one of BBC Online's *Where I Live* websites:

The thing is to get as much user-generated copy in there as we can, to provide a place for people to react to local news. There is page after page after page of people on here talking about local issues, it's not like the selection of one or two letters for the letters page of a local paper. One of the challenges of working for this site is thinking how you can put an element of interactivity into stories. Increasingly the online audience doesn't just want to be told the story, it wants to be part of the story. We have a vote running most of the time. You want people, rather than just reading something, to *do* something.

Internet journalism has both similarities with and differences from other forms of journalism, he explains:

Some of the things we do are the same sort of things that a local newspaper would have: local news, local features, local sport, competitions. And there are a lot of similarities with local radio: it's local, it's fast, it's information and event-driven. What's different is the amount of interactivity, and the fact that we can use sound, vision and photo galleries as well. It's thinking

in a unique combination of newspaper, magazine and radio really – it is everything.

Unlike newspapers there is no deadline and the site is never 'full', and these factors can affect the way stories are covered:

There's more pressure to get something up immediately. Coming into a story a couple of hours after somebody else has done it is almost so late as to be no use. Writing for a newspaper, you pick one moment in time whereas we sometimes have an evolving story and we might go into a story four or five times in a day. And it's far easier to put background material *around* the story that you're doing. An internet site is never full and you never put it to bed. At any one time some bits are going out-of-date and need to be taken off.

In common with most news-based websites, stories on BBC Online tend to be shorter than those in newspapers: they rarely take up more than two 'screens' and are almost all one sentence per par. 'But it's written in the same way, with all the important stuff in the first paragraph,' explains Gibbons, who adds that this is even more important online than in print because many readers will go no further than the opening few lines before flitting elsewhere. He believes that the same fundamentals apply:

> '*I see a future where there are millions and millions of reporters.*'
> – Matt Drudge, cyberhack.

Internet journalism is journalism. It's about ideas, it's about what you're actually going to put on the page. What makes a good story makes a good story online, in a newspaper or on the radio. Our sources are the same, we check them the same, we put in the same calls, we ring up the same people. Just like TV, radio or print, you need to know who you're writing for. There is the unique ability to construct this web behind a story, and that's what people who use the internet like about it, but the same attributes should apply really.

These attributes, the basics of journalism as discussed throughout this book, include the ability to ask questions, to think laterally, to maintain curiosity, to check sources, to look for evidence, and to tell stories. Although online journalism has distinctive qualities such as immediacy, interactivity and links, as Gibbons says it shares the basics with print and broadcast journalism. For Mike Ward: 'The application of *core journalistic principles and processes* should inform all stages of online content creation and presentation, from the original idea to the finished page or site' (Ward 2002: 6; my emphasis). He identifies these processes as:

- *Identify* and find news and/or information which will attract and interest the key audience/readers;
- *Collect* all the materials needed to tell the story/provide the information;
- *Select* from the collection the best material; and
- *Present* that material as effectively as possible.

(Ward 2002: 30; my emphasis)

But it's not simply a one-way process of core journalism skills being used to inform online reporting. The innovations associated with the internet also influence how 'traditional' media report events. So, for example, we now have TV news and sports channels featuring split screens plus captions and tickers delivering many different strands of information at once. We have the speedy feedback and polling made possible by email. We have the increasing trend in print reporting of emulating the 'layered' approach of online journalism by breaking up information into different sections with boxes, background material and graphics. And, finally, print and broadcast reporters can use the web to place background material, original documents, full interviews, photo galleries, links and discussions that would not 'fit' into their reports.

> **'The internet is only the street corner meeting on a big scale.'**
> – Tony Benn, Labour politician.

A note of caution

The global reach and instant communication provided by the internet has brought countless benefits to journalists, users, and all points between. However, it can have its drawbacks. Witness the false story that went around the world in September 2001 alleging that CNN film of Palestinian children apparently celebrating the attacks on the World Trade Centre was actually footage filmed ten years previously (Urban Legends 2001). The story began as a posting to an internet discussion list and quickly took on a life of its own before being recanted by its originator, Marcio in Brazil:

I'll tell you the strangest story about information. My life has turned upside down these last days . . . I wrote the original post to this list called Fourth Power, about the Palestinian images. There I affirm that someone else (a teacher of mine) claimed to have a tape proving those images to be a fake. Due to the high response I received from the list (lots of emails asking for this tape), I spent last Thursday (September 13) looking for this teacher. To sum up, everyone who was involved (all who claimed to know something) denied vehemently their own words. I wrote then a second mail to this list, denying the information; I firmly believed that source, which proved to be untrustworthy. The problem is that some members of the list had already reproduced the original email in other lists. Yesterday (Friday September 14) I woke up with some guy (allegedly) from Austria calling me on the phone! He wanted to know whether I had the tape or not; I explained the whole story for him. Throughout the day I received over 100 emails (4 of them were bomb emails!), was called by 2 televisions and 2 newspapers! The original email I sent to this list has been translated to Spanish, back to Portuguese, and reached Brazil again, after a trip around the world. But it came back changed, modified, mutilated; some information said that I'm a famous Brazilian International Politics Annalist [sic], others said that a group of scholars in my University analysed the tape (supposedly I was among them), and so on. My name and the name of my institution were linked these days to a story that became bigger than I could think. It was the craziest day of my life . . . *(Media-Watch 2001)*

A warning against believing everything you read on the internet. And a cautionary tale about how ignoring the basics of journalism can result in inaccurate stories being spread and embellished. One final thought, before we move on to consider the wider challenges facing journalists in the concluding chapter. How do we know that the above account is any more accurate than the original tale?

Summary

Journalists are increasingly working across different media sectors. Broadcast and online journalism may differ in style and detail but they share certain core processes with each other and with print journalism: the identification of news, the collection of information, the selection of material, and the presentation of stories. Online journalism makes greater use of interactive elements, although interactivity is also a growing element within broadcast and even print journalism. The internet user's power to access primary sources, combined with the sheer volume of information available on the internet, has led to claims that the journalistic roles of gatekeeper and information filter are under threat.

Questions

What are the core skills that all journalists need?

Does television's reliance on pictures affect what stories are covered?

What do you think is the best medium for breaking news?

What do you think is the best medium for explaining the news?

Has the internet now made *everyone* a journalist?

Further reading

Boyd (2001) is an authoritative practical introduction to TV and radio reporting, plus a brief look at online journalism. Holland (2000) and Fleming (2002) look at the practices of broadcast journalists within the context of introductions to the wider TV and radio industries respectively. See Ward (2002) for a practical guide to journalism on the internet; tips for writing news on the web are also to be found in Rich (1999). A useful introduction to academic analysis of broadcast journalism and the public sphere can be found in both Harrison (2000) and Bromley (2001), while Hall (2001) offers a polemical account of the impact of online journalism.

Notes

Sources for soundbites: Eliot cited in Briggs and Burke 2002: 107; McQuail 2000: 38; Reith cited in Briggs and Burke 2002: 221; Fowler cited in Salwen 2001: 635; Marr cited in Brockes 2002; Brown 2000: 185; Drudge cited in Boyd 2001: 400; Benn cited in Cottle 2001.

Chapter Thirteen

Conclusion: the challenge for journalism

Key terms

Constraints

Ethical responsibility

Public sphere

Citizens

Consumers

Reflective practitioner

Political economy

Agency

We have heard from many journalists in the preceding 12 chapters and we have seen something of the good and bad of journalistic practice in the real world. In the process, we have considered a range of influences that impact on the work of journalists. Some may be interpreted as positive, even liberating, influences rather than simply as **constraints**. For example, although the National Union of Journalists' Code of Conduct or the Press Complaints Commission's Code of Practice can be seen as constraining the behaviour of journalists, they may also help journalists to *resist* what they see as unethical behaviour and to *defend* journalistic integrity (Harcup 2002a and 2002b).

As HG Wells put it in a message to his fellow NUJ members back in 1922:

> We affect opinion and public and private life profoundly, and we need to cherish any scrap of independence we possess and can secure. We are not mere hirelings; our work is creative and responsible work. The activities of rich adventurers in buying, and directing the policy of, groups of newspapers is a grave public danger. A free-spirited, well-paid, and well-organised profession of journalism is our only protection against the danger. *(Quoted in Mansfield 1945: 518)*

> '*The best reporter is somebody who's naturally nosy.'*
> – Brian Whittle.

Ethical responsbility

The challenge for journalists is to take seriously the 'ethic of responsibility' that goes with the job, argues Jake Lynch. An international TV and print reporter, he believes that the emphasis on entertainment-driven 'news-lite' and simplistic notions of 'news you can use' have damaging consequences both for our work and for the world we report on:

> In this information age, journalists are not disconnected observers but *actual participants* in the way communities and societies understand each other and the way parties wage conflict . . . We live in a media-savvy world. There's no way of knowing that what journalists are seeing or hearing would have happened the same way – if at all – if no press was present. This means that policies are born with a media

Constraints

In Chapter Two we came across David Randall's suggested 'disclaimer' that should be printed in all newspapers. Perhaps we might now rewrite it along the following lines:

> This newspaper has been produced by underpaid and overworked journalists who were recruited from a small section of the population before being socialised into the routines and news values of journalism. Much of the material originated from press officers and public relations professionals working on behalf of well-resourced organisations. Many news items were selected to meet the perceived interests of audiences thought to be most desirable to our advertisers. The paper was produced against the clock to a deadline, and things may have changed since then. Stories have been made to fit largely arbitrary word limits determined by decisions on format and design. In the processes of research, writing and editing, stories may have been simplified and made more dramatic. The sources consulted may not have known the full story and/or may have had their own interests to promote, and some of the journalists may have been concerned not to jeopardise relations with some sources. The journalists involved may have their own opinions on the subject of news stories, and these opinions may or may not have influenced the finished product. The journalists may also have been influenced in story selection and construction by the attitudes of their proprietors, editors and colleagues. They will have been mindful of legal constraints and regulatory rules, knowing how far things can be pushed and who is most likely to complain or take legal action. They will also have been aware of what will impress their current and prospective employers. By the time you read this disclaimer this newspaper will have lost interest in many of these stories, even though they may not be resolved, and will have moved on a fresh selection.

It's become a bit long now, so we could sub it down to:

Don't believe everything you read in this newspaper.

It could go next to the corrections column.

strategy built in. There's nothing pejorative in that, it's a condition of modern life; but it closes the circle of cause and effect between journalist and source. The only way anyone can possibly calculate journalists' likely response to what they do is from their experience of previous reporting. Every time facts get reported, it adds to the collective understanding of how similar facts will likely be reported in future. That understanding then informs people's behaviour. This is the feedback loop. *It means every journalist bears some unknowable share of the responsibility for what happens next.* (Lynch 2002; my emphasis)

> *'We should have been dodging bricks, but the adrenalin gets you.'*
> – Lindsay Eastwood.

This returns us to the point made in Chapter 1 – that journalism is not simply an interesting job, journalism *matters*. Journalism matters because it informs discussion in the **public sphere**. This social role in informing citizens means that a good journalist will be a **reflective practitioner** and will be aware that he or she is not simply an entertainer or a story-teller.

Despite all the constraints discussed in this book – and despite the fact that most journalists work for monolithic corporations – journalists retain some **agency**. The actions of journalists, individually and collectively, can *make a difference to people's lives*.

Journalists make choices every day – what stories to cover, which sources to consult, whose door to knock on, what questions to ask, who to believe, what angles to take, what quotes to use, how much context to include, what words to use, what pictures to use, what to leave out . . . They may not be entirely free choices, they are not taken in a vacuum, and sometimes they will be orders from on high, but for the most part they are still *choices*. The journalist whose choices are not anchored in *some* sense of ethical responsibility will simply be blown this way and that by prevailing economic and political winds. As Lynette Sheridan Burns writes:

> *'The best journalists go into a situation with an open and absorbing mind.'*
> – Martin Wainwright.

> Professional integrity is not something you have when you are feeling a bit down at the end of a long week. It is a state of mindfulness that you bring to everything you write, no matter how humble the topic . . . Put

Public sphere

The concept of the public sphere is a potent one in discussion of the role of journalism in society. A space in which informed citizens engage in critical reflection is an ideal against which journalism has come to be measured and is often found to be wanting, as Brian McNair notes:

> Analysts and critics may dispute the extent to which Britain *has* a properly functioning 'public sphere' . . . but all agree that such a space *should* exist, and that the media are at its core. (McNair 2000: 1; first emphasis in original; second is mine)

The concept of the public sphere is associated with the writings of Jurgen Habermas, who located in the Britain of the late 17th and early 18th centuries, 'the advent of a public sphere of reasoned discourses circulating in the political realm independently of both the Crown and Parliament' (Allan 1997: 298). Although this public sphere was a conceptual space, it also had physical manifestations, for example in the coffee houses of London where this 'reasoned discourse' would take place, albeit among a limited section of the (male) population. Habermas also points to the existence of multiple or competing public spheres, including a 'plebian public sphere' with its own radical press (Habermas 1989: xviii; 425; 430; Habermas 1992: 425–7; see also Downing 2001: 27–33; and Harcup 2003).

The idea of journalism serving an informed citizenry is undermined by a tendency to treat audiences as nothing more than consumers, argues Granville Williams. He locates this as one of a series of key oppositions, signifying very different ways of viewing the world:

● Society v Market.
● Citizen v Consumer.
● Need v Want.
● Value v Price.
● Community v Globalism.
● Regulation v Efficiency.

(Williams 1996: 2–3)

simply, given the power that you have to do good or harm by virtue of the decisions you make, under pressure each day, the least you can do is think about it. *(Sheridan Burns 2002: 11)*

Not just to *think* about it but also to *talk* about it and even occasionally to *do something* about it (Harcup 2002a and 2002b).

'Don't lose your sense of curiosity'

If that is the challenge for journalism as a whole, the challenge for people starting out as journalists is to become part of an established journalistic culture without losing their early spark. What words of wisdom do some of our experienced hacks have for new recruits to journalism?

> *'I see myself as a reporter rather than a writer.'*
> – Jane Merrick.

For Martin Wainwright of the *Guardian*, 'the best journalists go into situations with open and absorbing minds'. He adds: 'The great virtue of a journalist is curiosity – a constant interest in what makes people tick, why has this happened, what is going on?' Similarly, news agency editor Brian Whittle feels that 'naturally nosy' people make the best reporters: 'You want somebody who's nosy, somebody with enthusiasm, somebody who wants to do it more than anything else.'

At the Press Association, Jane Merrick stresses the importance of learning 'the basics' such as shorthand and law. She points out that a humble attitude is also an attribute:

> Never think that you know more than the lowest journalist on the newspaper or agency, or wherever you start. Take *everything* on board. There's a balance between giving your newsdesk the confidence that you can do the job, and being level-headed. It's a matter of getting that balance right. Journalists will respect somebody prepared to take it all on board.

Even those doing the job they have always wanted, and who recognise its social role, can get down-hearted, warns Abul Taher:

> I was attracted to journalism because I had always wanted to be a writer. Journalism is easily the most widely read type of literature in modern societies, beating novels, books and poetry. There is a huge

For Williams, such competing world views impact on journalism in the following way:

> There are basically two views about the function of the mass media in society. One puts a commercial value on everything, turning citizens into consumers; children into vulnerable merchandising targets via video games, magazines, film and television; and information into 'infotainment' . . . Such a view assigns the media merely the role of a commodity, to be manufactured and assessed by market criteria . . . Counterpoised to this is a view of the media as a liberating force for human enlightenment and progress, informing, entertaining, nurturing creative talent and being financially and editorially independent from powerful vested commercial or political interests. At the heart of this view is a respect for diversity and pluralism, and a recognition that unchecked media power can undermine democracy. *(Williams 1996: 2–3)*

Reflective practitioner

If journalists are not to absolve themselves of all social responsibilities then they must become reflective practitioners, argues Lynette Sheridan Burns (2002: 11). Journalists should reflect critically on what they do, because 'a journalist who is conscious of and understands the active decisions that make up daily practice is best prepared to negotiate the challenges involved' (Sheridan Burns 2002: 11). That does not mean taking time off and sitting back in leisurely contemplation; rather, it means 'an active commitment in journalists to scrutinise their own actions, exposing the processes and underlying values in their work *while* they are doing it' (Sheridan Burns 2002: 41–4; emphasis in original).

Arguing along similar lines, Pat Aufderheide talks of the need to cultivate 'a more self-aware journalistic culture' (Aufderheide 2002: 14). Writing in the context of US television after the attacks on the World Trade Centre in 2001, Aufderheide argues that journalists need 'time, money and imagination to experiment with the kind of reporting that gives viewers an understanding of large conflicts and issues in the world, before they become the stuff of catastrophe', adding:

pleasure from writing a good, well-researched article, and you really do get a unique window into society through journalism. Journalism informs and educates people about the world beyond their own personal experience. It is a good profession, but it is also one where there is very little financial reward unless you are at the top. Money is the biggest problem for journalists like me, and it is especially hard if you have moved to London and are having to pay rent as well as student loans. It is also very hard to rise in the industry because it is so competitive. In a profession that is impatient, pacy and full of to-the-minute developments, it takes a while to get to a satisfactory position. I have a lot of friends who have become sick of finding that elusive break and want to do other things in life. I am slightly disillusioned by the job and the poor pay, but I haven't lost my enthusiasm.

> '*It's a daily ritual of moral and intellectual compromise – it is a good job, but it is hard.*'
> – Abul Taher.

Some weeks after this interview Abul got his break and left the *Eastern Eye* for the *Daily Mail*.

For a last word, I turned to Paul Foot – the veteran reporter, investigator and columnist – and asked what advice he had for aspiring young journalists in the 21st century. This is what he said:

I think people should join the NUJ and if there isn't a union where they work they should do their best to try and form one. That's the first thing. The other thing is, don't lose your sense of curiosity or your sense of scepticism. Understand the way the industry works and do your best to apply yourself against that. The last thing I mean is young people rushing in and telling their editors how to run the world, that's absolutely fatal. There's nothing worse than the arrogant young person – who knows *everything* – going and telling people what to do. Even if they're right, which often they are, that's not the way to behave. That's the way to get sacked. You've got to keep your head, you've got to bite your lip, and you've got to do what you're told a lot of the time. Nine times out of ten it's better to go ahead and do what you are told, but there's a tenth time when it is worth resisting. The main thing is to keep your sense of independent observation as to what's happening around you, and to

> '*Whatever you see, there's a story behind it.*'
> – Paul Foot

They need ways to bring other voices into their coverage, and to explain the implications and differing readings of US government behaviour. They need a relationship with viewers that permits them to introduce disturbing and conflicting perspectives, to go beyond the two masks of sentimental patriotism and coolly objective fact-vending. *(Aufderheide 2002: 12–13)*

It could be argued that *all* journalism would benefit from such a willingness to report conflicting perspectives, to offer differing readings, and to disturb the assumptions of audiences and journalists alike. In short, by working the other side of the street.

Agency

As introduced in Chapter 1, agency means the extent to which individual journalists can *make a difference*. Many academic theorists and commentators have been criticised for a tendency to downplay the room for agency in the production of journalism; so, for example, the *political economy* model emphasises the determining role played by economic power and material factors in creating media products. In the view of Peter Golding and Philip Elliott: 'News changes very little when the individuals that produce it are changed' (quoted in Curran and Seaton 1997: 277). That may be true when we look at the big picture but does it tell us the whole truth about the work of journalists?

Stuart Hall argues that the media have 'relative autonomy from ruling class power in the narrow sense', within certain ideological limits (Hall 1977: 345–6). But his emphasis is on the 'relative', because he argues that journalism *tends* to reproduce society's prevailing ideology. This is not because of the 'conscious intentions and biases' of individual journalists, but as 'a function of the discourse and of the logic of social processes', including sourcing strategies that privilege the powerful (Hall 1982: 88). For John O'Neill, however, individual journalists retain the power to resist the demands of the market, even if only

try to use what ability you have to get those things into print. Whatever you see, there's a story behind it. There is a truth and there's no doubt there are facts. Facts are facts, you can't bend them.

As good a note as any on which to conclude a book on the principles and practice of journalism. Over to you.

by resigning from their jobs. He argues that the relationship between journalistic 'virtues and vices' can be more fluid than is portrayed in the depiction of journalists as either heroes or villains:

> Many, I suspect, find themselves forced to compromise the constitutive values of journalism, while at the same time insisting that some of the standards be enforced . . . Journalists, like other workers, are not totally passive in their attitude to their own faculties. *(O'Neill 1992: 28)*

Put another way, agency may be limited by economic and social structures, but it exists. Journalists work in a field that is (ostensibly) constituted by a professional commitment to ethics and truth telling, yet at the same time journalists may be expendable employees expected to produce stories to sell in the marketplace (Harcup 2002b: 103; O'Neill 1992: 27–8). Discussion of agency needs to take account of the tension between journalists' different identities as individual professionals, as socially responsible citizens, as factors of production at the whim of management, and as workers with, potentially at least, a sense of collective identity (Harcup 2002b: 101–14). If journalism matters, then the actions of journalists matter too.

Summary

The social role of journalism in informing citizens, and the impact of journalism on people's lives, means that journalists have an ethical responsibility to engage in a process of critical reflection on their practice. Despite the structural forces and constraints that bear down on journalists, individuals and groups of journalists retain elements of choice in their work. Recruits to journalism are advised to learn everything they can from more experienced journalists without ever losing their own sense of curiosity and independent observation.

Questions

Who is journalism for?

What is journalism for?

Where is journalism practised?

When is journalism challenging?

Why are journalists not trusted?

How might journalism change?

Further reading

For historical context behind the practice of journalism, Curran and Seaton (2003) and McChesney (2000) offer informative and critical perspectives from the UK and US respectively. Sheridan Burns (2002) and Randall (2000) are good places to start for critical reflection on journalism, while Sanders (2003) Keeble (2001b) and Frost (2000) discuss many ethical issues facing journalists. For discussion of contemporary communication theories, try Stevenson (2002) in addition to McQuail (2000). Relevant academic research is published in the peer-reviewed journals *Journalism Studies* (Routledge) and *Journalism: Theory, Practice and Criticism* (Sage), while many discussion articles by practitioners can be found in *British Journalism Review* (Sage), *The Journalist's Handbook* (Carrick Media) and *Press Gazette* (Quantum Business Media). *Free Press*, journal of the Campaign for Press and Broadcasting Freedom, publishes thought-provoking and critical material on the media in general and journalism in particular, while the views of the National Union of Journalists can be found in the union magazine *Journalist*. Information and advice on journalism training and careers is also available from the NUJ (2003). Contact details on media companies, training courses, and much more can be found in Peak (2002), updated annually. Foot (2000), Wheen (2002), and Palast (2002) all demonstrate what can be achieved with a combination of journalistic flair, a questioning attitude, and a cantankerous insistence on getting at 'the facts'. You will find some relevant websites listed in Appendix Two. Finally, don't forget to read the papers – every day.

Bibliography

ABC (2002) 'National newspaper circulation', Audit Bureau of Circulations monthly report, August 2002, http://www.abc.org.uk/cgi-bin/gen5?runprog=nav/abc&noc=y.

ACPO (2001) *Guide to Meeting the Policing Needs of Asylum Seekers and Refugees*. London: Association of Chief Police Officers.

Adams, Catherine (2001a) 'Inside story', *Guardian*, 13 March 2001.

Adams, Sally (2001b), with Wynford Hicks, *Interviewing for Journalists*. London: Routledge.

Adams, Sally (1999) 'Writing features' in Wynford Hicks (1999) with Sally Adams and Harriett Gilbert, *Writing for Journalists*. London: Routledge, pp. 47–98.

Addicott, Ruth (2002) 'Magazines warned not to ignore financial watchdog', *Press Gazette*, 17 May 2002.

Aitchison, James (1988) *Writing for the Press*. London: Hutchinson.

Akbar, Arifa (2001) 'TV watchdog criticises ITN for footage of World Trade Centre set to music', *Independent*, 12 November 2001.

Allan, Stuart (1998) '(En)gendering the truth politics of news discourse', in Cynthia Carter, Gill Branston, and Stuart Allan (eds) (1998) *News, Gender and Power*. London: Routledge, pp. 121–37.

Allan, Stuart (1997) 'News and the public sphere: towards a history of objectivity and impartiality', in Michael Bromley and Tom O'Malley (eds) (1997) *A Journalism Reader*. London: Routledge, pp. 296–329.

Ananova (2002) 'Chinese paper apologises for printing satirical story as fact', www.ananova.com, 13 June 2002.

Arlidge, John and Cole, Sandra (2001) 'Jon Snow slams ITV's "crazy" cut in news budget', *Observer*, 2 December 2001.

Arlidge, John (1999) 'Nuts and sluts in TV fakery', *Observer*, 14 February 1999.

Armitstead, Claire (2002) 'Write the same thing over and over', *Guardian*, 31 January 2002.

Atton, Chris (2002) *Alternative Media*. London: Sage.

Aufderheide, Pat (2002) 'All-too-reality TV: challenges for television journalists after September 11', *Journalism: Theory, Practice and Criticism* Vol 3, No 1, pp. 7–14.

Austin, Tim (2003) *The Times Style and Usage Guide*. London: Times Books.

Bailey, Sally and Williams, Granville (1997) 'Memoirs are made of this: journalists' memoirs in the United Kingdom, 1945–95', in Michael Bromley and Tom O'Malley (eds) (1997) *A Journalism Reader*. London: Routledge, pp. 351–77.

Bakhtin, Mikhail (1935) 'The Dialogic Imagination', extract printed in Pam Morris (ed) (1994) *The Bakhtin Reader: Selected writings of Bakhtin, Medvedev and Voloshinov*. London: Edward Arnold, pp. 74–80.

Barber, Lynn (1999) 'The art of the interview', in Stephen Glover (ed) (1999) *The Penguin Book of Journalism*. London; Penguin, pp. 196–205.

Barnett, Steven and Seymour, Emily (2000): *From Callaghan to Kosovo: Changing trends in British television news 1975–1999*. London: University of Westminster.

Barrett, Michele, Corrigan, Philip, Kuhn, Annette, and Wolff, Janet (eds) (1979) *Ideology and Cultural Production*. London: Croom Helm.

BBC (2002) *The Message*, BBC Radio Four, 15 February 2002.

BBC (1999) 'UK politics: Old Bailey hearing for Aitken', http://news.bbc.co.uk/hi/english/uk_politics/newsid_257000/257826.stm, 19 January 1999.

Beaman, Jim (2000) *Interviewing for Radio*. London: Routledge.

Beaumont, Peter (2001) 'Straw hits out at Mugabe over threats to foreign reporters', *Observer*, 25 November 2001.

Beckett, Andy (2001) 'Mail order', *Guardian*, 22 February 2001.

Behr, Edward (1992) *Anyone Here Been Raped and Speaks English?* London: Penguin.

Bell, Allan (1991) *The Language of News Media*. Oxford: Blackwell.

Bell, Martin (2002) 'Glamour is not good news', *Independent*, 19 February 2002.

Bell, Martin (1998) 'The Journalism of Attachment', in Matthew Kieran (ed) (1998) *Media Ethics*. London: Routledge, pp. 15–22.

Belsey, Andrew (1998) 'Journalism and Ethics: can they co-exist?', in Matthew Kieran (ed) (1998) *Media Ethics*. London: Routledge, pp. 1–14.

Belsey, Andrew and Chadwick, Ruth (eds) (1992) *Ethical Issues in Journalism and the Media*. London: Routledge.

Bennett, Catherine (2001) 'The waste of space that is Lord Wakeham', *Guardian*, 5 July 2001.

BJR (2002) 'Quotes of the Quarter' in *British Journalism Review* Vol 13, No 2, 2002.

BJTC (1996) *Recognition for Broadcast Journalism Courses*. London: Broadcast Journalism Training Council.

Blumler, Jay (1999) 'Political communication systems all change: a response to Kees Brants', *European Journal of Communication* Vol 14, No 2, pp. 241–49.

Bonnington, Alistair J, McInnes, Rosalind, and McKain, Bruce (2000) *Scots Law for Journalists*. Sweet and Maxwell.

Boorstin, Daniel (1963) *The Image: Or what happened to the American Dream*. Harmondsworth: Pelican.

Bourdieu, Pierre (1998) *On Television and Journalism*. London: Pluto.

Boyd, Andrew (2001) *Broadcast Journalism: techniques of radio and television news*. Oxford: Focal.

Boyer, JH (1981) 'How editors view objectivity', *American Journalism Quarterly* No. 58, 1981, cited in James Watson (1998) *Media Communication: An introduction to theory and process*. Hampshire: MacMillan, p. 98.

Brants, Kees (1999) 'A rejoinder to Jay G Blumler', *European Journal of Communication* Vol 14, No 3, pp. 411–15.

Brants, Kees (1998) 'Who's afraid of infotainment?', *European Journal of Communication* Vol 13, No 3, pp. 315–35.

Brennen, Bonnie (2003) 'Sweat not melodrama: reading the structure of feeling in "All the President's Men"', *Journalism: Theory, Practice and Criticism* Vol 4, No 1, pp. 113-31.

Briggs, Asa and Burke, Peter (2002) *A Social History of the Media: From Gutenberg to the internet*. Cambridge: Polity.

Bright, Martin (2000) 'I'm handing nothing over', *Journalist*, May/June 2000, p. 11.

Brockes, Emma (2002) 'I'm a hack not a celebrity', *Guardian*, 4 November 2002.

Bromley, Michael (ed) (2001) *No News is Bad News: Radio, television and the public*. Harlow: Longman.

Bromley, Michael (1997) 'The end of journalism? Changes in workplace practices in the press and broadcasting in the 1990s', in Michael Bromley and Tom O'Malley (eds) (1997) *A Journalism Reader*. London: Routledge, pp. 330–50.

Bromley, Michael and Cushion, Stephen (2002) 'Media Fundamentalism: the immediate response of the UK national press to September 11', in Barbie Zelizer and Stuart Allan (eds) (2002) *Journalism After September 11*. London: Routledge, pp. 160–77.

Bromley, Michael and O'Malley, Tom (eds) (1997) *A Journalism Reader*. London: Routledge.

Bromley, Michael and Stephenson, Hugh (eds) (1998) *Sex, Lies and Democracy: The press and the public*. Harlow: Longman.

Brown, Andrew (2000) 'Newspapers and the internet', in Stephen Glover (ed) (2000) *The Penguin Book of Journalism*. London: Penguin, pp. 177–85.

Burchill, Julie (2003) 'Don't mess with the press', *Guardian*, 11 January 2003.

Calhoun, Craig (ed) (1992) *Habermas and the Public Sphere*. London: MIT Press.

Cameron, Deborah (1996) 'Style policy and style politics: a neglected aspect of the language of the news', *Media, Culture & Society* Vol 18, pp. 315–33.

Carroll, Rory (2002) 'Yes, prime minister', *Guardian*, 1 April 2002.

Carter, Cynthia, Branston, Gill and Allan, Stuart (eds) (1998) *News, Gender and Power*. London: Routledge.

Castells, Manuel (1998) *End of Millennium: Volume 3 of The Information Age: Economy, society and culture*. Oxford: Blackwell.

Castells, Manuel (1997) *The Power of Identity: Volume 2 of The Information Age: Economy, society and culture*. Oxford: Blackwell.

Castells, Manuel (1996) *The Rise of the Network Society: Volume 1 of The Information Age: Economy, society and culture*. Oxford: Blackwell.

Chambers, Deborah (2000) 'Critical approaches to the media: the changing context for investigative journalism', in Hugo de Burgh (ed) (2000) *Investigative Journalism: Context and practice*. London: Routledge, pp. 89–107.

Chandler, Raymond (1984) *Raymond Chandler Speaking*. London: Alison and Busby.

Channel 4 (1998) *The Real Rupert Murdoch*, broadcast 21 November 1998.

Chantler, Paul and Harris, Sim (1997) *Local Radio Journalism*. Oxford: Focal.

Chesterton, GK (1981) 'The Wisdom of Father Brown: the purple wig', in *The Penguin Complete Father Brown*. Harmondsworth: Penguin, pp. 244–55.

Chippindale, Peter and Horrie, Chris (1992) *Stick It Up Your Punter! The rise and fall of the Sun*. London: Mandarin.

Clement, Barrie and Grice, David (2001) 'Secret ministry email: "Use attack to bury bad news"', *Independent*, 9 October 2001.

Cohen, Nick (2002) 'The hero they tried to muzzle', *New Statesman*, 11 February 2002, pp11–14.

Cohen, Stanley (1972) *Folk Devils and Moral Panics: The creation of the Mods and Rockers*. London: MacGibbon and Kee.

Cohen, Stanley and Young, Jock (eds) (1973): *The Manufacture of News: Deviance, social problems and the mass media*. London: Constable.

Colston, Jane (2002), 'Reporting restrictions', in Tom Crone (2002) *Law and the Media*. Oxford: Focal, pp. 133–65.

Conboy, Martin (2002) *The Press and Popular Culture*. London: Sage.

Cottle, Simon (2001) 'Television news and citizenship: packaging the public sphere', in Michael Bromley (ed) (2001) *No News is Bad News: Radio, television and the public*. Harlow: Longman, pp. 61–79.

Cottle, Simon (2000) 'Rethinking news access', *Journalism Studies* Vol 1, No 3, pp. 427–48.

Covell, Mark (2001) 'Genoa: summit of rage', *Journalist*, September 2001, pp. 22–24.

Critcher, Chas (2002) 'Media, government and moral panic: the politics of paedophilia in Britain 2000–1', *Journalism Studies* Vol 3, No 4, pp. 521–35.

Crone, Tom (2002) *Law and the Media*. Oxford: Focal.

Curran, James (2000) 'Press reformism 1918–98: a study of failure', in Howard Tumber (ed) (2000) *Media Power, Professionals and Policies*. London: Routledge, pp. 35–55.

Curran, James (1990) 'Culturalist perspectives of news organisations: a reappraisal and a case study', in Marjorie Ferguson (ed) (1990) *Public Communication the New Imperatives: Future directions for media research*. London: Sage, pp. 114–34.

Curran, James and Gurevitch, Michael (eds) (1991) *Mass Media and Society*. London: Edward Arnold.

Curran, James and Seaton, Jean (2003) *Power Without Responsibility: the press, broadcasting and new media in Britain*. 6th edition. London: Routledge.

Curran, James and Seaton, Jean (1997) *Power Without Responsibility: The press and broadcasting in Britain*. London: Routledge.

Curran, James, Ecclestone, Jake, Oakley, Giles, and Richardson, Alan (eds) (1986) *Bending Reality: The state of the media*. London: Pluto.

Curran, James, Gurevitch, Michael and Woollacott, Janet (eds) (1977) *Mass Communication and Society*. London: Edward Arnold.

Dahlgren, Peter and Sparks, Colin (eds) (1992) *Journalism and Popular Culture*. London: Sage.

Daily Express (2001) 'For decades the Daily Mail has piously preached about patriotism and family values but what is the truth about the aristocrats behind it?', *Daily Express*, 21 February 2001.

Daniel, Isioma (2003) 'I lit the match', *Guardian*, 17 February 2003.

D'Arcy, Mark (2000) 'Local power and public accountability: an example from the East Midlands', in Hugo de Burgh (ed) (2000) *Investigative Journalism: Context and practice*. London: Routledge, pp. 213–30.

Day, Julia (2001) 'Hellier condemns Express "interference"', www.mediaguardian.co.uk, 6 September 2001.

de Burgh, Hugo (ed) (2000) *Investigative Journalism: Context and practice*. London: Routledge.

Deuze, Mark and Dimoudi, Christina (2002) 'Online journalists in the Netherlands: towards a profile of a new profession', *Journalism: Theory, Practice and Criticism* Vol 3, No 1, pp. 85–100.

Diamond, John (2001) *Snake Oil And Other Preoccupations*. London: Vintage.

Dixon, Sara (2002) 'The gentle touch', *Press Gazette*, 5 April 2002.

Dodson, Sean (2001) 'Hacks hit in drugs war', *Guardian*, 25 June 2001.

Doig, Alan (1997) 'The decline of investigatory journalism' in Michael Bromley and Tom O'Malley (eds) (1997) *A Journalism Reader*. London: Routledge, pp. 189–213.

Dorril, Stephen (2002a) 'Secrets and lies', *Free Press* No 127, March/April 2002, p. 1.

Dorril, Stephen (2002b) 'Suspicious incidents', *Free Press* No 126, January/February 2002, p. 2.

Dorril, Stephen (2000) 'What is investigative journalism?', *Free Press* No 116, May/June 2000, p. 6.

Dovey, Jon (2000) *Freakshow: First person media and factual television*. London: Pluto.

Downing, John (2001), with Tamara Villarreal Ford, Geneve Gil and Laura Stein, *Radical Media: Rebellious communication and social movements*. London: Sage.

Doyle, Gillian (2002) *Understanding Media Economics*. London: Sage.

DTLR (2001) *News Release 388: Consultation begins on council allowances*. London: Department for Transport, Local Government and the Regions. September 11 2001.

Economist (2000) *Style Guide*. London: Profile Books.

Engel, Matthew (2002) 'American media cowed by patriotic fever, says network news veteran', *Guardian*, 17 May 2002.

Engel, Matthew (1997) *Tickle the Public: One hundred years of the popular press*. London: Indigo.

Evans, Harold (2000) *Essential English for Journalists, Editors and Writers*. London: Pimlico.

Ferguson, Marjorie (ed) (1990) *Public Communication the New Imperatives: Future directions for media research*. London: Sage.

Fiske, John (1989) *Reading the Popular*. London: Routledge.

Fleming, Carole (2002) *The Radio Handbook*. London: Routledge.

Flett, Kathryn (2001) 'Something of Severus Snape about him . . . ', www.politics.guardian.co.uk, 31 May 2001.

Foley, Michael (2000) 'Press regulation', *Administration* Vol 48, No 1, Spring 2000, pp. 40–51.

Foot, Paul (2000) *Articles of Resistance*. London: Bookmarks.

Foot, Paul (1999) 'The slow death of investigative journalism' in Stephen Glover (ed) (1999) *The Penguin Book of Journalism: Secrets of the press*. London: Penguin, pp. 79–89.

Forde, Eamonn (2001) 'From polyglottism to branding: on the decline of personality journalism in the British music press', *Journalism: Theory, Practice and Criticism* Vol 2, No 1, pp. 23–43.

Fowler, HW (1983) *A Dictionary of Modern English Usage*. Oxford: Oxford University Press.

Fowler, Roger (1991) *Language in the News: Discourse and ideology in the press*. London: Routledge

Franceskides, Rebecca (2002) *Portraying Difference in the Media and Expanding your Market: A training manual*. IRIS asbl www.iris-asbl.org/outlook.

Franklin, Bob (1997) *Newszak and News Media*. London: Arnold.

Franklin, Bob (1994) *Packaging politics: Political communications in Britain's media democracy*. London: Edward Arnold.

Franklin, Bob and Murphy, David (eds) (1998) *Making the Local News: Local journalism in context*. London: Routledge.

Frayn, Michael (1995) *The Tin Men*. London: Penguin. (First published 1965.)

Frost, Chris (2002) *Reporting for Journalists*. London: Routledge.

Frost, Chris (2000) *Media Ethics and Self-Regulation*. Harlow: Longman.

Galtung, Johan and Ruge, Mari (1965) 'The structure of foreign news: the presentation of the Congo, Cuba and Cyprus crises in four Norwegian newspapers', *Journal of International Peace Research* 1 (1965), pp. 64–91.

Gans, Herbert J (1980) *Deciding What's News: A study of CBS evening news, NBC nightly news, Newsweek and Time*. London: Constable.

Gibson, Owen (2001) 'The truth about that CNN email', *Guardian*, 24 September 2001.

Gieber, Walter (1964) 'News is what newspapermen make it', in Howard Tumber (ed) (1999) *News: A reader*. Oxford: Oxford University Press, pp. 218–23.

Gilbert, Harriett (1999) 'Writing reviews', in Wynford Hicks (1999) with Sally Adams and Harriett Gilbert *Writing for Journalists*. London: Routledge, pp. 99–123.

Glover, Mike (1998) 'Looking at the world through the eyes of . . . :reporting the "local" in daily, weekly and Sunday local newspapers', in Bob Franklin and David Murphy (eds) (1998) *Making the Local News: Local journalism in context*. London: Routledge, pp. 117–24.

Glover, Stephen (1999) 'What columnists are good for', in Stephen Glover (ed) (1999) *The Penguin Book of Journalism: Secrets of the press*. London: Penguin, pp. 289–98.

Glover, Stephen (ed) (1999) *The Penguin Book of Journalism: Secrets of the press*. London: Penguin.

Golding, Peter, and Murdock, Graham (1979) 'Ideology and the mass media: the question of determination', in Michele Barrett, Philip Corrigan, Annette Kuhn, and Janet Wolff (eds) (1979) *Ideology and Cultural Production*. London: Croom Helm, pp. 198–224.

Goodhart, David (1999) 'Dumb and dumber', *Guardian*, 19 February 1999.

Goodwin, Bill (1996) 'Safe sources', *Journalist*, April/May 1996, p. 21.

Gopsill, Tim (2001) 'The wages of spin', *Journalist*, April 2001, pp. 16–17.

Gramsci, Antonio (1971) *Selections from the Prison Notebooks*. London: Lawrence and Wishart.

Gransby, Aaron (2002) 'Biggest? Yes. Best? No way', *Press Gazette*, 15 November 2002.

Greenslade, Roy (2003) 'Their master's voice', *Guardian*, 17 February 2003.

Greenslade, Roy (2001) 'The feud', *Guardian*, 26 February 2001.

Grundberg, Peter (2002) 'The "new" right to privacy', in Tom Crone (2002) *Law and the Media*. Oxford: Focal, pp. 114–30.

Gurevitch, Michael, Bennett, Tony, Curran, James, and Woollacott, Janet (eds) (1982) *Culture, Society and the Media*. London: Methuen.

Habermas, Jurgen (1992) 'Further reflections on the public sphere', in Craig Calhoun (ed) (1992) *Habermas and the Public Sphere*. London: MIT Press, pp. 421–61.

Habermas, Jurgen (1989) *The Structural Transformation of the Public Sphere: An inquiry into a category of bourgeois society*. Cambridge: Polity.

Hale, Don (2002) *Town Without Pity*. London: Century.

Hall, Jim (2001) *Online Journalism: A critical primer*. London: Pluto.

Hall, Sarah (2002) 'Paper fined for Leeds case error', *Guardian*, 20 April 2002.

Hall, Stuart (1986) 'Media power and class power', in James Curran, Jake Ecclestone, Giles Oakley, and Alan Richardson (eds) (1986) *Bending Reality: The state of the media*. London: Pluto, pp. 5–14.

Hall, Stuart (1982) 'The rediscovery of "ideology": return of the repressed in media studies', in Michael Gurevitch, Tony Bennett, James Curran, and Janet Woollacott (eds) (1982) *Culture, Society and the Media*. London: Methuen, pp. 56–90.

Hall, Stuart (1977) 'Culture, the media and the "ideological effect"', in James Curran, Michael Gurevitch, and Janet Woollacott (eds) (1977) *Mass Communication and Society*. London: Edward Arnold, pp. 315–48.

Hall, Stuart (1973) 'The determinations of news photographs', in Stanley Cohen and Jock Young (eds) (1973): *The Manufacture of News: Deviance, social problems and the mass media*. London: Constable, pp. 176–90.

Hall, Stuart, Critcher, Chas, Jefferson, Tony, Clarke, John, and Roberts, Brian (1978) *Policing the Crisis*. London: Macmillan.

Hanna, Mark (2000) *British Investigative Journalism: Protecting the continuity of talent through changing times*. Paper presented to the International Association for Media and Communication Research, Singapore, 18 July 2000.

Harcup, Tony (2003) 'The unspoken – said. The journalism of alternative media', *Journalism: Theory, Practice and Criticism* Vol 4 No 3, pp. 356–76.

Harcup, Tony (2002a) 'Conduct unbecoming?', *Press Gazette*, 1 March 2002.

Harcup, Tony (2002b) 'Journalists and ethics: the quest for a collective voice', *Journalism Studies* Vol 3, No 1, pp. 101–14.

Harcup, Tony (2001) *Style Guide for Journalism*. Leeds: Centre for Journalism, Trinity and All Saints.

Harcup, Tony (1998) 'There is no alternative: the demise of the alternative local newspaper', in Bob Franklin and David Murphy (eds) (1998) *Making the Local News: Local journalism in context*. London: Routledge, pp. 105–16.

Harcup, Tony (1996) 'More news means worse news, conference on media ethics told', *Broadcast*, 27 September 1996.

Harcup, Tony (1994) *A Northern Star: Leeds Other Paper and the alternative press 1974–1994*. London and Pontefract: Campaign for Press and Broadcasting Freedom.

Harcup, Tony and O'Neill, Deirdre (2001) 'What is news? Galtung and Ruge revisited', *Journalism Studies* Vol 2, No 2, pp. 261–80.

Hardt, Hanno (2000) 'Conflicts of Interest: newsworkers, media, and patronage journalism' in Howard Tumber (ed) (2000) *Media Power, Professionals and Policies*. London: Routledge, pp. 209–24.

Harris, Geoffrey and Spark, David (1997) *Practical Newspaper Reporting*. Oxford: Focal.

Harrison, Jackie (2000) *Terrestrial TV News in Britain: The culture of production*. Manchester: Manchester University Press.

Hartley, John (1982) *Understanding News*. London: Methuen.

Hecht, Ben and MacArthur, Charles (1974) *The Front Page*. A U-I film.

Helmore, Ed (2001) 'Meet the enforcer', *Observer*, 3 June 2001.

Hencke, David (2001) 'No news is bad news', *Guardian*, 5 March 2001.

Hencke, David and Evans, Rob (1999) 'Byers' adviser quits after TV expose', *Guardian*, 21 October 1999.

Herman, Edward (2000) 'The propaganda model: a retrospective', *Journalism Studies* Vol 1, No 1, pp. 101–12.

Herman, Edward and Chomsky, Noam (1988) 'Manufacturing consent', in Howard Tumber (ed) (1999) *News: A reader*. Oxford: Oxford University Press, pp. 166–79.

Hetherington, Alastair (1985) *News, Newspapers and Television*. London: Macmillan.

Hicks, Wynford (1999), with Sally Adams and Harriett Gilbert, *Writing for Journalists*. London: Routledge.

Hicks, Wynford (1998) *English for Journalists*. London: Routledge.

Hicks, Wynford and Holmes, Tim (2002) *Subediting for Journalists*. London: Routledge.

Hinsliff, Gaby, Bright, Martin, Beaumont, Peter, and Vuliamy, Ed (2003) 'First casualties in the propaganda firefight', *Observer*, 9 February 2003.

Hodge, Robert and Kress, Gunther (1993) *Language as Ideology*. London: Routledge.

Hodgson, F W (1993) *Subediting: A handbook of modern newspaper editing and production*. Oxford: Focal Press.

Hodgson, Jessica (2001) 'Why Wombles won't speak to journalists', *Guardian*, 7 May 2001.

Hold The Front Page (2002) 'Paper stripped from shelves after sex depot splash', www.holdthefrontpage.co.uk, 18 May 2002.

Holland, Patricia (2000) *The Television Handbook*. London: Routledge.

Holland, Patricia (1998) 'The politics of the smile: "soft news" and the sexualisation of the popular press', in Cynthia Carter, Gill Branston and Stuart Allan (eds) (1998) *News, Gender and Power*. London: Routledge, pp. 17–32.

Hollingsworth, Mark (1986) *The Press and Political Dissent: A question of censorship*. London: Pluto.

IFJ (2003a) *Media Victims of the War in Iraq*, International Federation of Journalists, www.ifj.org.

IFJ (2003b) *Journalists and Media Staff Killed in 2002*, International Federation of Journalists, www.ifj.org.

IFJ (2003c) *After 1,100 killings in ten years and heavy toll in Iraq: launch of International News Safety Institute*, International Federation of Journalists, 2 May 2003, www.ifj.org.

IFJ (2002) *Journalists and Media Staff Killed in 2001*. International Federation of Journalists www.ifj.org.

Isaacs, Dan (2002) 'Fatwa issued on Miss World journalist', *Daily Telegraph* 27 November 2002.

Johnston, Don (2002) 'He wouldn't last long on my desk', letter in the *Journalist* December 2002, p. 6.

Journalism Training Forum (2002) *Journalists at Work: Their views on training, recruitment and conditions*. London: Publishing National Training Organisation/Skillset.

Journalist (2002) 'Another triumph for low-paid as Guardian group gives in', *Journalist*, June/July 2002.

Karim, Karim (2002) 'Making sense of the "Islamic Peril": journalism as cultural practice', in Barbie Zelizer and Stuart Allan (eds) (2002) *Journalism After September 11*. London: Routledge, pp. 101–16.

Keeble, Richard (2001a) *The Newspapers Handbook*, third edition. London: Routledge.

Keeble, Richard (2001b) *Ethics for Journalists*. London: Routledge.

Keeble, Richard (1998) *The Newspapers Handbook*, second edition. London: Routledge.

Kelso, Paul (2001) 'We have known about this for 15 years. The media should have exposed this man a long time ago', *Guardian*, 23 July 2001.

Kieran, Matthew (ed) (1998) *Media Ethics*. London: Routledge.

Kiley, Sam (2001) 'The Middle East's war of words', *Evening Standard*, 5 September 2001.

Knightley, Phillip (2002) 'The creation of public enemy No 1', *Evening Standard*, 11 September 2002.

Knightley, Phillip (2001) 'The disinformation campaign', *Guardian*, 4 October 2001.

Knightley, Phillip (2000) *The First Casualty: The war correspondent as hero and myth-maker from the Crimea to Kosovo*. London: Prion.

Knightley, Phillip (1998) *A Hack's Progress*. London: Vintage.

Krajicek, David J (1998) 'The bad, the ugly and the worse', *Guardian*, 11 May 1998.

Kuhn, Raymond (2002) 'The first Blair government and political journalism', in Raymond Kuhn and Erik Neveu (eds) (2002) *Political Journalism: new challenges, new practices*. London: Routledge, pp. 47-68.

Larsson, Larsake (2002) 'Journalists and politicians: a relationship requiring manoeuvring space', *Journalism Studies* Vol 3, No 1, pp. 21–33.

Lipton, Eric (2002) 'Death toll is near 3,000, but some uncertainty over count remains', *New York Times*, 11 September 2002.

Lipton, Eric (2001) 'Toll from attack at Trade Center is down sharply', *New York Times*, 21 November 2001.

Lord, Robert and Morgan, Byron (1931) *Five Star Final*. A Warner Brothers film.

Ludlam, Joanna (2002) 'Breach of confidence', in Tom Crone (2002) *Law and the Media*. Oxford: Focal, pp. 89–103.

Lule, Jack (2001) *Daily News, Eternal Stories: The mythological role of journalism*. New York: Guilford Press.

Lynch, Jake (2002) 'Reporting the world: How ethical journalism can seek solutions', www.mediachannel.org, 23 January 2002.

Manning, Paul (2001) *News and News Sources: A critical introduction*. London: Sage.

Mansfield, FJ (1943) *Gentlemen, the Press! Chronicles of a Crusade: official history of the National Union of Journalists*. London: WH Allen.

Mansfield, FJ (1936) *The Complete Journalist: A study of the principles and practice of newspaper-making*. London: Sir Isaac Pitman and Sons.

Marsh, David and Marshall, Nikki (eds) (2002) *The Guardian Style Guide* available at www.guardian.co.uk/styleguide, updated September 2002.

Marx, Karl and Engels, Friedrich (1965) *The German Ideology*. London: Lawrence and Wishart.

Mayes, Ian (2001a) 'News travels', *Guardian*, 22 September 2001.

Mayes, Ian (2001b) 'City limits', *Guardian*, 30 June 2001.

Mayes, Ian (2000) *The Guardian Corrections and Clarifications*. London: Guardian Newspapers.

McCafferty, Nell (1984) *The Best of Nell: A selection of writings over fourteen years*. Dublin: Attic Press.

McCafferty, Nell (1981) *In the Eyes of the Law*. Dublin: Ward River Press.

McChesney, Robert (2002) 'The US news media and World War III', *Journalism: Theory, Practice and Criticism*, Vol 3, No 1, pp. 14–21.

McChesney, Robert (2000) *Rich Media, Poor Democracy: Communication politics in dubious times*. New York: New Press.

McCombs, Maxwell and Shaw, Donald (1972) 'The agenda setting function of mass media', in Howard Tumber (ed) (1999) *News: A reader*. Oxford: Oxford University Press, pp. 320–28.

McKay, Peter (1999) 'Gossip', in Stephen Glover (ed) (1999) *The Penguin Book on Journalism: Secrets of the press*. London: Penguin, pp. 186–95.

McLaughlin, Greg (2002a) 'Rules of engagement: television journalism and NATO's "faith in bombing" during the Kosovo crisis, 1999', *Journalism Studies* Vol 3, No 2, pp. 257–66.

McLaughlin, Greg (2002b) *The War Correspondent*. London: Pluto.

McNair, Brian (2000) *Journalism and Democracy: An evaluation of the political public sphere*. London: Routledge.

McQuail, Denis (2000) *McQuail's Mass Communication Theory*. London: Sage.

McQuail, Denis (1992) *Media Performance: Mass communication and the public interest*. London: Sage.

Media Lawyer (2002) '*S Mirror* fined £75,000 for interview', *Media Lawyer* No 39, May/June 2002, pp. 18–19.

Media-Watch (2001) 'Re: Palestinians celebrating?', email by Marcio, Brazil, circulated on *Media-Watch* discussion list, 18 September 2001.

Millar, Stuart (2001) 'Robot reporter "to write news in future"', *Guardian*, 9 August 2001.

Mirsky, Jonathan (2001) 'In bed with the Reds', *Spectator*, 10 November 2001.

Morgan, Jean (2002a) '"Lack of humanity" over Soham led to Herald sacking', *Press Gazette*, 6 September 2002.

Morgan, Jean (2002b) 'Never ever sign copy deals, says freelance in singer row', *Press Gazette*, 22 March 2002.

Morgan, Jean (1999) 'Reporter who refused death-knock loses job fight', *Press Gazette*, 17 December 1999, p. 4.

Morris, Pam (ed) (1994) *The Bakhtin Reader: Selected writings of Bakhtin, Medvedev and Voloshinov*. London: Edward Arnold.

NCTJ (2002) *Syllabus in Newspaper Journalism: Writing*. Harlow: National Council for the Training of Journalists.

Neveu, Erik (2002) 'The local press and farmers' protests in Brittany: proximity and distance in the local newspaper coverage of a social movement', *Journalism Studies* Vol 3, No 1, pp. 53–67.

Northmore, David 'Investigative reporting: why and how', in Richard Keeble (2001) *The Newspapers Handbook*. London: Routledge, pp. 183–93.

Norton-Taylor, Richard (2000) Bombing in Iraq an 'undeclared war' *Guardian*, 11 November 2000.

NUJ (2003) *Careers in Journalism*. London: National Union of Journalists.

NUJ (2002) *Definition of the Public Interest*, Ethics Council. National Union of Journalists Circular No 55, February 2002.

Observer (2002) 'Talking about my generation', *Observer*, 21 July 2002.

O'Malley, Tom (2002) 'A safety net for proprietors . . . The Press Complaints Commission 1991–2001', *Free Press* No 127, March-April 2002, p. 6.

O'Malley, Tom (1997) 'Labour and the 1947–9 Royal Commission on the Press' in Michael Bromley and Tom O'Malley (eds) (1997) *A Journalism Reader*. London: Routledge, pp. 126–158.

O'Malley, Tom and Soley, Clive (2000) *Regulating the Press*. London: Pluto.

O'Neill, Gilda (2000) *My East End*. London: Penguin.

O'Neill, John (1992) 'Journalism in the Market Place', in Andrew Belsey and Ruth Chadwick (eds) (1992) *Ethical Issues in Journalism and the Media*. London: Routledge, pp. 15–32.

Orwell, George (1946a) 'Decline of the English murder', in George Orwell (1965) *Decline of the English Murder and Other Essays*. Harmondsworth: Penguin, pp. 9–13.

Orwell, George (1946b) 'Politics and the English language', in George Orwell (1962) *Inside the Whale and Other Essays*. Harmondsworth: Penguin, pp. 143–57.

O'Sullivan, Kevin (2001) 'Kate Winslet disappears up her a***', *Daily Mirror*, 27 November 2001.

O'Sullivan, Tim, Dutton, Brian and Rayner, Philip (eds) (1998) *Studying the Media*. London: Arnold.

Palast, Greg (2002) *The Best Democracy Money Can Buy: An investigative reporter exposes the truth about golobalisation, corporate cons, and high finance fraudsters*. London: Pluto.

Panorama (2002) *A Licence to Murder*, BBC, June 2002, http://news.bbc.co.uk/1/hi/programmes/panorama/2019301.stm.

PCC (2003) '2002: statistics and review of the year', www.pcc.org.uk/statistics_review.html.

PCC (2002a) '2001 annual review', www.pcc.org.uk/2001/index.html, 20 June 2002.

PCC (2002b) 'Morley Advertiser', *Report No 58/59*, Press Complaints Commission, April-September 2002, p. 24.

PCC (1992) 'Editorial', *Report No 7*, Press Complaints Commission, March 1992, pp. 2–3.

Peak, Steve (ed) (2002) *The Guardian Media Guide 2003*. London: Atlantic Books.

Perkins, Anne (2001) 'Hands up who fell off the career ladder as they hit motherhood', *Guardian*, 31 May 2001.

Peterson, Sophia (1981) 'International news selection by the elite press: a case study', *Public Opinion Quarterly* Vol 45, No 2, pp. 143–63.

Peterson, Sophia (1979) 'Foreign news gatekeepers and criteria of newsworthiness' *Journalism Quarterly* 56, pp. 116–25.

Pew Research Centre (2000) 'Self censorship: how often and why. A survey of journalists in association with Columbia Journalism Review', www.people-press.org/jour00rpt.htm.

Philo, Greg (2002) 'Television news and audience understanding of war, conflict and disaster', *Journalism Studies* Vol 3, No 2, pp. 173–86.

Philo, Greg (ed) (1995) *Glasgow Media Group Reader Vol 2: Industry, economy, war and politics*. London: Routledge.

Philo, Greg (1991) 'Audience beliefs and the 1984/5 miners' strike', in Greg Philo (ed) (1995) *Glasgow Media Group Reader Vol 2: Industry, economy, war and politics*. London: Routledge, pp. 37–42.

Philo, Greg and McLaughlin, Greg (1993) 'The British Media and the Gulf War', in Greg Philo (ed) (1995) *Glasgow Media Group Reader Vol 2: Industry, economy, war and politics*. London: Routledge, pp. 146–56.

Pilger, John (2001) 'This war of lies goes on', *Daily Mirror*, 16 November 2001.

Pilger, John (1998) *Hidden Agendas*. London: Vintage.

Porter, Roy (2000) *Enlightenment: Britain and the creation of the modern world*. London: Allen Lane.

Powell, James (2001) 'The allure of foreign affairs', www.mediaguardian.co.uk, 30 October 2001.

Press Gazette (2002) 'Coventry paper wins name-ban challenge', *Press Gazette*, 18 January 2002.

Press Gazette (2000a) 'PA reporter stops identification ban on dead baby', *Press Gazette*, 28 July 2000.

Press Gazette (2000b) 'On and off the record', *Press Gazette*, 21 January 2000.

Private Eye (2001) 'Hackwatch: the big story', *Private Eye*, 26 January 2001.

Pulford, Cedric (2001) *JournoLISTS: 201 ways to improve your journalism*. Banbury: Ituri.

Purvis, Stewart (2002), 'ITN is on the front line, whatever Martin Bell says', *Independent*, 26 February 2002.

Randall, David (2000) *The Universal Journalist*. London: Pluto.

Reah, Danuta (1998) *The Language of Newspapers*. London: Routledge.

Rich, Carole (1999) *News Writing for the Web*, available at www.members.aol.com/crich13/poynterstudy.html.

Richardson, John (2001) 'British Muslims in the broadsheet press: a challenge to cultural hegemony?', *Journalism Studies* Vol 2, No 2, pp. 221–42.

Rocco, Fiammetta (1999) 'Stockholm Syndrome: journalists taken hostage', in Stephen Glover (ed) (1999) *The Penguin Book of Journalism*. London; Penguin, pp. 48–59.

Rose, David (2003) 'Wake up or face privacy law, warns Rusbridger', *Press Gazette*, 14 March 2003.

Ross, Karen (2001) 'Women at work: journalism as engendered practice', *Journalism Studies* Vol 2, No 4, pp. 531–44.

Roth, Eric and Mann, Michael (1999) *The Insider*. A Forward Pass film.

Rowland, Jacky (2002) 'Milosevic trial: I saw it as my duty', *Ariel*, 3 September 2002, p. 4.

Roy, Kenneth (2002) 'One pair of eyes: Jon Snow, presenter of Channel 4 News, laments the decline and fall of the broadcasting characters', interview published in *The Journalist's Handbook* No 71, Autumn 2002, pp. 33–8.

Ruddock, Alan (2001) 'Hello! Have redtops said goodbye to politics?', *Observer*, 26 August 2001.

Rusbridger, Alan (2000) 'Versions of seriousness', *Guardian*, 4 November 2000.

Sanders, Karen (2003) *Ethics & Journalism*. London: Sage.

Salwen, Michael (2001) *Book review* of 'The Business of the Media: corporate media and the public interest' by Croteau and Hoynes, *Journalism Studies* Vol 2, No 4, November 2001, pp. 634–36.

Schlesinger, Philip (1990) 'Rethinking the sociology of journalism: source strategies and the limits of media-centrism', in Marjorie Ferguson (ed) (1990) *Public Communication the New Imperatives: future directions for media research*. London: Sage, pp. 61–83.

Schlesinger, Philip (1987) *Putting 'Reality' Together*. London: Routledge.

Schudson, Michael (2001) 'The objectivity norm in American journalism', *Journalism: Theory, Practice and Criticism* Vol 2, No 2, pp. 149–70.

Schudson, Michael (1991) 'The sociology of news production revisited', in James Curran and Michael Gurevitch (eds) (1991) *Mass Media and Society*. London: Edward Arnold, pp. 141–59.

Schudson, Michael (1989) 'The sociology of news production', *Media, Culture and Society* Vol 11, pp. 263–82.

Schudson, Michael (1978) 'Discovering the news: a social history of American newspapers', in Howard Tumber (ed) (1999) *News: A reader*. Oxford: Oxford University Press, pp. 291–96.

Seib, Philip (2002) *The Global Journalist: News and conscience in a world of conflict*. Oxford: Rowman and Littlefield.

Sergeant, John (2001) *Give Me Ten Seconds*. London: Macmillan.

Sheridan Burns, Lynette (2002) *Understanding Journalism*. London: Sage.

Shoemaker, Pamela (1991) 'Gatekeeping', in Howard Tumber (ed) (1999) *News: A reader*. Oxford: Oxford University Press, pp. 73–8.

Shukman, David (2000) 'Watching them watching me', *Independent*, 7 November 2000.

Slattery, Jon (2002) 'Journalism must halt drift into "unintended apartheid"', *Press Gazette*, 12 July 2002, p. 5.

Spark, David (1999) *Investigative Reporting: A study in technique*. Oxford: Focal.

Sparks, Colin (1999) 'The press', in Jane Stokes and Anna Reading (eds) (1999) *The Media in Britain: Current debates and developments*. Basingstoke: MacMillan, pp. 41–60.

Sparks, Colin (1992) 'Popular journalism: theories and practice', in Peter Dahlgren and Colin Sparks (eds) (1992) *Journalism and Popular Culture*. London: Sage, pp. 24–44.

Stephenson, Hugh (1998) 'Tickle the Public: consumerism rules', in Michael Bromley and Hugh Stephenson (eds) (1998) *Sex, Lies and Democracy: The press and the public*. Harlow: Longman, pp. 13–24.

Stevens, Mary (2002) 'All about party girl Eva', *Press Gazette*, 11 October 2002.

Stevens, Mary (2001) 'The new doorstep challenge', *Press Gazette*, 15 June 2001.

Stevenson, Nick (2002) *Understanding Media Cultures*. London: Sage.

Stokes, Jane and Reading, Anna (eds) (1999) *The Media in Britain: current debates and developments*. Basingstoke: MacMillan.

Sullivan, Andrew (2002) 'Out of the ashes, a new way of communicating', *Sunday Times*, 24 February 2002.

Susman, Gary (2001) 'Tales of the junket', *Guardian*, 5 October 2001.

Tench, Dan (2001) 'Don't pull the dog's teeth', *Guardian*, 23 July 2001.

3WE (2002) *Losing Reality: Factual international programming on UK television, 2000–2001*. 3WE, www.epolitix.com/forum/3we.htm.

Thom, Cleland (2002) 'Spoon-fed and overspun', *Press Gazette*, 5 July 2002.

Tomlin, Julie and Morgan, Jean (2001) 'Poll voted a turn-off by viewers and readers', *Press Gazette*, 8 June 2001.

Traynor, Ian (2001) 'Taliban offer £30,000 a head to kill reporters', *Guardian*, 30 November 2001.

Tuchman, Gaye (1972) 'Objectivity as a strategic ritual: an examination of newsmen's notions of objectivity', *American Journal of Sociology*, Vol 77, No 4. Reprinted in Howard Tumber (ed) (1999) *News: A reader*. Oxford: Oxford University Press, pp. 297–307.

Tumber, Howard (ed) (2000) *Media Power, Professionals and Policies*. London: Routledge.

Tumber, Howard (ed) (1999) *News: A reader*. Oxford: Oxford University Press.

Tunstall, Jeremy (2002) 'Trends in news media and political journalism', in Raymond Kuhn and Erik Neveu (eds) (2002) *Political Journalism: New challenges, new practices*. London: Routledge, pp. 227-41.

UK Metric Association (2002) *Measurement Units Style Guide*. Available from www.metric.org.uk

Urban Legends (2001) 'False footaging', www.snopes.com/inboxer/outrage/cnn.htm, 17 September 2001.

Ursell, Gill (2001) 'Dumbing down or shaping up? New technologies, new media, new journalism', *Journalism: Theory, Practice and Criticism* Vol 2, No 2, pp. 175–96.

Vasterman, Peter (1995) 'Media hypes' www.journalism.fcj.hvu.nl/mediahype/mchype/hype_article.html (article first published, in Dutch, in magazine *Massacommunicatie*, September 1995).

Walker, David (2002) 'Low visibility on the inside track', *Journalism: Theory, Practice and Criticism*, Vol 3, No 1, pp. 101–10.

Walker, David (2000) 'Newspaper power: a practitioner's account', in Howard Tumber (ed) (2000) *Media Power, Professionals and Policies*. London: Routledge, pp. 236–46.

Ward, Mike (2002) *Journalism Online*. Oxford: Focal.

Waterhouse, Keith (1994) *English Our English (and how to sing it)*. London: Penguin.

Waterhouse, Keith (1993) *Waterhouse on Newspaper Style*. London: Penguin.

Watkins, Alan (2001) *A Short Walk Down Fleet Street: From Beaverbrook to Boycott*. London: Duckbacks.

Watson, J (1998) *Media Communication: An introduction to theory and process*. Hampshire: MacMillan.

Waugh, Evelyn (1943) *Scoop*. London: Penguin.

Weitz, Katy (2003) 'Why I quit the *Sun*', *Guardian*, 31 March 2003.

Wells, Matt (2002) 'BBC Zimbabwe line colonial, say staff', *Guardian*, 12 March 2002.

Wells, Matt (2001a) 'ITN cuts jobs and shifts towards lifestyle news', *Guardian*, 22 November 2001.

Wells, Matt (2001b) 'BBC's "brighter" news to beat rising rival, *Guardian*, 18 January 2001.

Wells, Matt (2001c) 'Decline in investigative reporting blamed on out-of-touch reporters', www.mediaguardian.co.uk, 16 November 2001.

Welsh, Tom and Greenwood, Walter (2003) *McNae's Essential Law for Journalists*. 17th edition. London: Butterworths.

Welsh, Tom and Greenwood, Walter (2001) *Essential Law for Journalists*. London: Butterworths.

Wheen, Francis (2002) *Hoo-Hahs and Passing Frenzies: Collected journalism 1991–2001*. London: Atlantic Books.

White, David Manning (1950) 'The gatekeeper: a case study in the selection of news', in Howard Tumber (ed) (1999) *News: A reader*. Oxford: Oxford University Press, pp. 66–72.

Whittaker, Brian (1981) *News Ltd: Why you can't read all about it.* London: Minority Press Group.

Williams, Granville (1996) *Britain's Media: How they are related.* London: Campaign for Press and Broadcasting Freedom.

Williams, Kevin (1992) 'Something more important than truth: ethical issues in war reporting', in Andrew Belsey and Ruth Chadwick (eds) (1992) *Ethical Issues in Journalism and the Media.* London: Routledge, pp. 154–70.

Williams, Raymond (1980) *Problems in Materialism and Culture.* London: Verso.

Wilson, John (1996) *Understanding Journalism: A guide to issues.* London: Routledge.

Winch, Samuel P (1997) *Mapping the Cultural Space of Journalism: How journalists distinguish news from entertainment.* Westport: Praeger.

Winchester, Simon (2001) 'My tainted days', *Guardian*, 22 May 2001.

Wykes, Maggie (2001) *News, Crime and Culture.* London: Pluto.

Younge, Gary (2002) 'Temples for tomorrow', *Guardian*, 9 December 2002.

Younge, Gary (2001) 'Bradford needs hope, not teargas', *Guardian*, 10 July 2001.

Zelizer, Barbie and Allan, Stuart (eds) (2002) *Journalism After September 11.* London: Routledge.

Appendix one
National Union of Journalists (NUJ) Code of Conduct

1 A journalist has a duty to maintain the highest professional and ethical standards.

2 A journalist shall at all times defend the principle of the freedom of the press and other media in relation to the collection of information and the expression of comment and criticism. He/she shall strive to eliminate distortion, news suppression and censorship.

3 A journalist shall strive to ensure that the information he/she disseminates is fair and accurate, avoid the expression of comment and conjecture as established fact and falsification by distortion, selection or misrepresentation.

4 A journalist shall rectify promptly any harmful inaccuracies, ensure that correction and apologies receive due prominence and afford the right of reply to persons criticised when the issue is of sufficient importance.

5 A journalist shall obtain information, photographs and illustrations only by straightforward means. The use of other means can be justified only by overriding considerations of the public interest. The journalist is entitled to exercise a personal conscientious objection to the use of such means.

6 A journalist shall do nothing which entails intrusion into anybody's private life, grief or distress, subject to justification by overriding considerations of the public interest.

7 A journalist shall protect confidential sources of information.

8 A journalist shall not accept bribes nor shall he/she allow other inducements to influence the performance of his/her professional duties.

9 A journalist shall not lend himself/herself to the distortion or suppression of the truth because of advertising or other considerations.

10 A journalist shall mention a person's age, sex, race, colour, creed, illegitimacy, disability, marital status, or sexual orientation only if this information is strictly relevant. A journalist shall neither originate nor process material which encourages discrimination, ridicule, prejudice or hatred on any of the above-mentioned grounds.

11 No journalist shall knowingly cause or allow the publication or broadcast of a photograph that has been manipulated unless that photograph is clearly labelled as such. Manipulation does not include normal dodging, burning, colour balancing, spotting, contrast adjustment, cropping and obvious masking for legal or safety reasons.

12 A journalist shall not take private advantage of information gained in the course of his/her duties before the information is public knowledge.

13 A journalist shall not by way of statement, voice or appearance endorse by advertisement any commercial product or service save for the promotion of his/her own work or of the medium by which he/she is employed.

The Public Interest

The above Code of Conduct uses the concept of 'the public interest' as a yardstick to justify publication of sensitive material. This is the definition of the public interest drawn up by the NUJ Ethics Council:

1 The public interest includes:

   a Detecting or exposing crime or a serious misdemeanour;

   b Protecting public health and safety;

   c Preventing the public from being misled by some statement or action of an individual or organisation;

   d Exposing misuse of public funds or other forms of corruption by public bodies;

   e Revealing potential conflicts of interest by those in positions of power and influence;

   f Exposing corporate greed;

   g Exposing hypocritical behaviour by those holding high office.

2 There is a public interest in the freedom of expression itself.

3 In cases involving children, journalists must demonstrate an exceptional public interest to override the normally paramount interests of the child.

(www.nuj.org.uk)

Appendix two *Some useful websites*

Here are some websites you may find useful for researching stories and/or for exploring debates in and around journalism. Most of these sites will have their own links worth trying out. Not included are search engines such as *Google* and the most popular mainstream media sites such as the *BBC* and the *Guardian's News Unlimited*, because they are easy to find if you haven't come across them already. Websites come and go, and addresses change, but the following were all operational in 2003.

www.alternet.org (Alternative news)
www.uk.indymedia.org (Alternative news)
www.schnews.org.uk (Alternative news)
www.altpress.org (Alternative Press Centre)
www.absw.org.uk (Association of British Science Writers)
www.bbc.co.uk/radionewsroom (BBC radio news scripts, style and more)
www.bbctraining.co.uk (BBC training)
www.britcoun.org (British Council)
www.bjr.org.uk (British Journalism Review)
www.bjtc.org.uk (Broadcast Journalism Training Council)
www.cfoi.org.uk (Campaign for Freedom of Information)
www.cpbf.org.uk (Campaign for Press and Broadcasting Freedom)
www.tasc.ac.uk/cfj (Centre for Journalism)
www.charity-commission.gov.uk (Charity information and links)
www.childrens-express.org (Children's news service)
www.cjr.org (Columbia Journalism Review)
www.cjr.org/owners (CJR guide to media owners)
www.cpj.org (Committee to Protect Journalists)
www.companieshouse.gov.uk (Company information)
www.contactsbook.com (Contacts and links)
www.courtservice.gov.uk (Court information and listings)
www.dnotice.org.uk (Defence Advisory Notices)
www.diversity-online.org (Diversity online)
www.192.com (Directory enquiries, electoral register and much more)
www.politicallinks.co.uk (Dod's UK politics site)
www.drugscope.org.uk (Drugs information)
www.foe.org.uk (Environmental news)
www.cec.org.uk (European Commission)
www.ejc.nl (European Journalism Centre)

www.europarl.eu.int (European Parliament)
www.fair.org (Fairness and Accuracy in Reporting)
www.honk.co.uk/fleetstreet (Fleet Street Forum)
www.globalreview.btinternet.co.uk (Global Journalism Review)
www.tagish.co.uk/links (Government, health, education and other links)
www.number-10.gov.uk (Government news)
www.gnn.gov.uk (Government News Network)
www.hse.gov.uk (Health and Safety Executive)
www.holdthefrontpage.co.uk (Hold the Front Page)
www.facsnet.org (Improving journalism through education)
www.ifj.org (International Federation of Journalists)
www.coldtype.net (International journalism)
www.newssafety.com (International News Safety Institute)
www.usus.org (Internet guide for journalists)
www.ire.org (Investigative Reporters and Editors, Inc)
www.journalismuk.co.uk (Journalism links)
www.journalismnet.com/uk (Journalism links, tools and tips)
www.upmystreet.com (Local details and maps)
www.lgiu.gov.uk (Local Government Information Unit)
www.mediachannel.org (Media Channel)
www.presswise.org.uk (Media ethics charity)
www.mediaguardian.co.uk (Media Guardian)
www.aukml.org.uk (Media librarians)
www.mediauk.com (Media links)
www.wrx.zen.co.uk/britnews.htm (Media links)
www.medialens.org (Media watchdog)
www.wales.gov.uk (National Assembly for Wales)
www.nctj.org.uk (National Council for the Training of Journalists)
www.nhs.uk (National Health Service)
www.nuj.org.uk (National Union of Journalists)
www.ananova.com (News)
www.2dayuk.com (News agencies)
www.newsnow.co.uk (News and links)
www.newsdesk-uk.com (News, links and contacts)
www.thebigproject.co.uk/news (Newspaper and broadcasting links)
www.newspapersoc.org.uk (Newspaper Society)
www.ni-assembly.gov.uk (Northern Ireland Assembly)
www.nujtraining.org.uk (NUJ training)
www.ofcom.gov.uk (Ofcom, Office of Communications)

www.ukpress.org   (Online forum)
www.journalism.co.uk   (Online news for journalists)
www.gregpalast.com   (Greg Palast's site)
www.ppa.co.uk   (Periodical Publishers Association)
www.ppa.co.uk/ptc   (Periodicals Training Council)
www.police.uk   (Police links)
www.epolitix.com   (Political news)
www.poynter.org   (Poynter Institute)
www.responsesource.com   (PR contacts)
www.pamediapoint.press.net   (Press Association Mediapoint)
www.pcc.org.uk   (Press Complaints Commission)
www.presscouncils.org   (Press councils internationally)
www.pressgazette.co.uk   (Press Gazette)

www.pro.gov.uk   (Public Records)
www.ramproject.org.uk   (Refugees, Asylum Seekers and Media project)
www.scotland.gov.uk   (Scottish Executive)
www.scottish.parliament.uk   (Scottish Parliament)
www.ukeditors.com   (Society of Editors)
www.soliciters-online.com   (Solicitors database from Law Society)
www.statistics.gov.uk   (Statistics galore)
www.tuc.org.uk   (Trade union news)
www.georgeviner.org.uk   (George Viner Memorial Fund)
www.parliament.uk   (UK parliament including Hansard)
www.webring.org   (Websites listed by subject)

Index

abbreviations 128, 130
access to news *see* news access
accuracy 12, 60, 103, 169
'active audience' 2, 6, 63, 144
active voice 107, 114, 128
Adams, Sally 98, 104, 119, 126
adjectives 107
advertisers 12, 14, 15, 19, 117, 152
Afghanistan 20, 54, 63, 64–65
Agence France-Presse 8
agency 6–7, 17–18, 34, 116–117, 153–154, 155–156
agenda setting 63, 64, 71, 144
Aitken, Jonathan 20, 23, 76, 81, 83
Ali, Naher 4
All the President's Men 74, 75
Allan, Stuart 62, 66, 153
alternative media 6, 15, 45, 47, 145, 153
Amanpour, Christiane 65
America – *see* United States
analysis 90, 121–122, 123, 124
Ananova 33–34
anecdotes 118, 119, 121–122, 123–124
Angola 18
animals 31, 35, 36, 89, 90
AOL 144
apologies and corrections 94, 152, 169
apostrophes 128, 130, 134
Arab-Israeli conflict 12
Archer, Jeffrey 23, 81
Armstrong, Stephen 121, 124–125
Arnold, Matthew 88
Associated Press 60–61, 94–95
asylum seekers 13, 65, 67, 68
attribution 65, 68, 101, 109, 112, 113
audience 12, 18–20, 56, 63, 86, 91, 109, 110, 113, 119, 120, 122, 128, 130, 143–145, 146–147, 152, 153, 155
audio 76, 86, 142, 146, 147
Aufderheide, Pat 154–155
authority 87–88, 92, 123

backgrounders 116, 147
bad news 24–25, 36, 37, 48
Bakhtin, Mikhail 109–110, 114
balance 60, 61, 62, 76, 109
Baldwin, Stanley 13–14
Barber, Lynn 96, 97, 99, 118
Barnett, Steven and Seymour, Emily 87–88
Baudrillard, Jean 60
BBC 3, 5, 15, 16, 18, 25, 31, 38, 39, 57, 62, 65, 87, 89, 99, 140, 144, 146

BBC Online 5, 147
Beaman, Jim 104
Beaverbrook, Lord 14
Beckett, Andy 67, 122, 123, 125
Behr, Edward 8, 57, 118, 123
Beijing Evening News 69
Bell, Allan 31, 44, 97, 106, 109, 110, 114, 128, 140
Bell, Martin 61, 65, 87
Benn, Tony 95, 98–99, 148
Bennett, Catherine 24
Bennett, James Gordon 61
Berkowitz, Dan 106
Berlusconi, Silvio 14
bias 6–7, 64, 65, 71, 109
Billington, Michael 120
Birmingham Evening Mail 102, 111
BJTC *see* Broadcast Journalism Training Council
Blackpool Evening Gazette 6
blogs 146
Bloody Sunday 117
Boorstin, Daniel 16, 94
Bosnia 54, 65
Bourdieu, Pierre 4, 45, 86, 90, 92
Bower, Tom 75
Boyd, Andrew 41, 71, 104, 116–117, 140, 142–143, 149
Boyer, J H 60
Bradford riots 144–145
Brants, Kees 88
Brazil 148
breach of confidence 21
Bright, Martin 4, 23–24
broadcast interviews 54, 99–100, 104, 144, 146, *see also* interviewing
Broadcast Journalism Training Council (BJTC) 6, 8
Bromley, Michael 8, 149
Bromley, Michael and Cushion, Stephen 107
Bromley, Michael and O'Malley, Tom 10, 71
Brown, Andrew 146
Bucktin, Chris 102
Burchill, Julie 9

Calendar see Yorkshire Television
calls 48–49
Cameron, Deborah 128–129, 140
Cameron, James 64, 70
Campaign for Press and Broadcasting Freedom 157
Campbell, Alastair 16
Carey, James 90
'carnivalesque' 92, 114
Cassidy, Denis 102

Castells, Manuel 144–145
Cavendish Press 6
CBS 26
celebrity, celebrities 25, 35, 36, 87, 88, 89–90, 95
censorship 4, 24, 60, 62, 63, 169
Chambers, Deborah 75
Chandler, Raymond 134
Channel Five News 38
Channel Four 80
Channel Four News 69, 87, 146–147
Chantler, Paul and Harris, Sim 142, 143
Chesterton, GK 3
China 12–13, 69
Chippindale, Peter and Horrie, Chris 20
Chomsky, Noam and Herman, Edward 14, 27
chronology 106, 110
'churnalism' 3–4
citizens 12–13, 92, 143, 153–154, 156
class 5, 12, 18, 25–26, 65, 86
cliches 131–132
CNN 65, 148
Cockburn, Claud 79
codes of conduct 12, 23, 24, 152, 169
Coelho, Mario 4
Cohen, Stanley 63–64
Cole, Peter 25
Colston, Jane 21
columns, columnists 44, 116, 117–118, 119, 122, 128
comedians 80
comment 60, 63, 108
common sense 65, 68
communication theories 2, 10, 157
Companies House 77, 78, 79
'computer-assisted reporting' 77
Conboy, Martin 86–87, 88, 92, 114
concentration of ownership 4
conflict 5–6, 17, 18, 26, 36, 37, 62–67, 86, 148, 152–153, 154–155, *see also* war
conflicting loyalties 12–13
constraints 4–5, 6, 9, 11–27, 33–34, 49, 64, 74, 75, 76, 152, 153
construction of news 6, 32–33, 114
contacts, contacts books 45, 47–49, *see also* sources
contempt of court 21
Cook, Roger 80
copy approval 25, 95–96
Cottle, Simon 45, 106
councils 48, 51, 132
courts 20–21, 39–40, 51, 129
Cowley, Jason 91
Craftsman 60
Craven Herald, Skipton 5
Crick, Michael 81
crime 34, 39, 65, 67, 80, 87, 89, 90, 96, 107–108, 169
Critcher, Chas 71
Crone, Tom 27
Curran, James 8
Curran, James and Seaton, Jean 33, 157

current affairs 80
Cushion, Stephen and Bromley, Michael 107
cuttings 31, 51, 94, 123

Daily Express 13, 13, 35, 44, 61, 67, 69, 90, 110
Daily Mail 6, 17, 35, 37, 38, 39, 44, 61–62, 67, 69, 155
Daily Mirror 5, 14, 35, 37, 52, 61, 64–65, 77, 89, 98, 111, 112, 122
Daily Record 5
Daily Sketch 6
Daily Star 6, 62, 89
Daily Telegraph 26, 44, 63, 90, 97, 120, 121, 123, 124
Daily Tribune, Sioux City 112
Daniel, Isioma 4
D'Arcy, Mark 83
databases 74, 77, 123, 146
Davies, Nick 79, 80, 101
Dawson, Jayne 120
deadlines 15–16, 147, 152
death knocks 17–18, 96, 101–102
deaths of journalists 4
de Burgh, Hugo 76, 83
defamation *see* libel
Defence of the Realm 74
Defence, Press and Broadcasting Advisory Committee 24
Delane, John Thaddeus 2
democracy 4, 15, 76, 81, 83, 87, 117, 153–154
description 112, 113, 120, 121, 132
Desmond, Richard 13, 90
Deuze, Mark and Dimoudi, Christina 143–144
dialogic 7, 109–110
Diamond, John 68
Dimbleby, Jonathan 97
Dimoudi, Christina and Deuze, Mark 143–144
Dixon, Sara 97
D-Notices *see* Defence, Press and Broadcasting Advisory Committee
documentary 19, 80, 80
'dodgy dossier' 146
Doig, Alan 83
doorstepping 78–80, 100, 101–102
Dorril, Stephen 64, 74, 75
Dovey, Jon 62, 87–88, 92, 117–118, 126
Doyle, Gillian 13
drama 34, 36, 37, 86, 103, 111, 113
Drudge, Matt 147
'dumbing down' 80, 86–87, 88, 91, 92, 154

Eastern Eye 6, 155
Eastwood, Lindsay 5, 16, 24, 90–91, 143–145, 153
Economist 134, 140
Eliot, George 142
elitism 62, 76, 83, 87, 88, 90–91
Elliott, Philip and Golding, Peter 142, 155
email 16, 51, 95, 98, 146, 147, 148
Engel, Matthew 92, 101
Engels, Friedrich and Marx, Karl 5
Engineer magazine 23

Enlightenment, the 60
entertainment 19, 35–37, 62, 80, 83, 85–92, 116–117, 152, 153
ethics 6, 9, 17–18, 21, 23–25, 57, 62–67, 69, 74, 75, 78, 91,
    95–96, 97, 101–102, 103, 104, 152–157, 169, *see also*
    reflective practitioner
Evans, Harold 130, 140
Evening Standard, London 6, 26, 54
exclamation marks 133

face to face interviews 98–99, *see also* interviewing
facts 9, 23, 32–33, 60, 61, 62, 63, 65, 68–70, 71, 75–76, 89, 91,
    95, 106, 108–109, 111, 112, 113, 116, 118, 119, 122,
    123, 145, 153, 156, 157
fakery 69
Falklands 26, 94
fax 16, 95, 98
features 89, 95, 108, 115–126
Ferguson, Euan 122
Financial Times 89
first person voice 117–118, 121
Fisk, Robert 26
Fiske, John 66
Five Star Final 12
five Ws 2, 8, 31, 100, 109, 110, 121
Fleming, Carole 149
Foley, Michael 13, 16–17
follow-ups 36, 38, 44
Foot, Paul 5, 14, 18–19, 26, 56, 64, 74, 76–77, 81, 82, 83, 98,
    155–156, 157
Forde, Eamonn 16, 95
fourth estate 3, 5, 60
Fowler, HW 140
Fowler, Mark 145
Fowler, Roger 117, 140
France 8, 49
Franklin, Bob 16, 78, 86, 87, 88, 92, 117
Frayn, Michael 32–33, 106, 113
free press model 4–5, 13
Front Page 109
Frost, Chris 58, 61, 71, 86, 96, 104, 157
fuel protests 38, 101

Galtung, Johan and Ruge, Mari 30–31, 33, 41
Gans, Herbert 41, 44–45
gatekeepers 16, 33–34, 39, 41, 144, 149
gender 12, 18, 19, 25, 62, 129, 169
Gentlemen's Magazine 60
George, Lloyd 62
Gibbons, Trevor 5, 147–148
Gibson, Jeremy 89
Gieber, Walter 33, 37
Gilbert, Harriett 126
Glover, Mike 19, 78
'golden age' 4, 76
Golding, Peter and Elliott, Philip 142, 155
Golding, Peter and Murdock, Graham 27
good news 25, 36, 37
Goodhart, David 91

Goodwin, Bill 4, 23, 26
Gopsill, Tim 12
grammar 130–139, *see also* style
Gramsci, Antonio 65
Granada Television 19, 20
Gransby, Aaron 15
Greenwood, Walter and Welsh, Tom 20–21, 23, 27
Grubb, Jon 25
Guardian 5, 6, 15, 16, 17, 20, 31, 32, 34, 35, 38, 44, 53–54, 63,
    81, 94–95, 111, 119, 120, 122, 124, 125, 140, 142, 147,
    154
Guerin, Veronica 4
Gumbel, Andrew 120, 123, 124
Guru-Murthy, Krishnan 146–147

Habermas, Jurgen 4, 60, 153
Hale, Don 4, 81, 82, 83
Hall, Jim 144, 145, 149
Hall, Stuart 5–6, 31–32, 41, 45, 47–48, 58, 64, 155
Hallin, Daniel 108
Hamilton, Neil 23
Hanna, Mark 74, 75, 76
Hanson, Lord 102
Harcup, Tony and O'Neill, Deirdre 35–39, 41, 89, 90
Hardt, Hanno 117
Hardy, Simon 111
Harris, Sim and Chantler, Paul 142, 143
Harrison, Jackie 17, 41, 75, 117, 143, 149
Harrogate Advertiser 35, 68
Harrogate Herald 6
Harrow Observer 15
Hartley, John 31, 61
Hastings, Max 26
Hazan, Sophie 112
hegemony 65, 71
Helliwell, David 5–6, 16, 19, 37, 39–40, 51, 89
Hencke, David 80, 82
Herald, Glasgow 117–118
Herbert, Susannah 120
Herman, Edward and Chomsky, Noam 14, 27
Hetherington, Alastair 34–35
Hicks, Wynford 108, 109, 114, 134, 140
Hicks, Wynford and Holmes, Tim 103, 128, 140
Hill, Peter 89
Hillsborough disaster 19–20
Hird, Christopher 77, 78
Hodge, Robert and Kress, Gunther 129, 137
Holland, Patricia 89, 142, 149
Holmes, Tim and Hicks, Wynford 103, 128, 140
Honeyman, Steve and Ullmann, John 74
Hopkins, Nick 111
horizontal communication 145
Horrie, Chris and Chippindale, Peter 20
house style *see* style
human interest 19, 35–37, 60, 75, 116
human rights 21, 23
humour 35, 36, 86, 89
hyphens 134

ideology 5–6, 17, 18, 31–32, 41, 64, 108, 129, 137, 140, 155
'imagined community' 106
impartiality 60, 61–62, 65, 71, 76, *see also* objectivity
inaccuracies 16–17, 69, 94–95, 148, 169
Independent 6, 13, 26, 30, 34, 89, 120, 121, 123, 124, 128
Independent on Sunday 33
industrial disputes 5–6, 66–67
'infotainment' *see* 'dumbing down'
Ingham, Sir Bernard 16
Insider, The 74
Institute of Public Relations 25
interactivity 144, 146–148, 149
International Federation of Journalists 4
internet 3, 5, 7, 8, 57, 79, 123, 142–149, 171–172
interviewing 79, 93–104, 123
intro 108, 109, 110–112, 116, 120–122
'inverted pyramid' 108, 110, 112, 126
investigative reporting 2, 14, 23–24, 73–83, 86, 87
Iraq 2, 13, 60, 62–64, 146, 147
Ireland 57, 80, 117, 129
Irish Times 129
Italy 14
ITN 8, 65, 86, 87, 146

Jardine, Cassandra 121
Jelbert, Steve 122
Johnson, Dr Samuel 117
Johnston, Don 128
Jones, Nick 16
'journalism of attachment' 65, 71
Journalism Training Forum 3, 7, 8, 25, 26
Junor, John 90

Kashmir 54
Keeble, Richard 10, 27, 58, 62, 65, 98, 104, 109, 112, 113,
    114, 126, 131, 157
Kelso, Paul 111
Kenyon, Paul 80
Kieran, Matthew 62, 71
Kiley, Sam 12
Kipling, Rudyard 118
'KISS and tell' 108–110
Knightley, Phillip 27, 38, 63–64, 81
Knutsford Guardian 54
Kosovo 17, 65
Krajicek, David J 90
Kress, Gunther and Hodge, Robert 129, 137

Lancashire Evening Post 5–6
language 62–63, 91, 107–108, 109–110, 113, 114, 123,
    128–140
Larkin, Philip 118
Larsson, Larsake 48
Lasswell, Harold 2
lateral thinking 32, 52, 79–80, 147
law 8, 20–24, 27, 152, 154
Lazenby, Peter 45, 55
legislation *see* law

legwork 79–80
Lewthwaite, Jim 100
libel 20, 21, 23
lifestyle journalism 19, 87, 88, 116, 117, 123
linking words 113, 125
Lippmann, Walter 9, 32
listeners *see* audience
Liverpool dockers 66–67
Lloyd, David 80
local government *see* councils
London Evening Post 12
Los Angeles Times 76
Ludlam, Joanna 21
Lule, Jack 32–33, 106–108, 114
Lynch, Jake 26, 152–153

MacEwen, Arthur 37
MacIntyre, Donal 80
MacLeod, John 117–118
magnitude 36, 37–38
Manchester Guardian see Guardian
Manning, Paul 15, 17, 47, 48, 58, 75, 76, 88, 142
Mansfield, F J 47, 91, 96
'manufacture of news' 32–33, 142
Marcio 148
market forces 4–5, 12, 13, 14, 27, 88, 153–154, 155–156
Marr, Andrew 97, 146
Marsh, David 122
Marsh, Geoff 111
Marx, Chico 69
Marx, Karl and Engels, Friedrich 5
Marxist perspectives 5, 71, 155
Matlock Mercury 4
Maxwell, Robert 5, 14, 23
Mayes, Ian 67
McCafferty, Nell 117, 129
McChesney, Robert 8, 17, 19, 27, 32, 157
McCombs, Maxwell and Shaw, David 63
McLaughlin, Greg 17, 71
McLaughlin, Greg and Philo, Greg 62
'McLurg's Law' 38
McNair, Brian 88, 92, 153
McQuail, Denis 2, 4, 5, 10, 12, 13, 15, 17, 27, 57, 61, 63, 109,
    110, 143, 157
McRae, Kim 111
media agenda 36, 38–39
Mercury news agency 6
Merrick, Jane 6, 39, 53, 54, 56, 69, 101, 102, 103, 107, 113, 154
Milne, James 111
Milne, Seumas 20, 147
miners' strike 66, 99
'miracle' stories 37, 87
Mirsky, Jonathan 12–13
miscarriages of justice 77, 81
Moore, Jo 24–25
Moore, Suzanne 119
moral panic 63–64, 67, 71
Morrow, Fiona 120

Municipal Journal 142
Murdoch, Rupert 12–13, 14, 61, 66, 86
Murdock, graham and Golding, Peter 27
myth 32–33, 106–108, 114

'name and shame' *see* paedophiles
Nation 95
National Council for the Training of Journalists (NCTJ) 6, 103, 108–109
National Enquirer 6
National Union of Journalists (NUJ) 6, 23, 75, 102, 152, 155, 157, 169
NCTJ *see* National Council for the Training of Journalists
Neil, Andrew 13
Netherlands 144
neutrality 6, 60, 61, 69–70, 109, 129
'new journalism' 2, 86–87, 88
New York Daily News 90
New York Herald 61
New York Tribune 94
news access 25, 45, 47, 58
'news actors' 44, 106
news agencies 6, 16, 31, 32, 39, 53, 79–80, 102, 103
News of the World 4, 38, 71, 74, 102
'news pegs' 31, 32
news releases 16, 24, 25, 31, 53, 57, 94
news values 6, 29–41, 106, 112, 142, 152
Newsnight 25, 99–100
Nicholson, Michael 65
Nigeria 4, 38
Northern Echo 61
Northmore, David 79, 83
notebooks, note-taking 66, 94–95, 103, *see also* shorthand
Nottingham Evening Post 25
NUJ *see* National Union of Journalists
numbers 34, 37, 69, 71, 77, 136

objectivity 13, 26, 59–71, 94, 109, 129, 155, *see also* impartiality
Observer 2, 6, 23–24, 95–96, 122
off-the-record 57, 99, 101
O'Hagan, Martin 4
O'Malley, Tom 3
O'Malley, Tom and Bromley, Michael 10, 71
O'Malley, Tom and Soley, Clive 27
O'Neill, Deirdre and Harcup, Tony 35–39, 41, 89, 90
O'Neill, John 155–156
O'Neill, Paul 107
Onion, The 69
online journalism *see* internet
Open Rugby magazine 5
opinion 5, 9, 60, 64, 89, 117, 118, 123, 124, 152
Orwell, George 64, 65, 90, 128, 129, 140
Osborn, Andrew 111
owners 4, 6, 12–15, 61, 152

paedophiles 38, 67, 71
Palast, Greg 74, 75, 83, 157

Panorama 74, 80
Panter, Steve 4
Pantic, Milan 4
paragraphs 108, 112, 113, 114, 125, 147
passive voice 128
patriotism 12, 26, 155
Paxman, Jeremy 96, 99
pay (of journalists) 2–3, 155
payoff 124–125
PCC *see* Press Complaints Commission
Peak, Laura 111
Peak, Steve 157
Perkins, Anne 18, 25
Periodicals Training Council 8
petrol crisis *see* fuel protests
Philo, Greg and McLaughlin, Greg 62
pictures 14, 33, 35–37, 39, 52, 76, 80, 89, 90, 119, 120, 142, 143–145, 146, 147, 148, 169
Pilger, John 64–65, 67, 70, 71, 77
police 23, 39, 48–49, 54, 136–137
political economy 155
politics and politicians 16–17, 18–19, 35, 48, 53, 54, 55, 61–62, 63, 86
polysemic 109–110
postmodernity and postmodernism 60, 71, 118
power elite 35, 36
PR *see* public relations
predictability 31, 33, 38, 106
Press Association 6, 101, 103, 107, 113, 154
Press Complaints Commission (PCC) 21, 24, 27, 51, 75, 94, 102, 152
press conferences 55, 94
Press Council 94–95
Press Gazette 21, 101, 119
press officers *see* public relations
press releases *see* news releases
primary definers 47–48, 49, 58, 64
Prince, Rosa 111
privacy 21, 91, 94, 96, 169
Private Eye 5, 39, 50, 56, 77, 81, 98, 119
privilege 23
profiles 116, 121, 123
propaganda model 14, 27
proprietors *see* owners
protection of sources 4, 23–24, 66, 74, 82, 169
'pseudo-events' 16, 33, 94–95
public interest 75–76, 169
public relations 16–17, 24–25, 45, 48, 55, 95–96, 152
public service broadcasting 14
public sphere 4, 13, 45, 87, 143, 144, 149, 153–154
pubs 32, 55, 60
Pulford, Cedric 95, 129
punctuation 130–139
Pursehouse, Mark 129
Purvis, Stewart 87

questions 76, 94, 95, 97, 98, 99, 100
quotes 94, 97, 103, 112, 113, 119, 121, 122, 123, 125, 137

race 12, 18, 25, 47, 62, 64, 129, 169
Radio B92, Belgrade 69
Radio Four 119
Radio Leeds 5
Radio Merseyside 20
Radio One 38
Radio Times 119
Randall, David 3, 10, 12, 41, 44, 71, 75, 77, 103, 104, 112,
    113, 114, 116, 117, 121, 123, 126, 152
Rather, Don 26
Raven, Charlotte 20
readers *see* audience
Reah, Danuta 114
reconstructions 80
reflective practitioner 8, 10, 57, 153, 154–155, 157, *see also*
    ethics
reflexivity 66, 87, 118, 126
regulation 12, 24, 61, 143, 152, 153, *see also* self-regulation
Reith, John 144
'relative autonomy' (of journalists) 75, 155
relevance 36, 38
reported speech 97, 113, 137
Reuters 8
reviews 116, 126, 137
Rich, Carole 149
Robertson, Geoffrey 18
Rocco, Fiammetta 95
Ross, Karen 18, 19
routines 6, 9, 12, 14–18, 67, 142, 152
Rowland, Jacky 65–66
'rows' 37, 49, 44
Ruge, Mari and Galtung, Johan 30–31, 33, 41
Rusbridger, Alan 89

safety 4, 20, 144–145
salaries *see* pay
San Francisco Examiner 37
Sanders, Karen 157
scandal 30, 34
Scargill, Arthur 99, 100
Schlesinger, Philip 38, 41
Schudson, Michael 53, 60–61, 94–95
Scott, C P 63
Seaton, Jean and Curran, James 33, 157
secret filming 80
Seib, Philip 62, 66
Selby rail crash 16, 37, 142
selection of news 9, 30, 31–32, 34–35, 39–40, 41, 61, 67, 143,
    152, *see also* news values
self-censorship 14, 24
self-regulation 18, 24, *see also* regulation
sentences 107–108, 112, 113, 114, 116, 122, 125, 130
September 11 attacks 20, 24, 26, 32, 54, 63, 69, 86, 121, 137,
    148, 154
Serbia 26, 66
Sergeant, John 8, 34, 95, 99
sex 34, 35, 36, 80, 88, 89, 90, 91
Seymour, Emily and Barnett, Steven 87–88

Sharpe, Martyn 111
Shaw, Donald and McCombs, Maxwell 63
Shayler, David 23–24
Sheridan Burns, Lynette 110, 153–154, 157
Shipman, Dr Harold 79–80
Shoemaker, Pamela 34, 41
shorthand 8, 103, 154, *see also* notebooks
Shukman, David 18
Simpson, Eva 122
Simpson, John 62
Sky News 26
Snow, Jon 69–70, 87
Snow, Peter 100
social environment 17–19, 25–26
social responsibility 2–3, 7, 152–154, 156, 157
socialisation 17–18, 26
Socialist Worker 5, 62
Soham 90, 118
Soley, Clive and O'Malley, Tom 27
sound *see* audio
sources 9, 12, 17, 23–24, 43–58, 68, 74, 82, 94–103, 109, 119,
    123, 143–144, 145, 147, 152, 155
Spark, David 75–76, 83
Sparks, Colin 4–5, 6–7, 15, 110
spin and spin doctors *see* public relations
sport 5, 7, 56, 60–61, 89, 148
statistics *see* numbers
statutory regulation *see* regulation
Stephen, Leslie 5
Stevenson, Nick 4, 6, 18, 63, 71, 144, 157
Stoke Sentinel 17–18
stories 31–34, 86, 91, 106, 107, 114, 147
story-telling 9, 32, 86, 106, 142, 153
'strategic ritual' 64–65, 67–68, 71
structural factors 6–7, 12, 18, 27, 33–34, 76, 83, 156, 157
style 12, 15, 107–108, 112, 118, 122, 125, 127–140, 143
subbing, subs 7, 15, 26, 77, 103, 108, 110, 119, 120, 124
subjective reporting 66, 70, 117–118
Sullivan, Andrew 146
Sun 6, 16, 19–20, 24, 35, 38, 61, 63, 64, 69, 88, 89, 94–95,
    100, 111, 119, 129
Sunday Express 90
Sunday Format 118
Sunday Mirror 21, 80
Sunday People 6
Sunday Telegraph 121
Sunday Times 13, 81, 140
surprise 34, 36, 37, 119
Susman, Gary 95
Sweden 54, 146
synergy 13–14

tabloidisation *see* 'dumbing down'
Taher, Abul 6, 26, 54, 69, 154–155
Telegraph and *Argus*, Bradford 6, 111
telephone manner 97–98
text 109–110, 113
Thalidomide babies 81

Thom, Cleland 45
Thomas, Mark 80, 81
Thomsen, Alice 121, 123, 124
threats to journalists 4, 20, 74, 81, 147
three-source rule 69
time 12, 15–17, 30, 44, 74, 75, 77, 96, 122, 123, 143, 147,
    154
Times 2, 12–13, 69, 88, 90, 111, 112, 134, 140
Today newspaper 128–129
Today programme 17, 54
tragedy 36, 37, 111
training (of journalists) 6, 8, 10, 26, 119, 128, 157
transmission model 2
Tremayne, Charles 19
truth 2, 4, 57, 60, 62, 64, 65, 67, 68, 71, 74, 76, 87, 108, 118,
    126, 129, 140, 156, 169
Tuchman, Gaye 64, 67–68
Tumber, Howard 27, 41, 58, 71
Tunstall, Jeremy 4
twenty-four-hour news 142–143

Ullmann, John and Honeyman, Steve 74
undercover reporting 78, 80
United States 14, 18, 20, 26, 30, 33, 34, 38, 60–61, 63, 64, 69,
    77, 94–95, 117, 124, 145, 147, 154–155, 157
Ursell, Gill 75, 88
Utley, Tom 97

Vague News 109, 113
Vallely, Paul 89, 121
Vasagar, Jeevan 111
Vasterman, Peter 33
victims 90, 96, 102, 107–108
Vietnam 108
viewers *see* audience

Wade, Rebekah 24
Wainwright, Martin 6, 16, 35, 37, 53–54, 70, 75, 76, 96–97,
    142, 153, 154
Walker, David 7, 13, 16–17, 145–146
Wanstead and Woodford Guardian 97
war 4, 7, 26, 27, 62–66, 71, *see also* conflict
war crimes tribunals 65–66

Ward, Mike 77, 83, 146, 148, 149
Ware, John 80
Washington Post 34
Waterhouse, Keith 112, 113, 133, 140
Watford Observer 5
Watkins, Alan 17
Waugh, Evelyn 39
websites *see* internet
Weitz, Katy 64
Wells, H G 152
Welsh, Tom and Greenwood, Walter 20–21, 23, 27
Wharfedale Observer 53–54
Wheen, Francis 23, 116, 118, 121, 157
whistleblowers 74, 82
White, David Manning 33
White, Sue 102
Whittaker, Brian 51
Whittle, Brian 6, 15–16, 32, 35, 45, 48, 52, 53, 54, 79–80, 102,
    103, 118–119, 152, 154
who, what, where, when, why and how *see* five Ws
Wild, Leah 119
Williams, Granville 153–154
Wilson, John 63
Winch, Samuel 86
Winchester, Simon 57
'winter of discontent' 5–6
world wide web *see* internet
writing features 115–126
writing news 91, 105–114
Ws *see* five Ws
Wykes, Maggie 32

Yelland, David 19
Yorkshire Evening Post 5, 33, 34, 37, 39–40, 45, 51, 53, 89, 90,
    111, 112, 120, 122
Yorkshire on Sunday 78–79
Yorkshire Post 34, 54, 78
Yorkshire Sport 60
Yorkshire Television 5, 24, 75, 90, 143–145
Younge, Gary 25, 47

Zaire 57
Zakir, Waseem 3–4